Blind Impressions

MATERIAL TEXTS

BLIND IMPRESSIONS

METHODS AND MYTHOLOGIES
IN BOOK HISTORY

※

Joseph A. Dane

PENN

UNIVERSITY OF PENNSYLVANIA PRESS

PHILADELPHIA

Published by
University of Pennsylvania Press
Philadelphia, Pennsylvania 19104-4112
www.upenn.edu/pennpress

Printed in the United States of America on acid-free paper
10 9 8 7 6 5 4 3 2 1

Library of Congress Cataloging-in-Publication Data

Dane, Joseph A.
 Blind impressions : methods and mythologies in book history / Joseph A.
Dane. — 1st ed.
     p.   cm. — (Material texts)
 Includes bibliographical references and index.
 ISBN 978-0-8122-4549-3 (hardcover : alk. paper)
 1. Bibliography—Methodology. 2. Bibliography—Methodology—History.
3. Printing—History. 4. Printing—Historiography. 5. Type and type-founding—
History. 6. Type and type-founding—Historiography. I. Title. II. Series:
Material texts.
Z1001.D23   2013
010'.44—dc23   2013011245

In memory of Jaenet Guggenheim

CONTENTS

Introduction

To write on print culture, one might start by selecting a monumental book from the presumed history of that culture: it might be the Gutenberg Bible; it might be an edition of Aldus Manutius, Shakespeare's First Folio, the French *Encyclopédie*. We might choose less grand things as well: a run-of-the-mill edition of an Elizabethan play, a fragment of an early grammar book. One of these books, or a set of its characteristics, might epitomize whatever print culture is. The book might mark a point in the history of print culture, a stage in its development perhaps, or, to invoke a nineteenth-century phrase no longer in fashion, the growth and progress of this thing or entity.

We could single out this book as marking a transformation in the history of printing, a crisis, if that is what our critical language calls for. For the first time, in this singular book, or once again, or now and for all, the function of books or The Book has changed: books are no longer transparent things; they are not these run-of-the-mill repositories of texts (so rarely discussed in histories of printing) to be "looked through"; they have lost their representational aspect and no longer transmit the text, thought, or intentions we once imagined are the raisons d'être of these things we call books. They are, rather, markers in a cultural history that the author and publishers only dimly imagined. Or so we might think.

As bibliographers or book historians, we perform our work by changing the function of the objects we study. We rarely pick up an Aldine edition to read one of the classical texts it contains. No one reads the Bible in Gutenberg's version, and as for books by Koberger, staples of histories of early printing, we don't read the texts they contain at all, and perhaps would not even recognize them. Bentley's *Milton* has nothing to do with Milton, nor does the mythology surrounding it have much to do with Bentley,[1] and no one learns Latin by reading Donatus. Print culture, under this notion, is not a medium for writing or thought, but a historical object of study; our bibliographical field, our own concoction, becomes the true referent of the objects we define as at its foundation.

When we consider print culture in this way, as a significant subject of investigation rather than an event in history, the singular book that initiated our thinking becomes less important. That book, whether an abstraction (the Shakespeare First Folio) or a material object (my copy of this book), is just one member of a series. The First Folio is only one of many editions; my copy is interchangeable with any other copy. Print, in a bibliographical sense, produces editions, as manuscripts can never do; and editions eliminate the singularity of the individual object, the book-copy we are holding now. Our book is repeatable, a mere exemplar of something else. Editions too are in some sense repeatable. This is what a book is. This is what print culture is. Even as I outline these sometimes contradictory possibilities, I can see that the privileged beings in these histories are not those who produced the textual and bibliographical material (book-makers and writers); the privileged beings are bibliographers, particularly contemporary ones, and most specifically ourselves. Book history? It is us.

Yet the singularity of that material book asserts itself. And perhaps this is a way out of the self-reflective circularity of the above paragraphs. The physicality and materiality of the individual book-copy—that must be other than a pure reflection of our thinking. Perhaps our book, selected and seen as the epitome of book culture, print culture, literary culture, or some sort of culture (always in the West) can be seen as something else again: not the epitome of this abstraction of culture (however we define it) but its antithesis, the thing that marks the limits of the abstraction, or perhaps the line in the sand where the abstraction loses force. This object defines our abstractions more rationally in a negative sense. To single out a particular book-copy is to define what such a copy is not. It reveals our abstractions only by insisting in its very materiality that those abstractions do not exist "out there" in the culture or history or series of events we claim to be interested in. Whatever it is, this material object, this book-copy is not "the" abstraction we (or some of us, or some of you) think of when the phrase "print culture" is uttered. The copy does not represent, illustrate, or epitomize print culture or anything else. Even the attributes of its materiality—its weight, its smells, the texture of its leaves—these are things in and of themselves, and no scholar of the twenty-first century would make the mistake of losing them in aesthetic abstractions or, even worse, waxing nostalgic about them. After all, the sensory attributes of the object likely reflect only those of the libraries that house it and the peculiarities of individual sense organs; they cannot be generalized.

As a bibliographer, I hold this book and I try to ignore this wilderness of paradox as well as all its dilettantish aspects, smells, colors, textures. I try to look through this book to other things, even though I cannot look through these books as they were intended to be looked through by their producers, and I do not want to look through them in ways that other scholars insist I should. I ignore what I claim their functions must be. I see through them to other abstractions—the suspect categories of bibliographers, the unwritten articles and notes I might construct—using the book once again only as a mirror to what I might call the internal methods of bibliography, or at least my version of it.

*   *   *

The following study concerns the history of printing as known by bibliography, or rather by my own sense of what bibliography is. How are the histories of printing and bibliography related, and what are the most obvious rifts between the two that I have encountered or created for myself? There are no detailed studies of individual book-copies here because, as I have conceded elsewhere, I have begun to feel that I know exactly what I will say about any book-copy well before I begin to examine it: each will be exceptional, anomalous, and a challenge to the grand abstractions of book history and bibliography.[2]

The chapters below are not designed to offer up a neat and orderly bibliographical argument: there is no narrative arc or subtle progression here. There are rather certain conceptual and verbal details that provide enough formal structure to make this a unit, among them the very covers of the book itself. Because this is an academic book, there is a table of contents, and thus how this book is organized should be clear before you begin. You can thus easily see what the structure of this is before you begin reading it, and you can also see the obvious analogues.

I am not attempting to formulate a thesis or enforce an argument or lead anyone step by step toward a conclusion. Bibliographers are unlikely to change their ways of thinking because of anything I say or discover, whether the apparent subject is Caxton, early printing, analytical bibliography, editing, or theories of representation. I am concerned, thus, largely with the

conventions of what we talk about, not the subjects. Do we really pay anything more than lip service to the presumed but ill defined and always
changing foundations of our talk: evidence, logic, knowledge, history? Or do
we simply adjust these evidentiary matters to conform to our conclusions,
much the way we inadvertently teach our own undergraduates to do in their
papers?

I recently attended a lecture by Nicholas Pickwood, entitled "Unfinished
Business," on incomplete or provisional bindings on early books.[3] These mod-
est bindings (or sewings) hold the book block together as a usable and readable unit, but do not include boards (at least not finished ones); they were
constructed and sold leaving the possibility open for buyers to rebind them in
standard bindings or simply use them "as is." For those of us who at one
point ascribed to the rule of E. Ph. Goldschmidt that early books were sold in
loose sheets and in no other form, the radical nature of this talk and accom-
panying examples was apparent.[4] Yet to others things are different. I brought
with me an extremely bright student, unschooled in the niceties of bibliography, and I neglected to explain to her the scholarly context and history of
Pickwood's argument. To her, the entire talk and discussion seemed elementary, like "Binding 101," she said: surely such provisional bindings were routine, and the notion of their very existence commonsensical. Why, she
asked, and why, I wondered, did Pickwood's examples and conclusions seem
so revolutionary to librarians and bibliographers? Was it because our assimi-
lation of the bibliographical cliché (even when we knew of works refuting it)
made it difficult if not downright impossible for us to see what any intelligent
amateur would see? [5]

Bibliographical Reasons and Bibliographical Reasoning

Bibliographical arguments operate within a closed system with a minimal set
of assumptions, and their circularity is likely ineradicable: there is a finite
set of objects called books, produced by a set of well-recorded procedures to
which a standard language can apply. And reorganizing that language occasionally runs parallel to reorganizing the objects to which it refers.[6] Critical
arguments can of course be advanced that are true, but most of them depend
on other statements: the statement $2 + 2 = 5$ can be critiqued under arithmeti-
cal systems, but an incisive critique is more or less useless if no one has actually advanced such an argument.

There is nothing scandalous or surprising about this. Many bibliographical arguments are mopping up in some sense: a book-copy is mis-described; it has been defined as constituting an edition although it does not meet the minimal standards of "edition-hood"; a major database needs correcting.[7] In my view, it is often more amusing to pursue such individual cases than to leave them alone once things are sorted out. These books are perhaps not anomalies; the systems that define book history and bibliography thus cannot be cleaned up. Exceptions do not "prove the rule," whatever that gnomic banality might mean, and whatever hearers think it means.

Furthermore, the conventionality of language (that gnomic bibliographical language at issue here) is so entrenched that a challenge is likely to do little to unsettle it. Just because scholars cannot explain categorically and convincingly what books or editions are does not mean they will be unable to talk about them, nor have I ever argued that they should stop talking about them, or that they should do so only in hushed, guilt-ridden tones.

In 2003, David McKitterick critiqued the bibliographical language of the New Bibliographers Bowers, McKerrow, and Greg as overly idealized.[8] It promoted, according to McKitterick, a notion of fixity that was not to be found in the real world of printed books, at least, not in the real world of books printed before the age of the "mechanized book," by which I believe he means books printed in the nineteenth century. McKitterick's "fixity" (whatever this word refers to) has become something of a bête noire for book historians (Elizabeth Eisenstein and Adrian Johns are two obvious examples of those who have attacked it). Yet it has a way of coming to life and reestablishing itself on a higher level of abstraction whenever it is presumably put to rest: "If, indeed there is a link between bibliography and social understanding of books, then we need to accommodate bibliographical practice and terminology to the requirements of more ordinary language" (165). I assume this means that bibliographical language needs to be changed to better reflect the social realities or the realities of material books to which it applies, and the way to do this is to adopt an idealized version of "ordinary language," which is somehow better suited to describe these realities. Pushed to an extreme, bibliographical language would be language that perfectly reflects the things of the world, an ideal of language we associate with the seventeenth and eighteenth centuries. I doubt this is how McKitterick would put it, but even in their weakest form, I can't agree with these sentiments. Of course bibliographical language is not the same as history; the term "ideal copy" (a particular target of McKitterick) does not imply anything special about what came out of the printers' house or what printers wanted to come out of their houses.[9] It deals only with descriptions of what came out of the printers' house; and these are two completely different things. There is always a gap between language and reality, and more deservedly characterized as a "will o' the wisp" than any bibliographical term is the idea that we should be shocked when history does not conform to this language. Why should it?

Organization and Subject Matter

This book is in three parts. "What Is Print?" deals with the essences of print as conceived by bibliographers; "On the Making of Lists" consists of three applications of classic bibliographical methodology; the concluding "Ironies of History and Representation," is a view of bibliography as I have experienced it in theme and variation form. The subject matter is of two kinds. Some sections deal in minutiae of bibliography and printing history: cataloguing decisions, the function of the catchtitle. Others deal with more general problems: paleography/typography.

Some of these subjects are central to modern Anglo-American bibliography: McKenzie's "Printers of the Mind" is for many bibliographers an article of faith. Editing methods and methodology have always been prominent in this field as well. To argue that the entire enterprise of what we call Anglo-American bibliography (the tradition from Greg, Bowers, and McKerrow onward) is editorial in nature, as are the principal bibliographical journals in this field (*Studies in Bibliography*, *PBSA*), would not be at all far-fetched. In Chapter 6, I attempt to discuss that facet of bibliography in its most basic and simple form, to move the discussion, say, from editing theory and methodology to the basic process at its core. In other chapters, subjects are those in which most bibliographers will have little investment: the composing stick, two-color printing, illustrations in scholarly articles. The advantage of choosing such subjects lies entirely in that disinterest: scholars can talk about these without worrying about defending or obscuring their methods or flaws in their methods; the consequences of error seem small, and there seem fewer moral dimensions to it, whether the errors are mine or those of scholars I discuss. Pressure. Vagueness about facts. The demands of style. Typographical errors. Conventions of scholarly presses.

In the late nineteenth century, Henry Bradshaw, one of the greatest English bibliographers, announced as a principle of bibliographical scholarship,

"Arrange your facts rigorously and get them plainly before you, and let them speak for themselves, which they will always do." Oddly and unaccountably, this was misread as "vigorously" in the memoir of Bradshaw by G. W. Prothero in 1888, a much more intriguing and subtle principle of scholarship.[10] As a novice bibliographer, I was once ordered to Cambridge University Library to check on this misreading; I said nothing about how much I hate reading old letters, particularly those that resemble familial ones of two generations ago. The archivists had done most of the important work before I got there, and all was relatively easy. There isn't the slightest question about what Bradshaw's letter reads: "rigorously." Of course. Just what you or I would say. And the fact that the error *vigorously* violates the sacred rule of *lectio difficilior*—so piously invoked by editors for more than two centuries—that's a problem for editorial theorists, not for bibliographers. I doubt a scholar like Prothero misread that, stumbling on an infinitely more intriguing bibliographical method than Bradshaw himself had formulated. I blame a typesetter, a careless proofreader. A monkey could thus have thus articulated a more profound bibliographical principle than Bradshaw did. I don't know what the consequences of such thinking might be.

Part II of this study is a practical tribute to what Bradshaw said, whatever it was he said, or whatever he is said to say. The chapters do not speak to the validity of his methodology in and of itself; by practical I mean only "how useful is Bradshaw's method in the hands of an ordinary scholar or a garden-variety bibliographer like myself?" And what sort of intellectual shenanigans (the perfect word for it) are required to make this method work? It is from the principles tested in Chapters 4–6 that the essays in Part I and the variations in Part III develop.

PART I

What Is Print?

CHAPTER I

Paleography Versus Typography

"Black-Letter Antiquity"

In 2011, in an introductory section entitled "No Leaners," I made a simple observation regarding the distinction between type and script. However we define type, it is distinguished from script by the discrete nature of the typecase: a typesort either is or is not in a type compartment of a typecase; a typefont has a finite and identifiable number of letterforms.[1] In this chapter, I will consider that in terms of the descriptive language used to apply to each field. To what extent does the language of typography exploit this distinction? And does the essential difference between the objects of description find an analogue in the language used to describe them?

I begin with Thomas Frognall Dibdin's introductory comments in *Typographical Antiquities*:

> Both Herbert and Rowe Mores appear to have been incorrect in supposing [de Worde] to have introduced the Roman letter into this country; as the honour of that tasteful mode of printing is first claimed by his contemporary Pynson. His Gothic type has been called, by the latter authority, "the pattern for his successors in the art. As to his being his own type-founder (the same writer observes) Mr. Palmer and Mr. Psalmanaazar give us a circumstance which induced them to think that he was his own letterfounder. We have no doubt but he was; yet we cannot own their reasoning convinces us of it" [quoting Mores, *Of English Founders and Founderies*, 4–5] . . . The type, which he used for the generality

of his books, has less resemblance to a foreign form than some of Pynson's: although it is evident that both Pynson and himself used the same form of letter in the greater number of their publications.[2]

Dibdin's comments, characteristically Dibdinesque yet perfectly intelligible both to his contemporaries and to modern bibliographers, assume a binary system of type, gothic/roman, a system reflecting the language of eighteenth-century type-specimen sheets and catalogues.

What blackletter opposes in these binary systems is, however, inconsistent. In type specimens, it distinguishes a specific typeface (generally called "English") from others, such as roman, italic, or even "gothick." In the casual language of printers, it opposes "the white" (that is, roman and italic).[3] For Dibdin, blackletter is more than a family of type. It is an icon of the past: his Advertisement to *Typographical Antiquities* speaks of a group of his readers as "resolute lovers of black-letter antiquity," a curious phase that seems to oppose "classical" to "antique" (however that might be imagined).

The oldest printed books do not and cannot exhibit this neat binary system. Until roman fonts became widely used, the very notion of blackletter type was impossible. And what we now call "semi-gothic," or "fere humanistica," that transitional type between the two basic classes we recognize, of course could not be recognized until the two main categories were established. Furthermore, distinctions that did exist in early type are obscured here: the slanted vernacular "bastarda" and the squarish "textura," so clearly in our view opposed, are subsumed under blackletter in this system; in most abstract typographical classification systems, they are considered different families. By the time roman type becomes reasonably well defined, its relation to such categories of type is less clear than Dibdin's language implies.

The most common categories of typeforms are not always pure: upper-case forms from one font can be used in another, and italic does not even have a coherent set of upper-case letters; typecases mix sorts from different families. The relation of fonts to each other is not symmetrical, and the fonts themselves are not comparable. Those attempts to apply traditional biological classification to these categories (with *classes* referring to the opposition of gothic/roman/italic, and *families* to categories within gothic) fail, since there are no coherent and easily distinguishable *orders* within any family but gothic.

The Language of Type Classification in Twentieth-Century English Typography

The most bibliographically significant attempts to classify early type (that is, type manufactured before the self-conscious standardization found in type-specimen catalogues) are by incunabulists of the late nineteenth and early twentieth centuries. Early incunabulists combined two systems based on different orders of criteria. The first is purely quantitative, based on measurement: how many mm per twenty lines (for manuscripts, this number is a codicological matter, that is, a function of format, not handwriting). The second is an abstract method of classification into broad categories that reflect or are defined by cultural and aesthetic factors: roman, italic, gothic, rotunda, semi-gothic.[4] The differences between these terms are not quantifiable, nor are the main categories on the same plane: rotunda, for example, is a form of gothic, roman opposes gothic. And of course there is no meaningful relationship among the types classed together by measurement, the one feature of these descriptions that was unique to typography.

Yet both incunabulists (those identifying typefonts for various cataloguing projects) and printing historians such as A. J. Johnson, Daniel Updike, and R. B. McKerrow maintained an allegiance to paleographical categories in the description of early type (the terms gothic, rotunda, fere-humanistica as opposed to purely typographical categories, such as Garamond, Caslon, Baskerville), even when that language was of minimal use in classifying typeforms and the boundaries particularly porous.[5]

Updike uses the neutral term "type-forms" and defines "three great classes" as what paleographers consider a formal hierarchy: "the formal, to which in type our capital letter answers; the less formal, to which our lowercase type is equivalent; and the epistolary or cursive, which is now rendered into type called 'italic'" (*Printing Types*, 1:57). That leaves for fifteenth-century type only "two classes": "Gothic (a corrupt national following of the Carolingian minuscule) . . . and Roman (a fairly faithful return to the Carolingian minuscule)" (1:59). The three "type-forms" within gothic repeat the variation of Updike's great formal classes: lettre de forme, lettre de somme, and lettre bâtarde. The nature of these forms depends on the nation (in Germany lettre de forme becomes Fraktur; bâtarde becomes Schwabacher): "These three type-forms were the black-letter equivalents of the formal, less formal, and cursive manuscript-hands of the Roman period" (1:60). Roman is divided more simply into "pure" and "transitional."[6]

Robert Proctor, whose identifications of fonts are basic to the modern study of fifteenth-century books, identifies type primarily by measurement; his vocabulary of typefaces is more descriptive than classificatory: square Church, ordinary German type, round text gothic, heading, very small gothic, curious roman, french text, rather large, of quite unrivalled beauty. BMC systematizes these descriptions: G (Gothic); GR (gotico-roman); B (bastard), R (roman). Johnson's categories are similar: textura (type used in the Gutenberg Bible); fere-humanistica (= gotico-antiqua); bastarda, and a fourth type "the Bolognese letter" or rotunda.[7]

All these classifications show the strain of national typeforms, or rather, the difficulty of combining two different criteria, one purely formal, the other cultural or historical. Fraktur is a national form, not generally found outside Germany; bâtarde (in the usual sense) is not found in Italy or Germany. Thus, there is no need to develop a universal classification of type that takes such forms into account: that is, someone within history (a fifteenth-century reader) does not need an intellectual or linguistic category that can distinguish, say, Fraktur from bâtarde, because that distinction is never encountered. The only person who might need to distinguish these is an international dealer in type, defying contemporary cultural boundaries, or, in the twentieth or twenty-first century, a typographer or bibliographer or teacher of these subjects. Classifications that attempt to place Fraktur or Schwabacher within a scheme that includes, say, italic and bastarda, have more to do with modern reception than with the early history of type.[8]

Paleography

Those of us for whom letterforms and classifications are anything but second nature find the taxonomies of paleography from which the basic categories of type are derived much more difficult. The very foundation of this classificatory language seems built on error: the humanists imagined that the Carolingian script they found in manuscripts of the classics was Roman; they reproduced it so skillfully that for many of us manuscript fragments in such script bound into early books might be dated hundreds of years apart.[9] Within this erroneous history, the central term *gothic* developed, not as a formal term but as a cultural one. Gothic was "other" than the scripts and variants imitated by and developed by the humanists.

In the mid-twentieth century, G. I. Lieftinck developed a system whereby the impressionistic differences distinguishing types of hands could be described objectively.[10] Lieftinck's system is based on two orders or measures of classification; as with typography, one is objective, the other cultural or impressionistic. Textualis, cursiva, bastarda (all book hands) are based on objective criteria: three letter forms: *a* (one or two stories), ascenders (with or without loops), *f* and long-*s* (with or without a tail).[11] The impressionistic order involves "levels of execution": formata, textualis (= libraria or media in later systems), currens. There are no objective criteria for this second set of distinctions. The language (as in much typographical language) is often equivocal: textualis (a formal category, describing script equivalent to what typographers call lettre de forme) reappears as a second order of execution (lower than formata). The obvious relation of currens to cursive again blurs formal categories with formal levels. Lieftinck's bastarda or hybrida (see his n21) implies a mixture, but this mixture has to do with origins, not forms. What is ordinarily described as bâtarde is something else.[12] In addition, many common scripts cannot be described in these categories, and are considered "hors-système" scripts—anglicana and various forms of semi-gothic or fere humanistica.[13]

In this system, there is a divorce of terminology (nomenclature) from the categories to which that terminology applies. A "universal terminology" is not the same as a "universal system of handwriting," and the meaning of these terms can change as the cultures to which they apply change. Lieftinck promotes a nomenclature that will be useful in distinguishing and describing scripts that develop historically and exist at different periods. Thus, say, in 1400, there will be a hierarchy of scripts that can be described as formata, textualis, currens, and at the same time, categories or classes of scripts that could be distinguished through the terms textualis, cursiva, bastarda. But the distinguishing characteristics might not be the same in all periods. It is thus designed as a means for those who already know the history of these scripts to communicate with others who also know that history: a "base internationale" (31) allowing paleographers to talk to each other.[14]

Among the paradoxes of these systems of classification and the problems they pose for typographers are those involved in the terms hybrid and bastarda.

The words imply impurity. But as a typographical category, bastarda seems reasonably well delineated: there is no blurring of a bastarda type with roman, no "semi-bastarda," "bastarda-formata," "bastarda-anglicana-formata," "bastarda-italica." It remains linked to its origins in Burgundian culture, and it is that aristocratic allusion that is maintained when it appears in Caxton's early books. By the early sixteenth century, the conceptual category bastarda seemed to have no function for English book producers. However distinct it may be, it is functionally the same as textura.[15] The same can be said of rotunda, or what is paleographically a form of "southern textualis." Typographers use this term for a completely unrelated type: a small, round type based on thirteenth-century scholastic manuscripts. Gotico-antiqua is certainly useful as a typographical term, but it refers to wide variety of scripts and forms classified together more on the basis of terminology than history.

When seen against the background, not of handwriting, but of paleographical nomenclature, printing seems to develop at the most inconvenient time, when what paleographers following Lieftinck refer to as "hors-système" scripts (fere humanistica) are most popular.[16] When these scripts become typeforms, they are inconsistently related to others for purely technical reasons. Within certain aesthetic bounds, scribes can vary the size of their scripts at will to conform to the format of the page they write on, just as they can vary script styles;[17] typesetters can do neither of these things. Thus in many books, a particular typefont will be opposed to another strictly in terms of size; differences in family are secondary or in some cases irrelevant. A typesetter is limited to what is in the printing house, where it is not economically feasible to represent all families by all sizes. The symmetries of our language of type classification thus cannot reproduce the material and economic realities of the typecases available in different printing shops.

The Depiction of Type: Typesort and Array

Theoretically, type is contained in a typecase, with each compartment holding interchangeable typesorts. But while typesorts may be indistinguishable, as material objects they are never identical, any more than two hand-drawn letters would be. Nineteenth-century typographers attempted to illustrate what they considered a typefont through the type array, a chart that showed both typical sorts (however imagined) and variant sorts. Figure 1 is a conventional array, showing the sorts used in Caxton's Type 2 and its variant 2*.

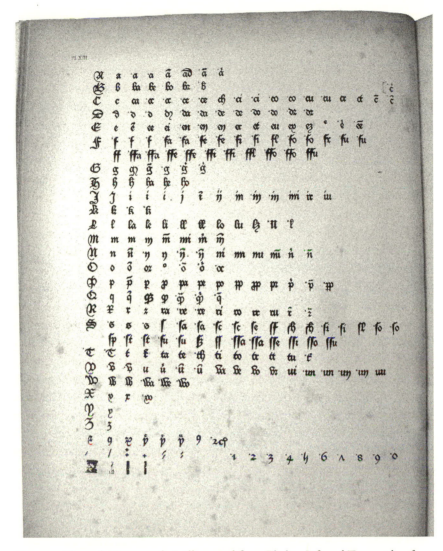

Figure 1. Caxton's Type 2 and 2*, illustrated from Blades, *Life and Typography of William Caxton*, Pl. XIII. Photo courtesy of the William Andrews Clark Memorial Library, University of California, Los Angeles.

Such arrays were a staple of scholarship on early printing at the turn of the last century, particularly in the works on early type produced by the Gutenberg Gesellschaft.[18] They illustrated and in certain cases defined typefonts, which incunabulists such as Henry Bradshaw considered the basic units of the history of printing. There are obvious problems with such an array, whether it is of type (where a single impression stands for an entire compartment of typesorts) or of a paleographical hand (where individual letters are shown isolated from their contexts). What is the technology of reproduction? What makes a particular impression typical? Is that impression considered by the printer to be typical? These questions lead to the more basic question: what exactly does the type array illustrate or depict? And what is the history that such an array implies?

Defending these arrays, we might claim that the historical narratives they imply are merely intellectual constructs superimposed on the chronological past (whatever that is), and that such narratives do not claim to represent anything historical: a typographical array is nothing more than a convenient shorthand, comparable to what a paleographer might use in constructing or selecting examples of the letterforms that constitute a particular script.[19] But this is certainly not the way nineteenth- and early twentieth-century bibliographers felt about this. These bibliographers were not creating artificial structures or shorthand definitions in such arrays, but rather, in Bradshaw's words, arranging facts. Their arrays are based on many unstated assumptions, and the incorporation of different forms of those assumptions undermines what the arrays are intended to represent.

Some of the most basic of typographical terminology (typefont, typecase, typesort) corresponds to an imagined or reconstructed version of the manufacturing process. In the classic description by Moxon in 1683, an artist designs a type and cuts that alphabetical set on punches.[20] These punches (patrices) are then struck into matrices. Each matrix is fitted into an adjustable hand-mold, and individual typesorts are produced from that (these typesorts are identical in the sense that they are stored in the same box of the typecase and the printer considers them interchangeable). Typographical categories respond to stages in this process:

(1) At the highest end, a type family or style (italic, roman, Caslon). Each letter in an alphabet is a member of a stylistic unit. This corresponds to the material set of punches, and would constitute a *typeface* or even *type family*.

(2) The set of letters determined by the matrices (meaning a trimmed and justified matrix). To most bibliographers, a set of these matrices is what is meant by a *typefont*. But the same set of matrices can produce two clearly distinct typefonts of different measurements.

(3) The set of physical pieces of type held and sold as a unit in a particular material case. This would be known as a *typecase*.[21]

Yet even the most scrupulous bibliographers will blur the distinctions, not due to carelessness but because the issues discussed move from one level to another. In addition, the nature of the evidence does not permit hard and fast distinctions here. The evidence for all such levels is the same: books, or reproductions of books, and the appearance of type on printed pages. The different levels and material units responding to those levels have to be abstracted from these physical type impressions. It is unreasonable to insist on a "typefont = matrix" equation, or "typecase = physical set of type" when there is not a single example of a physical matrix or physical typesort that can be associated with the type impressions of a particular book printed before 1600.

As if to finesse these problems, bibliographers use the word *type*. *Type* can refer to a material typecase (or imagined one), individual typesorts, the impressions made by these, the abstract notion of these impressions, a typefont, a class or family of type, any and all of these things, and at times it is impossible to construct a bibliographically coherent sentence without allowing for such slippage. But this linguistic slippage becomes implicated in the evidence. What is it that a type array really represents?

The type arrays of William Blades for Caxton (shown in Figure 1) or Gottfried Zedler for Gutenberg identify and illustrate all distinguishable typesorts in a font or case. The objects of these images are perhaps most accurately, albeit somewhat tortuously, described as "typesort types," since it is not always clear how many individual pieces of type (typesorts) might be indicated by the illustrated impression and could thus be classified as "the same" and in some way "distinct from" others in the same type compartment of a typecase. Furthermore, in the array, impressions with distinctive features that might enable them to be regarded as products of an individual and identifiable sort (I'll call it a "rogue sort") are depicted side by side with impressions or images that represent multiple sorts or a typical sort. This is related to, but not I think dependent on, the technical means of illustration, that is, whether the images in an array are produced by hand, by tracings, or photographically.[22]

Depending on how the type array is produced, the illustrated impressions are either generalizable or generalized in their very construction. What is indistinguishable is regarded as "the same"; differences that might be perceived but cannot be described or represented are also considered "the same," and the individual sorts of the type compartment become indistinguishable from the matrix that presumably produced them.

To argue for a historical (actual) relation of the variant to objective reality is to postulate a particular (likely accidental) setting of a matrix in a mold that produced one or possibly a set of variants with a distinctive and identifying characteristic visible in the impressions on a printed page. When Zedler reproduces the impression of such a sort, he is claiming it has characteristics that we can perceive but to which the printers themselves were indifferent, and further that all those letter sorts (producing the standard type impression and the variant) were produced by the same matrix at roughly the same time in the type foundry. I believe this is what is meant by a type variant, but the array often places these identifiable variants together: the differences between accidental impressions, accidental sorts, and standard impressions (what the printer intends) are not always made clear. The type array removes the context in which these impressions appear, and that context is the basis for evaluating them. What it displays, then, is not what occurred in history (its presumed object), but rather what can be perceived by someone examining that history. And what can be perceived is conditioned by all the preconceptions quantifiable evidence is supposed to eliminate.

Removal of Clutter

When navigators look at a radar screen, what they see is neither what is "out there," nor what is on a two-dimensional conventional navigational chart. What is on the screen is "something like" what is on the navigational chart, just as what is on the navigational chart is "something like" what exists in reality. Amateur navigators who grew up with conventional charts reduce the radar blips to the distorted version of reality found in these charts and sail accordingly. I am not certain what the next generation of navigators will do, but I suspect they too will translate these screens, not into reality, but into other screens, say, those that represent the contours of the depths they sail over. What remains after these translations can be significant. A blip may be formed by another boat moving into your path. Or it can be what is called clutter, equally real but of no navigational importance; clutter might be a simple electronic glitch on the screen, or the real but inconsequential foam blown off the top of a wave. It is important to understand these differences, to know which differences are important, and to act on what you think or assume you know.

Bibliographical clutter exists in the same way, but because it has few real-world consequences (no bibliographer has ever suffered bodily harm due to even the most egregious of errors), its definition and removal have more to do with the nature of the field than what that field is supposed to accomplish: defining clutter is a case of *petitio principii*. What a radar screen does for the navigator has little to do with the theory or operating principles of radar. But in bibliography, the definition of clutter defines a problem and reinforces assumptions that might well be in question.

When G. I. F. Tupper represented a typesort in an array for William Blades's work on Caxton, he selected what he considered a typical sort and idealized it, either through isolating it in the array, or physically cleaning up some of the defects of the impression.[23] But all these actions reinforced his assumptions concerning the existence of typical sorts. Sorts were products of matrices, and most achieved the typecaster's ideal of indistinguishability, just as the book-copies of an edition reproduced the printer's ideal of indistin-guishable copies. All we can perceive in a type array is an expression of what we (or the creator of the array) know already. Yet what is a much more diffi-cult and important task is to perceive or express things we do not know.

Caxton 2 Versus Caxton 2*: The Meaning of "Variant"

The word *recast* is often used in typographical studies and can refer to a num-ber of different things. To make the most logical sense, it should be used of a particular situation: a printer or typefounder owns a set of matrices that potentially constitutes a font. Those matrices are used in a hand-mold to pro-duce what bibliographers would describe as "font 1" or "typecase of font 1." They are then reused with a different mold or with different settings on the same mold to produce another typecase (or font) that is distinguishable in some way from the first: the 20-line measurement of the second casting may be different from the first, some matrices may be remade, or new letterforms added. What makes the two fonts variants or the product of a recasting in the bibliographical sense is the assumption or implication that there is some material continuity from one to the other (the same matrices? or punches? are used). But of course for early printing, there are no records of such an event taking place, no extant matrices associated with known typefonts, no descriptions of such a process taking place for any known typefont. The evidence consists of variations in the type impressions we see in books. While our word *recasting* seems to be the hypothesizing of an historical event, it is more accurately a metaphor that describes our analysis or perception of evidence, referring to the differences we perceive in the appearance of type impressions in two or more books.

The most important systematic and detailed study of Caxton types was Blades's two-volume *Life and Typography of Caxton* (1861) with facsimiles by Tupper, but the verbal descriptions by Blades and pictorial descriptions by Tupper (his facsimiles and imitations) are often at odds. Blades numbered Caxton's fonts sequentially to conform to their first appearance in books, and these numbers are now conventional: Type 1 is that used in the French *Recueil*; Type 2 is a bastarda type used in several books from 1476 to 1479, including the first edition of the *Canterbury Tales*; Types 3 and 5 are textura types; Type 4 is another bastarda, very similar in style to Type 2.[24] Two of these fonts show systematic variant sorts or forms, and Blades thus defined the variant fonts: 2* (a variant of 2) and 4* (a variant of 4).

Blades and Tupper did not make use of photography, even though it was available to them. Tupper made two kinds of plates, which he characterizes as "facsimiles" and "imitations." Facsimiles were made by tracing the images of typesorts; that is, the final image resulted from physical contact at each stage of production—page to tracing, tracing to final image on the plate. Imitations by contrast were idealizations, drawn freehand and subsequently cut into woodblocks.[25] Tupper's "facsimiles" show type impressions warts and all, including inking variations, even stray quads. His "imitations" are cleaned up; they reproduce what is imagined to exist in Caxton's mind or the mind of his typefounder. They are thus equivalent to the descriptive bibliographer's "ideal copy," the idealized standard against which all real exemplars of that edition can be compared. I believe, although neither Blades nor Tupper states this directly, that the type arrays are examples of what Tupper labels "facsimiles"; that is, they are made by tracings of individual letters, which are in turn taken from their contexts and arranged in a table.[26]

Blades's Plate XIII ("An Alphabet of Types Nos. 2 and 2*") shows 296 sorts, a number unsettlingly close to the number conventionally given for Gutenberg's B42 type (the type used in the Gutenberg Bible).[27] Although it is by no means obvious on looking at Blades's table, and barely visible at all in any reproduction (even commercial ones), it contains three kinds of characters: sorts marked [2] (=font 2); sorts marked * (=font 2*) and unmarked sorts (sorts presumably found in both font 2 and 2* (total = 296 plus 4 quads). To get at the ambiguity of this table I will say: the table thus serves as an illustration of two separate fonts although it may not actually illustrate those two fonts.

Blades distinguishes the two fonts of this "dashing, picturesque, and elaborate character" as follows:

> The general appearance of Type No. 2 is very different from that of No. 2*, many letters in the former having a bolder and thicker face than in the latter; and the fact of there being a perfect division of the books into two distinct classes prevents our attributing this differ-ence to either wear of type or faulty printing. The former of which would be gradual, the latter irregular. (2:xxxi)

He notes here *k* without loop, double *l* without loops, and sorts for *th wa we wo*—all associated with 2* only, and all easily seen by comparing pages of books printed in these fonts. These new sorts are the result of new matrices.[28] But the difference between the two fonts, according to Blades, is not simply the addition of new typesorts:

> the remainder, although often very nearly alike, so constantly pre-serve some peculiar slight characteristic in each section (which could not have been satisfactorily shown by single examples in the plate), that a minute examination of numerous instances, . . . leads to the conclusion that not any of the letters of the first section are abso-lutely identical with those of the second. (2:xxxii)

This states explicitly that the impressions of each typesort in one font are dis-tinguishable from those of the comparable typesort in the other font, even though these real differences cannot be represented visually. There is serious ambiguity in this formulation. The principle of "absolute identity" is not a principle at all, since no two type impressions or two entities of any kind can be "absolutely identical" with anything else. And if a "peculiar slight charac-teristic" is "constantly" preserved in each sort, I cannot see why that charac-teristic cannot be defined verbally and represented through an image (or series of images).

More important, it is not at all clear that Blades's facsimilist Tupper agrees with him. If none of the sorts are "absolutely identical" in the two fonts, the array (Plate XIII) is inaccurate or misleading, since it shows three kinds of sorts: those unique to 2, those unique to 2*, and sorts common to both fonts or whose variant forms are indistinguishable (Tupper does not identify which books serve as the source for these). The implication of the array is that some sorts in font 2 are the same as or indistinguishable from the sorts in font 2*, whether they are materially the same or the result of a recasting. If Blades is right that none of the sort-forms or letterforms in 2 are "absolutely identical" with their counterparts in 2*, there should be two separate and complete arrays, difficult though it may be to distinguish individual sorts in those arrays. And this is what Blades claims elsewhere: the complete font 2 contains 217 sorts; the complete 2*, 254 sorts.[29] This statement, requiring 471 distinguishable sorts, is contradicted by Tupper's array, which shows only 296.

Blades's description implies that the entire font was recast with a different set of matrices, that is, matrices that were materially distinct from the matrices of the original set, or matrices that were modified in some way (some of these matrices may have produced sorts indistinguishable from those produced by the first set of matrices). What Tupper's array implies is that the sorts marked [2] were removed (completely) from the typecase when the sorts marked * were introduced. Maybe the others were recast and maybe Blades could distinguish them, but Tupper could not.[30]

The most striking part of Blades's history, and one that seems to have overshadowed the contradictions between Blades and his facsimilist, is his suggestion that the new matrices were formed not from the old punches from type 2 but from the actual typesorts of 2. Caxton's 2* was "cast from matrices formed by the use of old casts of Type No. 2 as punches, after being trimmed by hand" (2:xxxv) (Blades's word "casts" refers to physical typesorts): "we find the conclusion inevitable that hard-metal punches were not used, and that even types themselves were used either as punches, or in some analogous way for the production of new founts" (2: xxv).[31]

The history, coherent as it seems, requires us to imagine that old sorts from Type 2 were good enough to be used as punches but not as type.[32] And although taking Blades's statements in their strongest sense makes the implications of his argument stand out most clearly, his phrase "or in some analogous way" shows he has reservations about this.

What Blades says about the analogous variants in Types 4 and 4* brings up further problems:

> Types No. 4 and 4* may be spoken of generally as *one*, there being the same intimate connection between them as between Nos. 2 and 2*; unlike them, however, there is a slight variation in the body, Type No. 4 being, as compared with the re-casting of it, or Type No. 4*, as 20 is to 19. . . . As is shown in the chapter on typefounding, the moulds and matrices as now used were unknown in those days. . . . Type No. 2* was, as already shown, cast from matrices formed by the use of old casts of Type No. 2 as punches, after being trimmed by hand. But for both Nos. 4 and 4* there is the strongest evidence of the same punches having been used. . . . The variation . . . is simply a fact. (2: xxxv)

Note that an array does not illustrate the "body" (height of cast letter). Therefore, according to this statement, the two types in their isolated impressions would be indistinguishable. Yet Tupper's Plate XVIII illustrating Types 4 and 4* is similar to Plate XIII illustrating Types 2 and 2*: it distinguishes three groups: sorts unique to 4, sorts unique to 4*, and sorts that presumably appear in both fonts (215 sorts, plus 6 quads).[33] Again, Blades's explicit statements and descriptions are at odds with the implications of these arrays.

In 1976, George Painter, in his biography of Caxton, returned to the question of variant fonts and derided Blades's theory as unworthy of consideration. "Blades had the preposterous notion that Caxton cast the new state himself, using the old type as punches to strike the matrices" (*Caxton: A Quincentenary Biography*, 95). Painter calls these variant fonts "states," and his notes imply that some physical sorts appear in both states (95 n3, upper-case *A*; he gives no examples of lower-case letters).[34] Painter may well be right, but he does not detail here or in his work with BMC why he believed Blades's theory to be "preposterous." He does not state whether he takes Blades's statements in their strongest sense or acknowledges the phrase "in some analogous way." He does not identify the evidence, however obvious it may be, or even the nature of the evidence that contradicts either the strong or weak version of Blades's theory.[35]

I assume Painter's dismissal of Blades is based on the assumption that the procedures for casting type in the fifteenth century were roughly those used in the seventeenth century, an assumption to which nineteenth-century bibliographers were not as committed as bibliographers in the early twentieth century and one Blades occasionally explicitly denied: "the moulds and matrices as now used were unknown in those days" (*Life and Typography of Caxton*, xxxv). Under these procedures, the hypothesized production of type is reflected in the categories of typographical terminology noted above. A typefounder cuts a piece of type in hard metal (a punch); this strikes a matrix in softer metal (copper), which in turn is the basis for casting type in even softer metal (lead/tin). Under this model of typefounding, Blades's notion is indeed not worthy of consideration, since it reverses the process: something in softer metal (typesort) is used to produce a matrix in a harder metal. If we do not accept that model, then Blades may well be wrong still, but more reasoning may be necessary to refute him.[36]

What could be called the traditional method of typefounding (the one described in typefounding manuals as early as the seventeenth century) was not accepted in the nineteenth century as an explanation for the earliest type, even though it was the most obvious way of interpreting the evidence. The hardening of views on typographical production (as shown in Painter's statement) is related to and may even be a product of the identification and classification of fifteenth-century books based on their typefonts. The association of books with printers proceeded most efficiently if one assumed as a guiding principle the association of a particular identifiable typefont with a single printer.[37] The autonomy and integrity of the typefont was essential to this work. Mixed or problematic typefonts made identification of printers difficult, as did notions of borrowed typefonts, recast typefonts, or anything of the kind. And typefonts recast with old typesorts? There is simply no room for such histories.

Blades Redivivus: BMC XI

The most important recent discussion of Caxton is in the latest volume of BMC XI: *England*. Lotte Hellinga accepts the distinction of Blades; there are two fonts, 2 and 2*.

> *Caxton Type 2*: A recasting of the type with the same measurement, appeared in 1479 in the Cordiale, Duff 109. In the recasting, designated as Type 2*: 135B, a number of new sorts are introduced: ligatures *th wa we wo*, plain *ll*, hooked *k*[2] as an alternative to looped *k 1*.

Capitals and 2 of Type 3 are found admixed. Double-bowled *a*, wide R^2 and flourished I^2 are now used more frequently. (BMC XI, 352)[38]

The same language is used for the difference between 4 and 4*:

Type 4*: Type 4 was recast on a larger body in 1483 or perhaps at the end of 1482; following conventions it is designated as Type 4*: 95(100)B.

The recast state can be distinguished not only by its taller measurement but also by the capital A that in the recast lost its hairline, which was not always visible in the first casting of the type.

There is some ambiguity to this formulation. But I believe it implies there are two separate castings of the type, exactly what Painter implies, even though some of the details in Painter's discussion contradict that. If this were done according to traditional methods, we would assume the two fonts were cast with the same (or identical) type mold with the same settings and the same matrices. In other words, the impressions made by the two sets of typesorts are indistinguishable except for "a number of new sorts introduced."[39]

Hellinga's description points out a basic problem with Blades's discussion. If Hellinga's description of the two fonts is correct (and likely what Blades himself believed, despite what he actually said), then certain statements by Blades are incorrect, for example, his reference to the "delicate features" of 2*. The "general appearance" of 2 is different from that of 2* not because all sorts are slightly different (which is what Blades seems to say), but rather because some of them are.[40]

To assume recasting in a traditional sense (I assume this is what Painter and Hellinga believe) raises a number of questions regarding Blades's observations. Is Hellinga denying Blades's explicit claim that the two fonts are distinguishable in each instance? Or does "general appearance" mean only that the introduction of new sorts changes the "general appearance" of a typeset page? Was the use of different metals somehow responsible for the "lighter" appearance? Were there changes in the matrices? Were the same punches used for different matrices? Was it possible to recut punches, reconstruct matrices, recast type, and still produce a typecase of the exact same vertical measurement of the first? If the new casting were done on the Continent, why would the 20-line measurement have been maintained in the case of 2 and 2* and not in the case of 4*? And why are the two fonts not "admixed"?[41]

One of the problems in BMC's discussion is that the bibliographical term *type* seems disembodied or abstracted from the material processes of type manufacture, even though the object of discussion often is the material history of typefounders, typecutters, their geographical locations, and the physical things they owned. Note in the following passages, concerning the history of Caxton's Type 3, how the word "type" and the pronouns seemingly referring to this word are equivocal and often have quite different real-world referents.

> It [Type 3] was undoubtedly designed in conjunction with Caxton's Type 2 . . . for several years Caxton was its sole user . . . He may even have acquired it in the first place for liturgical printing. . . . Caxton must have owned matrices of the type, but its ownership was not exclusive to him. (BMC XI, 337)

What is "designed" is a typeface. But what Caxton "acquires" and "owns" are matrices in which that design is embodied. These physical things, like punches or typesorts, can be owned; type (the abstraction) cannot.

> In 1484 Veldener himself began to use it in Louvain and it is undoubtedly through him that it was obtained in the same year by another printer in Louvain, who from then on used it regularly as a title type.

Design? Typesorts?

> In 1481 Caxton may have leased or lent matrices to Johannes Lettou when he was working for William Wilcock, and it continued to appear in books printed by him in partnership with William de Machlinia . . . probably in two separate castings; however, the possibility that the London printers obtained it directly from Veldener cannot be excluded.

> In *Fifteenth-Century Printing Types*, Hellinga states, I think categorically, that Veldener did not even use punches. Therefore, ownership can only involve sorts and matrices.

> Whatever the meaning of Veldener's pronouncements about typecutting, from the way in which he could develop his fount and

could vary it, and from the sheer quantity of his production in these years, the conclusion must be drawn that Veldener did not cut punches, but that he made his matrices by engraving. (1: 21n2)[42]

Such formulations run into difficulties. See the discussion on Veldener's "conversion of Type 1 to Type 3":

> What we see happening in Cologne is the modification of a type over a number of years by means of a series of small changes. Some sorts were replaced by others; variants, especially capitals, were added; and later on the number of variant sorts, capitals as well as lower case, was reduced by the elimination of those used to begin with. These last may, however, reappear if the compositor happens to be short of a particular letter. (1:18)[43]

But this discussion has its own attendant difficulties: how could the sorts be replaced gradually unless in the same typecase, and does this imply that a compositor deliberately chose (with each selection) only new sorts, until exhausting each compartment?

Decades of type analysis seem to have returned the question to the same ambiguous state it enjoyed when Blades and Tupper began to define the problem a century and a half ago.

Conclusion

Tupper's type arrays do not portray the facts Blades claims to perceive. These facts are produced through a history we do not know, and likely not by the processes described two centuries later in Moxon's *Mechanick Exercises*. When Moxon's language is used to describe early type production history, problems in the fit of language and history quickly emerge. A logical and elegant narrative can be applied to verbal descriptions of evidence, but that narrative is not necessarily consistent with the visual presentations of evidence.

The final answer is that I have no answer. I still do not know how Type 2* replaces Type 2, even though I agree with all Caxtonians that Caxton's books in these two types can be arranged, according to the principles of Robert Proctor, showing that bibliographically, this (whatever "this" means) did occur. I think I know one scholar who could explain this to me. If there are more of you, please identify yourselves.

Excursus 1: J. P. Gumbert: "Toward a Cartesian Nomenclature"

In 1976, J. P. Gumbert responded to criticisms of Lieftinck's classifications of letterforms.[44] The dispute cited by Gumbert as eliciting his article is a simple one: Lieftinck's paleographical classifications had been criticized because his nomenclature, it was claimed, is a matter of words, not of things; what is needed is an understanding of the things (the historical realities) to which the words apply.

Gumbert begins with the three characteristics used by Lieftinck to distinguish "categories" of hands or scripts:

single story *a* / two-story *a*
looped ascenders / unlooped ascenders
f/s feet / *f/s* extend below line

These define three categories (textualis, hybrida, cursive), which are combined with a hierarchy of formalism: formata, textualis, currens. Gumbert does not address problems in the words themselves (the use of the same term to represent both a category and a level of formalism, as noted above), but rather tries to show how the formal taxonomy can be used historically. To do this, he constructs a Cartesian diagram in three dimensions, the maximum we can visualize in space and thus the maximum we can at least imagine we can represent on a two-dimensional page surface (see Figure 2). Each axis is defined according to one of the features defined by Lieftinck: *a*-form for the *x*-axis; ascender-forms for the *y*-axis; *f/s* forms for the *z*-axis. Each real script can then be analyzed in terms of the three-dimensional grid, plotting its characteristics on each of the three axes.

Gumbert's analysis does not produce a name for each script, nor is that of any particular importance. The emphasis, thus, is on the apparent things, not the names for them. Nor, importantly, is the interest in single scripts. What his grid is intended to show is how historical scripts evolve. Plotting a number of fifteenth-century Dutch scripts, for example, will produce clusters on the diagrams indicating the change scripts undergo over a hundred years. Contemporaneous German scripts will form different clusters. The purpose

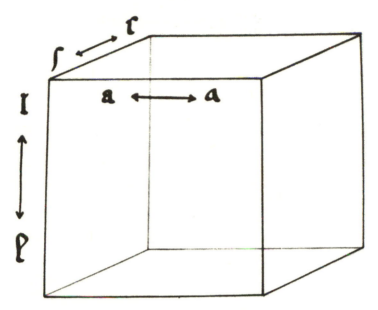

Figure 2. Gumbert, "Proposal," Figure 1.

of the nomenclature, then, is not to provide names for things but to illustrate the way things change through history.

There are a number of basic problems with this grid. (1) A paleographer knows before plotting the location of particular scripts most of the answers that might be sought, that is, the location and date of a particular script. (2) Gumbert never explains in detail how to plot each feature, for instance, an *a* of a particular script. Is a hand that mixes single- and two-story *a* (certainly a possibility if Gumbert's scheme were to be transferred from script to printing) to be classified on the same point of the *x*-axis as one that shows remnants of a two-story *a* in a single-story form? Gumbert's short article gives no examples here, although practically, this was clearly an issue he dealt with constantly. (3) Plotting a particular script in three dimensions and representing the results in two dimensions is not as straightforward as it seems. Note that, in Gumbert's own figures reproduced here, a point on the two-dimensional page surface can represent many points (an infinite number, I think) on the three-dimensional grid represented here. (4) Most important, the diagrams Gumbert prints in his article undergo a radical transformation from the simple, language-oriented (Cartesian?) grid (Figure 2 above) to what I'll call the historical grid (Figure 3). The transformation from formal

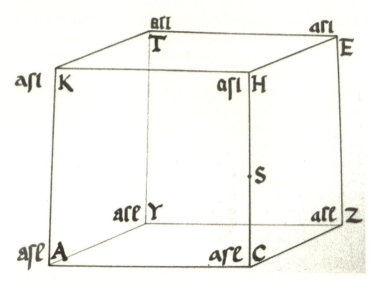

Figure 3. Gumbert, "Proposal," Figure 2.

taxonomy to historical reality is not one that is revealed (magically) as the research data are plotted on a neutral grid, but rather takes place in the scheme by which data are defined.

Among the conclusions noted by Gumbert is the "remarkable" absence of points in the center of the grid, which Gumbert effectively dismisses as "something that needs investigation." That investigation is far more central than Gumbert's discussion seems to claim. Lieftinck's terms were designed to analyze hands in such a way as to produce yes/no answers. That is, scripts showed *either* single-story *a or* two-story *a*. The features Lieftinck chose lent themselves especially to binary analysis; they do not suggest a continuum or reveal gradations. Such features will inevitably cluster points at the far ends of any axis constructed to represent them. Using multiple axes will compound this effect. The only way to produce points in the center of Gumbert's three-dimensional grid is for a script to prove exceptional, not in one of the categories (single-story versus two-story *a*), but in all of them. If the nature of the nomenclature positions points on the ends of an axis, then the absence of scripts in the center has nothing to do with the history of writing, but deals only with the nomenclature. What is really surprising is not that so few scripts or hands appear in the center of this imagined space, but that any of them do. (Note that this is not a critique of the system, but rather an indication that it works, at least as far as nomenclature is concerned.)

Furthermore, the printed diagrams are deceptive, since they represent the grids in two dimensions. Gumbert's examples of "clustering" give the illusion of three-dimensionality, but it won't take much visualization to realize that it is impossible simply to plot a point in the center of the space. No matter where a point is placed, and how that point is defined, it is always possible to interpret it as on one of the extreme planes. A single-story *a*, for example, is not a point on the *x*-axis as Gumbert defines it, but rather a plane encompassing all points on the left wall of Gumbert's cube. Looped ascenders are not the extreme point of the *y*-axis but rather the entire plane that serves as the base of the cube. And *s/f* with extension below the line is the entire near face of the cube. I believe the only unambiguous points in this two-dimensional representation are those on its outermost edges, that is, on the perimeter.[45]

Equally important are the transformations, unaccounted for, that occur in Gumbert's construction of the second figure (Figure 3), the one on which differences in real hands are to be plotted. It is this diagram, I assume, that provides the "historicization" of the terminology or nomenclature set out in the first cube. But the axes are defined differently. Here, looped ascenders occupy the base, and extended *s/f* occupies the near face. But the single-story *a*s that should occupy the right wall are quite different in form. The two-story *a*s that occupy the left wall are also quite different, at least to my eye; one of them (K) seems hardly a two-story *a* at all. Furthermore, the antithesis to the "extended *s/f*" in E is nowhere near the "footed form" in points T Y Z. The reason for this is that Gumbert's cube has been historicized to reflect actual hands rather than the idealized scripts defined in his first figure. The cube, thus, has been transformed, or at least misshapen, its walls bent and twisted, its extremes pulled in toward the center, such that the extremes are no longer extremes but realities.[46]

The conclusions Gumbert draws seem perfectly reasonable, and they are probably valid.

My impression is that hands outside the cardinal points, i.e.,—per definition—hands with fluctuations in their characteristics, are more frequent in the lower levels of the hierarchical scale, in periods of disintegration or in those of development (which is probably the most interesting case). Conversely, an isolated cluster at one of the cardinal points is likely to correspond to a highly formalised script which has lost contact with living development (such as the textualis of the fifteenth century). (49)

But these conclusions are not based on what one sees in the cubes, and Gumbert obviously did not have to plot his data to arrive at them.

Excursus 2: Vincent Figgins and Caxton's *Game of Chess* (1855)

In 1860, a year before the appearance of Blades's *Life and Typography*, Vincent Figgins produced a facsimile of the second edition of Caxton's *Game of Chess*, using type cast especially for this purpose.[47] Figgins cast type in traditional fashion, even though he believed Caxton himself did not:

> that Caxton used separate types . . . is undoubted. . . . and that the metal was cast in blocks ready to receive the letter from the hand of the engraver; but that each letter was so cut separately, is easily established by observing that throughout any book printed with these types, no two letters can be found exactly alike; whereas, if cast from a matrix, each perfect type must have been a facsimile of all the others. (3)

In 1861, Blades criticized this facsimile, referencing his own (erroneous?) theory of the way Caxton cast this type, using typesorts from Type 2 as punches:

> This trimming up [of soft metal punches], . . . may have had great effect in misleading the late Mr Vincent Figgins, the well-known typefounder, who, when examining the 2nd edition of the "Game and Play of the Chess," came to the erroneous conclusion that the whole book was printed from types cut separately by hand, a conclusion which he would never have adopted had he extended his examination to other works of Caxton in the same types. (*Life and Typography*, 2:xxvi)

Blades does not explain how and why Figgins's thinking would have changed by examining more books.

Figgins recognizes Caxton's fonts, as do Ames and later Blades. On page 3, he speaks of the "strong likeness" of the type in various books of Caxton printed in what we now speak of as Caxton 1 (*Recueil*, *Recuyell*, and the first edition of the *Game of Chess*) and an "exact similarity" in the paper used. A modern bibliographer would consider these examples of Type 1 "identical."[48] But under Figgins's theory, no Caxton types are truly identical: "Now I find so much difference in the earlier works of Caxton, that I am disposed to that each work had, if not altogether new type, at least a very large proportion recut" (3; see also 4).

Figgins does not seem concerned with what by our standards is an accurate image of the original (to us, this means a photographic one), and even concedes he does not have "the original before him" (7).

> Very few persons have ever had the opportunity of seeing any of the productions. . . . This reproduction of the first work printed by Caxton at Westminster, containing 23 woodcuts, is intended, in some measure, to supply this deficiency. . . . The Type has been carefully imitated, and the cuts traced from the copy in the British Museum. The Paper has also been made expressly, as near as possible like the original. ("Tribute")

When placed next to the original or a photographic facsimile, Figgins's Caxton is easily distinguishable from the original. It is not an image of Caxton, but an idealization of one.

Figgins's idealized history of Caxton isolates editions from their histories and typesorts from their contexts: each is an individual, just as were the individually cut typesorts Figgins imagined Caxton used, just as were the individual type images isolated in a typefont array by Tupper. To both Tupper and Figgins, individual sorts are subsumed under an abstraction: a typesort is not the thing that makes an impression on paper, but the abstraction that could account for all the imperfect impressions on the paper. For Tupper, this is the typesort represented in the array; for Figgins, it is the typesort he himself cut and subsequently cast in quantity that would represent the "individual sorts" he imagined in the Caxton.

Figgins defined and imagined typesorts (that is, historical reality) not in terms of what he saw, but in terms of the overly simplified typographical/paleographical language at his disposal:

> The fact that the original is printed from cut metal types . . . makes the work of reproducing by means of cast types from a single cut

punch somewhat difficult; but as I found the black letter and its ap-
proximations predominate, I have endeavoured, while keeping between the two styles, to adhere more closely to the black letter. (7)

Thus even the impressions on the page of Caxton's original, which we see as
clearly slanted right in what we might consider bastarda style, he can dismiss
as aberrations or departures from the "true" letters, more in the "black-letter
style" (that is, a style more along the lines of what we consider textura). The
letterforms he prints, therefore, must have existed in Caxton's mind, even
though to us they can only be seen in Figgins's own imitations.

CHAPTER 2

"Ca. 1800": What's in a Date?

When Rabelais and others characterized their own period as involved in "la restitution des bonnes lettres,"[1] they created what we now know as the Middle Ages, a period between two points of interest, Roman classical times and contemporary times, with both periods romanticized through a Renaissance or Early Modern perspective.

The medieval period was equivalent to the Dark Ages: inaccessible, empty, barbaric, devoid of interest. Even what should have been seen as its literary achievements were defined out of existence: humanists saw Carolingian script as classical. Gothicists invented their own version of medievalism, but for modern scholars interested in what they themselves imagined was the real Middle Ages, the limits of the period became increasingly restricted. W. P. Ker limited the Dark Ages to the second half of the first millennium. The High Middle Ages referred to something else. Occasionally, chronology was tangled to keep early modern ideology intact: Boccaccio was a medieval author, but Petrarch a Renaissance or early modern one. What was known then as The Renaissance established outposts in this territory: the Twelfth-Century Renaissance, the Carolingian Renaissance, the Ottonian Renaissance. All these scholarly notions further narrowed the field, whatever field it might now be. Was there a Dark Ages at all? Did "medieval" make sense? What were the eras for which this was a demarcation? And in what conceivable way were things changed when all was rechristened as whatever it was that preceded Early Modern?[2]

As a erstwhile medievalist, I was always amused by this narrowing of the field, a field generally defined not by medievalists, but by others disparaging the Middle Ages (whatever they or it was) either by dismissing this period and everything associated with it or by romanticizing it until no longer recognizable. So I was prepared to sense or imagine something analogous happening in the history of printing, the invention of which (at least in some histories) coincides perfectly with the emergence of the Early Modern. Printing too might seem peculiarly modern, exhibiting all those special virtues, self-reflection, for example, we ourselves possess;[3] it might be vilified as that strange Other, sullying the purity of the Oral or Scribal. Certain periods of printing might be romanticized, especially by those, such as William Morris, seeking to restore them, or by those who see an undefined threat in the rise of electronic culture.[4] Despite the supposed technological and material base that roots printing in chronology, the field Print might expand or contract as did the field Medieval, as scholars, whether interested in Print or whatever it is Print is Not, extracted for themselves what seemed of interest and left for mere "specialists" the bibliographical detritus.[5] Orality might permeate print; print might expand from a technology to a Culture.

Yet, in contrast to the elusiveness of the Middle Ages, printing, that is to say, the scholarly or bibliographical history of printing, has remained remarkably fixed. Printing (understood as the printing of things we call books) begins with the ineradicable and immovable fact of the invention of the printing press at some point in the mid-fifteenth century. A second demarcation has developed within this history, and that is the subject of my chapter here. The date 1800, or "ca. 1800" is used, particularly by bibliographers, to define a period of classic printing, a period marked by an assumed continuity of techniques and conventions. This continuity, or sense of it, leads to an equally tenacious continuity of bibliographical techniques and conventions that begin roughly when the presumed early period of printing ends. The field thus is both a historical event (or series of events) and an object of study, and there are various terms and phrases used to describe it: printing, early printing, the hand-press period. "Around 1800," everything (that is, both printing history and bibliographical history) changes.[6]

When writing my own introductory history in *What Is a Book?*, I saw no way around this date, even though my initial plan was to write a comprehensive history of books independent of what I considered arbitrary and traditional markers of this history.[7] The date kept reasserting itself, in the same way, I suppose, that the word *medieval* has seemed in the past three decades impervious to resounding critiques of it. And while I recognized that nineteenth-century technology and twentieth-century bibliographical methods certainly leak into the field of early printing, however that may be defined, they never seemed a direct part of that field; they were secondary, that is, works and events that were somehow about the field, not within it. The date 1800, I seemed to think, or thereabouts, terminates the field, and something else takes over: the iron press, stereotyping, self-reflection, or modern bibliography itself.

I look at printing history, 1450 to the present. But as I give that history my attention as a print historian or as a bibliographer, the field begins to change, or perhaps narrow in a gerrymandering way to exclude all the things I know or care nothing about. At first it seems to begin in 1450 or so and last until whenever it lasts until. Perhaps it lasts through the nineteenth century, or perhaps to the first electronic book. Yet electronic books, I think, exist in much earlier forms than those we refer to with that term today. Is a printed broadsheet essentially different from a wire story by a news service? I am suddenly overwhelmed by these early twentieth-century machines, whose nature and functioning I barely understand at all: linotype, monotype, and so on. They are things out of *Metropolis*, it seems, or maybe the twentieth-century version of the staggering industrial glories depicted in the French *Encyclopédie*. I go back to the iron press of William Morris, which I delude myself into thinking I understand perfectly. A model is on display in the former manuscript catalogue room of the Huntington. To many viewers, scholars of English literature and history in particular, it represents metonymically the most important rare books contained in this collection; but of course, it has nothing to do with those books. The nearly 6,000 incunables, the vast collection of STC books and even ESTC books—all were produced on the wooden machines that were rendered obsolete by this iron press. Print historians assert that this iron press, the one I am looking at with more than a little nostalgia, changes everything, industrializing printing in a way it had never been industrialized before, even though, paradoxically, this particular iron press was used by an ardent foe of industrialization.

I turn to the incunable period looking for the origins of printing, the earliest history of printing. But instead of finding something helpful there, all I find are the tangled myths of origins, entwined with the political and nationalistic myths they serve.[8] I find or imagine a set of conventions and an array of evidence that do not fit well with the traditional language of bibliography: all these monuments of early printing history; all these books we do not read and do not want to read, so unlike the literary glories of seventeenth-century English literature; and all produced by means we have neither defined nor perhaps imagined. The early books I look at most seriously do not fit the conventions of early printing at all; and all those printed after the date 1800, those that concern me so little, do not fit those conventions either.

This chapter considers why Anglo-American bibliographical history privileges this date, or more honestly, why I see book history constructed in this way, turning on a date that in retrospect seems so conveniently coordinated with other important events in Western history: the founding of America, the French Revolution, events and technologies of book history and bibliography such as the development of stereotype, the iron press, the closing of the German monasteries, the great incunable catalogues of Ludwig Hain and George Wolfgang Panzer, even the publications of Thomas Frognall Dibdin.[9] What are the bibliographical implications of this? Is that date just a product of periodization? an illusion generated by the base-ten system? an index of our intellectual attention spans? Something happens. Or so it seems. And is there any significant difference between these two statements?

Early Printed Books: Defined

Early printing is defined by print historians as beginning in 1450 ("printing") and terminating some time in the early nineteenth century ("early"). This period is also called, somewhat oddly, the hand-press period, a term that only makes sense if we use it metaphorically for "the wooden press," since nineteenth-century iron presses were surely operated by hand;[10] we also have to concede that we do not really know what the earliest presses looked like, how they were constructed, or even what they were made of. We all of course agree that these limits are porous, and no subfield of book history can be studied in any detail without encroaching on other fields; for example, a subfield such as "Bibles, 1660–1680," could not usefully be studied without consideration of such things as "Secular Printing, 1660–1680," "Bibles, 1600–1750." Any category defining a group of historical objects requires language that transcends or even violates the field: the study of early printing, whatever it is, incorporates in some way the study of manuscripts that preceded printed books, later developments in book illustration (planographic techniques), the very history of bibliography, electronic databases that enable us to find and even view early books or versions of them.

The simplest reason I respect this traditional terminating date for early printing is that I am less familiar with nineteenth-century books as objects of study than I am with books printed before 1800, and this is likely a consequence of the traditional cut-off date I seem to have internalized. In other words, my experience that is to some extent determined by the academic cliché begins to produce supporting evidence for the validity of that cliché. Abstractions lead to experience and material evidence supporting those abstractions. When I hold a book from 1730, I examine it physically or I ignore it; when I hold a book from 1850, my decision is different: I read it, or I don't.

It is easy to construct my bifurcated history of printing (printing before 1800/modern printing), since any presumed fact of printing can be made fit within this framework, whether legitimately or by a version of *petitio principii*. It is harder to invoke contradictory evidence, or even to imagine what contradictory evidence might be.

Paper as a Fundamental Unit of Printing: The Book as a Function of Format

Implicit in the definition of materials for early books is the notion of format: books are things constructed of pieces of handmade paper, all in manageable, handheld paper molds. Even the minimal descriptions in the print versions of STC (1926 and 1976) include this detail. Somewhat surprisingly, the ISTC catalogue of fifteenth-century books follows suit, including format in its brief descriptions but not type, even though type identification is the single most important factor in identifying these books, and its description easily quantifiable.[11]

Short-title catalogue definitions are based on the assumption that "printed book" means "codex-like object," formed of sheets of paper (or vellum) roughly the shape of paper made in a traditional hand-mold, a shape in turn roughly the same as animal hides. A book is something formed of complete or nearly complete sheets of handmade paper or its equivalent, whose shape is reflected in the codices that are its primary product. The size of a sheet of paper and the way it is folded are foundational to the definition of what a book is (or more accurately, what we will include in an enumerative catalogue).

In the earliest period, playing cards and independent engravings are excluded by this assumption, whereas the products of comparable printing projects such as indulgences and blockbooks are generally included.[12] By the eighteenth century, as such un-codex-like printing projects increase to unmanageable proportions, most are defined away. A book (that is to say, an item in ESTC, whether a codex or a broadsheet) has to incorporate a complete sheet (or half-sheet), not part of that sheet, and it has to be able to be described in terms of this sheet: among the first details in an enumerative catalogue is a statement of sheet format.

The introduction of machine-made paper changes the relation of paper to "objects of bibliographical consideration" from an essential to an arbitrary one. By the late nineteenth century, paper is made by machine. When paper is made by machine, rather than on a hand-mold, format becomes more decorative than essential. The size and shape of books must be defined as conventional, rather than as a function of materials; they reflect the rectangular shape of paper produced by the hand-mold, a shape we assume is in turn rooted in the material world of animal skins. Paper is produced and distributed in large rolls prior to being cut for anything we could recognize as a ream or even a book.[13]

One result has been a more careful distinction of bibliographical items in the Nineteenth Century Short Title Catalogue (see Introduction quoted below): "monographs" are distinguished from periodicals and ephemera. What we once considered books are now specific kinds of books. They are functions not of the materials at their base (paper size and format), but rather of shelving conventions. The producer yields to the library.[14]

Alternate Printing Techniques

Other more striking changes involve printing techniques, the most significant of which from a bibliographical standpoint is stereotyping. Stereotyping changes what a book or an edition is, and changes too the basic definitions bibliographers use to define these things.[15] In its simplest and earliest form, the stereotyping process begins with traditional typesetting. A forme is typeset and a mold is created over this form with papier mâché. That paper mold can then be stored, and new plates made from it at any time, plates which themselves can be destroyed without destroying the "edition." This means that a reprint no longer involves either the resetting of type or the retention of heavy, type-set pages and formes—actions basic to the traditional definition of what an edition is.

Convenient as this is for printers and publishers, it is calamitous for bibliographers. McKerrow, Bowers, Greg, STC bibliographers—all based their system of bibliography on a narrow and convenient definition of printing technology. All distinctions and the very definition of sameness and difference were based on the material state of particular locked formes of type that would produce impressions of those formes on pages; these impressions would have the same bibliographical name (formes) as the physical thing that produced them. An impression is what ends up on the paper (all the paper) imposed on that forme. A different forme of the same text or pages produces a new impression, a new state, and if extended to other pages and sheets, a new edition.[16]

The definitions of edition, state, variant, and with that all histories of printers and book distribution depend on these ideas. And thus all the basic reference material (bibliographies, printing histories, histories of individual printers) is organized accordingly. Without these ideas, we cannot really speak coherently about Shakespeare's First Folio, or Caxton's Chaucer, or Urry's Chaucer, or Pope's Iliad, or any of the other familiar and unfamiliar topics in English bibliography.[17]

It is easy enough to construct such lists. Critical technological inventions and developments appear wherever we look for them. Planographic techniques not only change the way that illustrations are made, they make possible the most pernicious of facsimiles and forgeries; in some sense, they create historical books that precede the invention of these techniques. End-cut wood blocks change both the technique of woodcutting and what is often called the "grammar" of the images. The white-line cuts of Thomas Bewick are constructed, and even described bibliographically, not as woodcuts but as engravings, where the incised line is the positive. Woodcuts after 1800 are apparently no longer woodcuts at all.[18] We can add to this list of significant technological changes things like color printing, steelcut engravings, and, of course, the Stanhope iron press. The materials involved in paper manufacture change (this by the later nineteenth century), and I assume, although I know nothing of this, that there are substantial changes in ink manufacture as well.

Something undefinable happens when print is invented (in 1450, was it?), transforming what was then that culture of script that didn't even know its own name or being into that culture of print barely defined until threatened in the late twentieth century. Something equally radical seems to happen in 1800; at least, it must happen if we accept the way bibliographers define their subject. But is our view of history just a product of the date we choose to define it? Wherever we place this date, and however we might choose that date in the future, there will always be plenty of evidence to support it.

The Banality of Counting

As I go through the technology of this apparent sea-change in book production, I do so in relation to various enumerative bibliographies, particularly STC and ESTC, whose principles were established in Anglo-American bibliography almost a century ago. It is as if the bibliographical categories defined there were the fundamental units of history, and not the facts or events of history, however those would be defined.

Walk into the library stacks of a large university library and head to the Zs, or perhaps to the reference room, if it's still there, containing select books in this range. If that library had any purchasing power in the 1990s, you will eventually come across a series of short-title catalogues. In English, the series will begin with STC (1450–1640), the single volume of 1926, the three-volume revision of 1976–1991; Wing (1640–1700), still three volumes, or four. You might find something that looks like a book, a plastic folder once known as ESTC, or that might be in the microfiche section, if the library still has such a thing. The early ESTC (= Eighteenth-Century Short Title Catalogue) was too large for codex form and was published in microfiche, a form more cumbersome to use than the dozens of imagined volumes it could replace. You will find that plastic microfiche folder on your shelves. Or perhaps this volume has been placed in storage, since the very acronym ESTC now refers to something else: not "Eighteenth-Century Short Title Catalogue," but "English Short Title Catalog," including all books in STC, Wing, and the Eighteenth-Century Short Title Catalog itself.[19]

Somewhere in this vicinity will be a series of red volumes taking up several shelves, many shelves, or maybe you will find reoccupied shelves where this set used to be: the *Nineteenth-Century Short Title Catalogue*. Those red volumes, once as unmanageable as the original ESTC microfiche, have now been replaced by an electronic version. You might find the original in offsite storage, where it will now be almost impossible to retrieve. You might find it listed in the catalog of a hopeful book dealer. I quote the promotional introduction to the electronic version here (the note speaks of the aims of the project as fixed, although clearly they must have changed as the possible ways it could be published changed):

Chadwyck-Healey's *Nineteenth-Century Short Title Catalogue* (*NSTC*) defines the printed record of the English-speaking world from the beginning of the nineteenth century to the end of the First World War. The project aims to index all printed works published in Britain, its colonies and the United States of America, all printed works in English wherever published, and all translations from English. In addition to providing an exhaustive survey of the complete spectrum of monograph publications in the period, the catalogue indexes thousands of periodicals, directories and other ephemeral publications.

NSTC brings together as one cross-searchable database NSTC Series I (1801–1815), Series II (1816–1870) and Series III (1871–1919), first published by Avero Publications between 1983 and 2002 in print and on two CD-ROMs. It comprises more than 1,200,000 cross-searchable records drawn from the catalogues of the Bodleian Library, the British Library, Harvard University Library, the Library of Congress, the Library of Trinity College, Dublin, the National Library of Scotland and the University Libraries of Cambridge and Newcastle.[20]

It is difficult to judge these claims without testing them. I do not know what sort of information I should get from a survey of over a million books (meaning in this case "bibliographical items"), and I thus am in no position to judge the quality of any results I would obtain by using this one. Even when I use book databases two orders of magnitude smaller than this one, I have found myself unable to assess the quality or in some cases even the nature of my results.[21]

The first STC by Pollard and Redgrave (1926) covered the years from the earliest printed English book (1476) to 1640; the 30,000 entries fit into one volume. Overall a reasonably consistent set of principles and standards was applied to each entry, since the same two bibliographers, with their same prejudices, wrote or edited each entry. The number of entries in NSTC, by contrast, is said to be 1,200,000, about 40 times the number for STC. In my rough calculations, an experienced bibliographer proofreading this and allowing fifteen uncritical seconds to each entry, working 40-hour weeks without break and taking two weeks vacation a year, would require two to two and a half years just to skim through it, with no time to give any extended

thought to the bibliographical materials (books and book-copies) these entries refer to. Comparing the entries with the books they denote or refer to, in
order to ensure the accuracy of each entry and the consistency of transcriptions, would of course be out of the question. There is little chance of a professional bibliographer imposing a uniform standard on this material such
that each entry might refer coherently to the object or abstraction it is meant
to describe. Nor is there a single notion of a book or an edition that could
describe the increasing number of codices, serial publications, advertise-
ments, and ephemera that are produced during this period and said to be
included in the catalogue.

When we look through the entries in the single-volume STC of 1926, we
know roughly what a book is. Although we may not know, say, the variant
edition of Chapman's *Bussy d'Amboise* (1608, STC 4967), if we have spent any
time in libraries of seventeenth-century materials we know books like that;
we also know about the Shakespeare First Folio, which really isn't much like
that at all, but can be described the same way, and perhaps we have seen some
broadsides (or at least seen them pictured), and know enough about early
paper manufacture to understand why they are included in this catalog
as well.

Furthermore, we know who the authorities are for determining all this
for us, and we know what basic works have been written in the same tradition. If you asked for the standard bibliographical works relevant to STC, a
legitimate answer (not a complete or even correct one) might be Katherine
Pantzer's introduction to the revised STC, Bowers, *Principles of Descriptive
Bibliography*, McKerrow, *Introduction to Bibliography*, Greg, *Bibliography
of Restoration Drama*, and Peter Blayney, *The Texts of King Lear and their
Origins*.[22] There is least some hope of common ground. I know what a
seventeenth-century book *is*, and so do you, or so we think, and all that is
required is some sort of uneasy convention or truce on what the meaning of
"is" is.

Although many bibliographers might feel equally at home in the nineteenth century, I don't. As a nonspecialist, I have no idea what a book comparable to any book I pick up from the nineteenth century might be, who
might be able to tell me this, and where I could find a typical or representative example. What are the key English monuments of this bibliographical
history? First editions of the dreaded Victorian Novel? Serial versions? Three-
deckers? Newspapers? Or any of the various encyclopedia projects? Do I
count commercial printing only? Or perhaps the distinction between public

and private printings cannot really be enforced, any more than it is enforced either for early books or for those produced in modern academic settings. Maybe nineteenth-century bibliographers know the answers to these questions, but I am not sure of that, since I have never to my knowledge exchanged so much as a bibliographical greeting with one. Considering the amount of time I have spent in rare book rooms, how can that have happened?

The genres of books (or book-objects) increase with the sheer number of items. If we were to extend this survey to the twentieth century, these problems multiply further. There are products of typewriters and mimeograph machines. Photo-reprints. Electronic editions begin to appear. And as these book-forms multiply, it becomes increasingly difficult to determine just what the entries in a short-title catalogue refer to, and equally difficult to determine what they should refer to: whether some new and tentative definition of books or editions, or simply pure bibliographical imaginings.

I look at the numbers of these books, or rather, the number of entries in the catalogues, and consider the difference between the manageable numbers of early catalogues and the unmanageable figures in the NCSTC. The number of entries in a union incunable catalogue (ca. 30,000) is roughly the same as the number of entries in the first STC. And there is that remarkable coincidence that the arbitrary century date of 1500 and the date of the English Revolution (1640) should combine with the dates of the origin of printing and various national and linguistic boundaries to produce such a number, when we know perfectly well that the things counted in these catalogues (whether books or editions) are not subject to the same defining principles, even in the single catalogue.[23]

What I earlier in this section called the calamitous situation for book history—those developments in all aspects of the book world that produced the corrosion of bibliographical language—seems not a calamity in history at all, but a pure function of the bibliographical assumptions that made it visible. Not history, but historians. Not the 1,200,000 books, but the arbitrary definitions of time frames and national and linguistic boundaries that produce this number in the first place. Perhaps we should revise that NCSTC project and rename chunks of it as the 1800–1815 STC, as the various "Series" described in the NSTC introduction imply has been done, working forward in increasingly smaller units (unlike these NSTC series) until we are able to think in terms of the units these diminishing units define. Yet no matter how we define these units, the mathematics will not produce the continuity we need; Achilles will never quite catch the tortoise.

I then return to the simple assumption that made these last paragraphs possible: there was a time when we all believed we knew what a book was. A time, that is, when books were made long ago: incunables, early English books. We knew what these were, whether in history or on our library shelves, even though, paradoxically, we were unsure, at least in the earliest period, how they were made. Yet I concede now that I know (or knew) what a book was not because of my experience of books, which I thought was extensive, but rather because of my experience with bibliographies. In some sense, I am back to square one; in other senses, I haven't even gotten back to that initial starting place.

The Printers' History of Printers' History

One of the key documents in the Anglo-American bibliography is Joseph Moxon's *Mechanick Exercises* of 1683. It is strange that this book should be of such importance for the field of bibliography, since it is not a bibliography at all, not like, say, Maittaire's *Annales typographici* of 1719 or the many purely bibliographical works that followed it.[24] The manual had a dual audience, or at least, Moxon implies it ought to have that dual audience. On the one hand, it is a technical manual, directed at professionals in the trade; on the other hand, it is simply a history or description of a technology, that is, a book for the amusement of amateurs and dilettantes.

Viewed from the standpoint of twenty-first-century bibliography, *Mechanick Exercises* seems seminal. As the first reliable description of the technology of printing, it establishes the modern history of printing; equally important, since it serves as the basis for later works, it establishes the genre of describing that history. The work and its reception are the basis for what I have called the myths of continuity regarding printing. The techniques described in Moxon were basic, even when early printers were said to use different techniques. And it served as the basis for many nineteenth-century manuals in their own descriptions of contemporary printing: all procedures were to be described through what became (somewhat arbitrarily) the classic work in the field.

I select three recent books or projects that have looked at this history and defined it, indirectly, in fundamentally different ways. David Pankow's *The Printing Manual: An Illustrated History* is a catalogue from an exhibition of printing manuals. David McKitterick, *Print, Manuscript and the Search for*

Order (1450–1830), defines his discussion as "Chronologically . . . before the introduction of machine printing in the nineteenth century." Finally, Gabriel Rummonds has two books, actually projects, dedicated to printing technologies and their description from the nineteenth century.[25]

Pankow's pamphlet catalogue shows the continuity in this history, one that is at least in part a product of his definition of his subject. When you define a set of books as printing manuals and arrange them chronologically, the implication or apparent conclusion will necessarily be one of historical continuity. But this continuity is simply the diachronic version of the defining (synchronic) assumption used to define the field. McKitterick and Rummonds, by contrast, organize their own histories according to the traditional date terminating early printing history in the early nineteenth century.

As a curator and archivist, Pankow can collect and present material that just happens to be at hand, that is, "what is there" in his library, and connected by some notion of genre or continuity in historical procedures. Such an exhibit would be legitimate whether or not the items were definitive or even representative of a particular historical period or field (it is not a thesis-driven exhibit such as becoming increasingly popular in libraries and in museums). McKitterick is a bibliographer; writing about these materials, he is thus compelled by the genre to do both: to argue or imply that the materials he selects are in fact representative (either of a general period or of a particular aspect of it), and furthermore, to claim that these materials possess a coherence, one articulated by the scholar and parallel to a coherence in the history he studies. There is certainly an argument to be made that the curator and archivist has a tremendous advantage here: the arbitrariness of the materials available and finally selected is much more likely to reflect the chaos of real history than the carefully defined corpus selected by bibliographers, who in conformity with the rules of the monograph genre must argue for the coherence of whatever materials they choose. Yet in terms of the present chapter, the result of these different approaches is oddly the same and reinforces the structure of history that is at their base: a bifurcated history turning on the magical date of 1800.

From Moxon to the *Encyclopédie*

Moxon's book is a compendium of printing techniques, describing the administration of the craft and the mechanics of it. You could not print a book after reading Moxon, but you could at least walk into a print shop and feel at home (or so we think), although no one I know or have read has ever claimed to have done this. The first wooden press I encountered looked, of course, exactly like its description in McKerrow, and was apparently designed in such a way that it could be operated by anyone with experience in the iron press developed in the nineteenth century. One could only conclude from operating it that things have not really changed all that much since the fifteenth century. It seems that physical support for the notion of continuity is produced by the myth of continuity.[26]

I have no idea how Moxon's manual was used initially, and those who had the opportunity to reprint it, but did not, in the first two centuries after its publication must have felt the same way. In the nineteenth century, it developed a better defined function: it became essential to the production of other printing manuals. With DeVinne's reprint, it became a foundational text for printing history.[27] More important, by the early twentieth century it became a central text in the field of Anglo-American analytical bibliography, as printing history was recast as a product of bibliographical assumptions and categories.

To Moxon, printing or typography is an art, like Architecture, not a manual craft:

> But whoever were the Inventers of this Art, or (as some Authors will have it) Science; nay, Science of Sciences (say they) certain it is, that in all its Branches it can be deemed little less than a Science: And I hope I say not too much of *Typographie*: For Dr. Dee, in his Mathematical Preface to *Euclids Elements of Geometrie*, hath worthily taken pains to make *Architecture* a Mathematical Science; and as a vertual Proof of his own Learned Plea, quotes two Authentique Authors, *viz. Vitruvius* and *Leo Baptista*, who both give their descriptions and applause of *Architecture*: His Arguments are somewhat copious, and the Original easily procurable in the English Tongue; therefore instead of transcribing it, I shall refer my Reader to the Text it self. . . .
>
> By a *Typographer,* I do not mean a *Printer*, as he is Vulgarly accounted, any more than Dr. *Dee* means a *Carpenter* or *Mason* to be an *Architect*: But by a *Typographer*, I mean such a one, who by his own Judgment, from solid reasoning with himself, can either perform, or direct others to perform from the beginning to the end, all the Handy-works and Physical Operations relating to *Typographie*. (*Mechanick Exercises*, Preface, 10–11)

Moxon is addressing not those who perform work, but rather those who imagine themselves supervising it. Architects, not builders. "First The *Master Printer*, who is as the Soul of *Printing*; and all the Work-men as members of the Body governed by that Soul subservient to him" (12).

The eighteenth-century works by Fournier and the encyclopedists at first glance seem quite different from Moxon's *Mechanick Exercises*. But these later works also reflect the notion of a reader who stands above the technical level of a worker. Fournier's *Manuel typographique* is a genial essay on printing. There is no sense that one could found type, operate a printing press, or even imagine doing so by consulting this. Printing is a "means of communication," and the manual a voyeuristic look at the craft, a substitute for getting involved in the craft, rather than an incitement to do so.[28]

> L'Imprimerie, regardée à juste titre comme un présent du ciel, pouvoit seule y remédier. Elle a été donné aux hommes pour diminuer leurs peines, soulager leur mémoire & procurer la facilité de se communiquer réciproquement leurs lumières, sans trop de soins ni de dépenses. (Fournier, *Manuel typographique*, 1:vii)

The work that dominates all others is the nearly contemporary *Encyclopédie*, and I cannot look at contemporary illustrations of printing without judging them through this standard. When we look for illustrations of the traditional hand press, these are the most detailed and these are the ones we will find reprinted. An unattributed plate from the *Encyclopédie* serves as the cover illustration for the paperbound Dover edition of Davis and Carter's reprint of Moxon, despite the many serviceable illustrations in the book itself.

The various plates from the *Encyclopédie* will not enable anyone to construct or operate the intricate tools or machines they illustrate. Neither from the *Encyclopédie*'s illustration of the hand-mold nor from Fournier's illustration could I construct such a thing or even operate it.[29] Such illustrations thus have little of the practical value that Moxon's manual purports to have. All I could understand from the illustration of the hand-mold in Pl. III is how it works, roughly the same thing I get from any of the other illustrations on technology. The *Encyclopédie* is a celebration and appreciation of modern industrial phenomena: its readers are observers, as are the readers of Fournier, not participants or would-be participants.

The detail of the *Encyclopédie* necessitates a change in the presentation of the material. Individual articles strive to be comprehensive, and the massive amount of material and detail in those articles eliminates the oversimplified narrative we find in Fournier, or the logical and sequential discussion in Moxon. It eliminates, that is, the genial myth of the typographer/architect—the dilettante workman or supervisor—even though it is just such a figure who is imagined as the reader. The narrative of procedures once found logically connected in Moxon is fragmented in the *Encyclopédie*, just as the labor of producing printed books is fragmented among specialists. It glorifies in its very form the complexity of the industry it celebrates, a complexity that applies to both production and distribution of the encyclopedia itself.[30]

Two English Histories: Timperley/Savage

There are a number of English works that could fill out this history, that is, "early histories of printing technology," but even Pankow states that between Moxon and 1800 there are only two "of any significance": Watson's *History of the Art of Printing* (1713) (more a history than a technical manual) and Philip Luckombe's *The History and Art of Printing* (London, 1771), discussed extensively by McKitterick as well.[31] After 1800, the number of works seems to explode. Pankow's exhibition catalogue contains some two dozen of these, and it is easy to turn up additional titles.[32] Like the *Encyclopédie*, these seem to be a celebration of modern or new technology; yet that embracing of modern technology is to some extent belied by a deeply conservative tendency that runs through all of them: if you want to learn to print, begin with the oldest of authorities.[33]

From these I choose Timperley, not because it is typical but because in it, the seams in the history I trying to understand are most visible. There are three works at issue: C. H. Timperley, *A Dictionary of Printers and Printing, with the Progress of Literature, Ancient and Modern* (London, 1839); *The Printer's Manual: containing instructions to learners, with scales of impositions, and numerous calculations, recipes, and scales of prices in the principal towns of Great Britain together with practical directions for conducting every department of a printing office* (London, 1838); and finally, the 1842 *Encyclopedia*, which is essentially a re-issue of the 1839 *Dictionary*: unsold copies of the 1838 *Manual* are bound in between the "Introduction on the Origin of Language" (32 pages) and the Dictionary proper beginning p. 33, sign. F. The section on the origin of language is a familiar feature in this genre and appears in Luckombe's 1771 *History and Art* as well. The independent manual (the second of the three major sections of the *Encyclopedia*) is a technical manual (although called by Pankow one of the briefest in this genre, it consists of 116 very densely printed pages). What is called the "Dictionary" is not a dictionary in the ordinary sense: it is rather an annals, that is, organized chronologically.

To indicate the nature of this work, it is enough to quote the title page (or part of it), garrulous even by the standards of the time:

> Encyclopaedia of Literary and Typographical Anecdote; being a chronological digest of the most interesting facts illustrative of the history of literature and printing from the earliest period to the present time. Interspersed with biographical sketches of eminent booksellers printers type-founders, engravers, bookbinders and paper makers, of all ages and countries, but especially of Great Britain. With bibliographical and descriptive accounts of their principal productions and occasional extracts from them. Including curious particulars of the first introduction of printing . . . An account of the origin and progress of language, writing and writing materials, the invention of paper, use of paper marks, etc. Compiled and condensed from Nichols's Literary Anecdotes, and numerous other authorities. . . . second ed. to which are added A continuation to the present time . . . and A Practical Manual of printing.

Timperley's *Encyclopedia* in its final 1842 version thus combines two narratives and two genres. The inserted manual is written according to the logic seen in Moxon's *Mechanick Exercises*, constructed for "the profession," that is, for "the inexperienced apprentice, or journeyman, who has not the means of purchasing more expensive works upon the art of typography." The Dictionary is a different kind of narrative, constructed not according to logic, but rather to reflect the serendipitous way the facts of history seem to emerge: the logical organization of the "origin and progress" genre has yielded to the more capricious Annals. X happened. Then Y.

William Savage, *A Dictionary of the Art of Printing* (London, 1841), is the first of these manuals or histories that dispenses with all these systems of organization. It is a true dictionary of printing, the first English example of this genre that is alphabetized. The major source is Moxon, the only work Savage cites in his preface, but the logical structure of Moxon is gone.[34] The massive history of printing, consisting of bibliography, anecdote, narrative, and technology, is made materially available by putting it into one physical book. But the work is so arbitrarily organized as to make that history inaccessible to one who does not know it already. As is the case with NCSTC, enumerating the editions of this period, the sheer volume of information makes that information impossible to assimilate.

The Modern Printer's Manual: Gabriel Rummonds

Gabriel Rummonds has compiled two works that are and will continue to be basic to the study of nineteenth-century printing and perhaps to hand-press printing generally: (1) *Printing on the Iron Handpress* (1998), a narrative summary of techniques; (2) *Nineteenth-Century Printing Practices and the Iron Handpress* (2004), a two-volume collection of nineteenth-century descriptions of printing procedures. Rummonds points immediately to the paradox of the term *hand press*, but seems to despair of a solution: "Printing on the iron handpress is not included in the historical period usually designated as the *hand-press period*, which traditionally covers only the years 1500–1800. Therefore, when I refer to the 'hand-press period,' it should be understood that I am talking about pre-nineteenth-century practices" (*Nineteenth-Century Printing Practices*, 1:4).

The material covered in these books is the same; the organization is also roughly the same, beginning with the physical nature of the printing press, then various basic operations at press (imposition, making register), followed by the description of more specialized procedures (printing in two colors, inking). This is more or less the organizational scheme used by McKerrow in his *Introduction to Bibliography* of 1926, one McKerrow got from Moxon, and one found in several of the manuals from which Rummonds's book is derived.

> When I first decided to make a compilation of readings describing nineteenth-century printing practices and the iron handpress, I found that Timperley's words closely coincided with my own aims for just such a product. My book, like his, should not be viewed as a *new work*, but as a ready-reference guide to "everything you always wanted to know about handpress printing as gleaned from pre-twentieth-century English-language printers' manuals." (*Nineteenth-Century Printing Practices*, 1:3)

> All of these writers, except Moxon, relied heavily on the manuals of their predecessors, and each added new technological information as it became available. The readings offered here are often lengthy and repetitive; sometimes to the point of exasperation. I have left some of these long-winded discourses intact in order to give my readers a feeling for the expository styles of these nineteenth-century manual writers. (1:5)

The fact of continuity seems so obvious, the choice of evidence is almost secondary.

> I have arranged the material in this book in what I believe to be a logical sequence, although after you have set up the press and printed your first form, you will no longer need to follow this sequence. (*Printing on the Iron Handpress*, xix)

The history of printing and typography, the history of the histories of typography and printing, these histories collide in Rummonds, who defines himself at the outset as the product, the last product, of these histories, and true to their real or stated purposes: to enable a reader to operate a press.[35] I am not sure that the purpose of many of the earlier manuals, particularly Moxon's, was to enable anyone to operate a press, since such instruction, if successful, would only result in the creation of competitors. And Rummonds may be the first printer for whom the creation of rivals was something to be desired. Nonetheless, you could never start printing from reading Rummonds, at least not without prior experience, any more than a seventeenth-century reader could set up a printing press after reading Moxon.

Rummonds is both the historian of and an expression of the manuals of the nineteenth century. He omits one set of narratives familiar from these manuals (the narrative of printing origins), but then recontextualizes the fragments he collects (an account of typesetting in one manual is interchangeable with the account in another), rebuilding them in a second narrative: a compendium of nineteenth-century printing compendia, organized according to his experiences as a twentieth-century printer. He creates in his own work another *grand récit* of the very process of fragmentation and specialization that took place in the nineteenth century.

The manuals and histories of the nineteenth century—these works saw nothing in the date 1800. They described, rather, their own period as the endpoint in a history whose major secondary documents (printing manuals and printing histories) promoted a history of continuity, relentlessly forming a tradition beginning with Moxon and running continuously through the next two centuries.

Yet when I look at this history, now with my viewpoint determined by assumptions of twentieth-century Anglo-American bibliography, I find something completely different. Rather than examples of continuity with the past of early printing, what the works of the nineteenth century appear to be are signs of a growing self-reflection on that history. But even as I say that, I recognize I am repeating yet another academic cliché: that printing itself, in the mid-fifteenth century, is what marks this tendency.

In all these histories, the date 1800 seems inescapable. Not because it is a real thing, or because the sections of printing history it describes are real, but because this is the way modern bibliography has made that history understood. And my only avenue to that history is through the clichés and schemata of the field in which I have chosen to work. The things that make that history at all intelligible or workable turn out to be things that also make counterexamples difficult to find or imagine. What exactly could be discovered that would refute the date that defines the fields?

Conclusion

Thinking about the date 1800 pointed me in two directions. It forced me first to consider the historical factors that justified that date (facts of history, facts of bibliography), and second to imagine a possible critique of that date. The first part of this chapter concerns the set of facts defined by modern history, in particular, the technological features of printing that are now incorporated into standard histories. But these facts do not seem quite adequate and were certainly not viewed as revolutionary by nineteenth-century historians. What I can see from a twenty-first-century perspective that nineteenth-century historians could not concerns the banality of numbers: the date today marks the difference between a corpus of material we can imagine (those 30,000 books) versus one that cannot be imagined or even investigated (the number of entries in NSTC, which by definition would not have been imaginable until the twentieth century and the coincident rise of what is considered Anglo-American bibliography, that is, the so-called New Bibliography of McKerrow, Greg, and Bowers).

This banality (those tens and tens of thousands of books) is a product of bibliographical clichés: it is a product of the privileging of that single "thing"—the book, the edition—that yields those numbers; that is, it is the product of the particular concern of New Bibliographers. Certainly, it would be imaginable that a field could be developed whose basic unit of concern was "the page" or "the typesort"; but when we speak of printing or bibliography, these units are not and cannot be what we mean.

Even historicizing this does no particular good. I assumed originally that the narratives and organization of histories of printing in the nineteenth century would undermine the now traditional 1800 date. And true, none of them shows the slightest concern for this apparent bibliographical sea-change, even though they are all far more aware of the consequences of the technological changes than we could ever be. The result, however, was a conclusion reinforcing the date I expected to critique: not "1800 means nothing, as witnessed by these works," but rather something along the lines "these works support the significance of that date by taking a self-reflective attitude toward the history they write." Unsatisfactory as that last formulation might be, I find it inescapable. If I discard it, another comes in its place: "What the nineteenth century histories did was establish a tradition, not of investigation, but of history itself."

Self-contradiction is not difficult—scholars do this all the time—but self-refutation is something else entirely. In the following chapters, I will look at other examples: how do we get beyond the clichés of a field, while staying within the bounds defined by the language of that field?

CHAPTER 3

Bibliographers of the Mind

One of the most influential articles written on bibliography in the past half century is D. F. McKenzie's "Printers of the Mind."[1] It is likely the compelling nature of the title and the implied thesis that have prevented me from reading or re-reading it as closely as I should, and I assume I am not alone in this. That title suggests there are two kinds of printers: (1) printers who existed and worked in the real world, slovenly, dirty, messy, inconsiderate and inconsistent, inefficient, and self-contradictory—more or less like all of us—and (2) Printers of the Mind, products of bibliographers and scholars—efficient, rational, consistent, reasonable, coherent—the types of people we imagine ourselves to be, or more accurately, the mask scholars are forced to assume when they write scholarship. Such Persons of the Mind are those our simplified language and scholarly abstractions project onto the real world we claim to be studying. Expressed in its most extreme way, McKenzie's article (or title) implies that the mischaracterizations of scholarship are evil, like racism, or perhaps just innocent wishful thinking. It is the intellectual self-justification of the scholar: because I wish it to be, therefore it is. Less extremely, it might be argued "so what?" Obviously, scholarly language (The World of the Mind) simplifies and makes coherent an otherwise complex and unintelligible natural world. That, it could be argued, is its function. Boyle's law, oversimplifying the complex and messy behavior of gases in varying temperatures, is no different: gases do not behave according to laws; rather, so-called laws are merely simplified descriptions of the erratic behavior of gases within certain narrow limits.

McKenzie targets that Anglo-American bibliographical field known conventionally as "analytical bibliography" ("Printers of the Mind," 1) and the subfield known as compositorial study; the careful examination of books, some bibliographers claim, reveals consistencies in the way historical individuals set type, or at least, their spelling habits, grammatical habits, tendencies toward arbitrary corrections. This, to the Anglo-American bibliographer, would then be part of the information available to document the transmission of the text, to many, including McKenzie, the most important role of bibliography.[2]

Against this claim, McKenzie sets the detailed records from Cambridge University Press and the eighteenth-century printer Bowyer, where compositors' stints were set out in detailed records of payment. These stints and patterns, he concludes, could not be determined by ordinary methods of analytical bibliography:

> It must suffice for the moment simply to observe that the patterns which emerge seem to me to be of such an unpredictable complexity, even for such a small printing shop, that no amount of inference from what we think of as bibliographical evidence could ever have led to their reconstruction. ("Printers of the Mind," 7)

With that, the article should write itself, or at least, the method of testing this thesis should do that: you would simply go to the books printed at Cambridge in the late seventeenth century or by Bowyer in the eighteenth century; you would apply in good faith the methods of analytical bibliography or compositorial study (or assign your graduate students to apply them or challenge fellow scholars to apply them); you would then compare the two sets of conclusions (those from the printing house records and those obtained from the methods of analytical bibliography), and you would draw your conclusions from that. What could be easier and more obvious? You would have tested the methods of one branch of analytical bibliography, and furthermore you would have in this the basis for practicing and teaching that method. I suspect it was thinking along these lines that led to my writing Chapter 6 below.

Yet this, to my knowledge, has not been done, despite all the discussion of McKenzie and even the general acceptance of his views among bibliographers. Nor am I about to do it here. I have never believed in the virtues of compositorial analysis, and thus I could not conduct such a study either competently or in good faith, nor could I explain to others how such a study would proceed. As far as I know, those who did believe in compositorial analysis continued to believe in it and apparently saw no need to have their methods tested. Looking through the indexes in the MLA Bibliography leads to the conclusion that the article that should have sounded the death knell on compositorial study only generated more of it.[3]

It is that "undone" testing of this theory that underlies the chapter here. Why has it seemed to bibliographers pointless, redundant, or unnecessary to perform what the article and theory requires and certainly would generate if this were in the field of science, so often invoked in the article (see, for example, p. 6)? Why would no one want to reproduce or test results and why am I so indifferent to doing so myself? And what implications does that have for the nature of the fields bibliographers define and study? Bibliographers often invoke science, yet they seem completely indifferent to scientific method and the tedious repetitiveness that method entails: the obsession with performing an experiment once, then performing it again.

Bibliography: Analytical, Enumerative, Descriptive

This tripartite scheme of bibliography is one I have assimilated so thoroughly that I cannot expunge it from my consciousness. I teach it, refer to it, and even distinguish key works in bibliography according to it. I have never had occasion to argue for it or defend it, and I was frankly surprised when I began to put together this chapter on McKenzie that I could find so few authorities for it. In fact, most of the obvious sources I found seemed to contradict the model I have kept in my head for decades in order to make the field negotiable and intelligible. Were my own bibliographical categories simply bibliographical categories of the mind? And did that, I wondered, thinking back to certain anthropological studies that affected me so profoundly thirty years ago, really make any difference?

I am not certain of the source of my error, or whether it is an error. The subject index for *The Library* lists as a heading "Analytical, Descriptive and Enumerative Bibliography," but I am sure this is the first time I have seen that. D. C. Greetham, *Textual Scholarship* (1992), seems to distinguish the three categories in his introduction the way I recall them, but the chapter divisions do not follow through on this, nor do his discussions suggest that his understanding of these terms is the same as the definitions given by those he cites.[4]

There are many variant schemes. In an article featured prominently on the website of the Bibliographical Society of America, Terry Belanger distinguishes "two main sorts" of bibliography: "enumerative (sometimes called 'systematic') and analytical"; analytical bibliography is divided into historical, textual, and descriptive bibliography (this in Belanger's scheme includes binding details). In a University of Illinois syllabus by Sidney E. Berger, there are five branches of bibliography: enumerative, analytical, descriptive, historical, and textual. I assume this is influenced by Belanger, although I am not certain of that.[5]

Fredson Bowers, who virtually defined descriptive bibliography as a field, sees it as a form of analytical bibliography: "A true bibliography is primary an analytical bibliography" (*Principles of Bibliographical Description*, 34). This statement is quoted by T. Howard-Hill in an article distinguishing two main branches: "enumerative and descriptive bibliography."[6] G. Thomas Tanselle, who has made a career out of systematizing obscure and contradictory material like this, seems to oppose descriptive to analytical bibliography in a recent book. In his widely distributed Syllabus for Scholarly Editing, only analytical bibliography has a category.[7] William Proctor Williams and Craig S. Abbott, in their *Introduction to Bibliographical and Textual Studies*, have chapters on analytical bibliography (chap. 2) and descriptive bibliography (chap. 3), although they claim that "in methodology and terminology the two fields are nearly identical" (13).[8] Yet the bibliographical journal once edited by Williams, *Analytical and Enumerative Bibliography*, implies two different basic bibliographical categories, the same two defined by Howard-Hill.

Peter Blayney's introduction to his study of Nicholas Okes is an obvious reference here.[9] But his discussion is much less helpful than one would suppose and much less comprehensive on this topic than I recalled. If I am reading this complex introductory section correctly, its primary purpose is to show the relationship between Anglo-American bibliography and textual criticism, as well as the formulation of that problem by W. W. Greg. It is not concerned (as I had hoped) with other schemes of bibliography and the way Blayney's own work fits those schemes. I will return to this point later.

Among the problems involved in separating these fields, one most of the above scholars note, is that few of the important works are pure examples, and the very definitions of the fields make such examples difficult to find. The categories are asymmetrical, and fields of bibliography are conflated with bibliographical approaches: obviously any real descriptive bibliography is the result of analytical practices (analytical bibliography), and enumerative bibliography is, in the case of STC for example, a compilation of the results of descriptive bibliography. Furthermore, the ordinary meanings of these terms get grafted onto the technical ones: any list becomes "systematic"; descriptive bibliography "describes" books; analytical bibliography "analyzes" them. The occasional inclusion in these schemes of the kind of pointless bibliographical exercises we give undergraduates and misdirected graduate students (creating a book list) only complicates things.

The Function of Anglo-American Analytical Bibliography

The fields traditionally defined in Anglo-American bibliography are in large part a function of the most important English bibliographical project of the twentieth century: the STC (1926; 1976–1991; now expanded to ESTC), a comprehensive catalogue of all books printed in England or in English to 1640.[10] STC is not, however, a catalog of what we normally think of as books, that is, material book-copies. It is a catalog of editions, and these are the units to which each entry refers. How to define these units is the question addressed by Bowers's *Principles of Bibliographical Description*. Descriptive bibliography uses the techniques of analytical bibliography in order to produce descriptions that are the basis of an enumerative bibliography like STC.[11] I don't think any bibliographer would disagree with that statement, although of course we might disagree about what it means.

The object of a descriptive bibliography is not a book-copy, but what Bowers defines as "ideal copy."[12]

> The collational formula and the basic description of an edition should be that of an ideally perfect copy of the original issue. A description is constructed for an ideally perfect copy, not for any individual copy. . . . Thus an *ideal copy* is a book which is complete in all its leaves as it ultimately left the printer's shop in perfect condition and in the complete state that he considered to represent the final and most perfect state of the book. (113)

The distinction is between books and book-copies, although that distinction is not I think specifically advanced by Bowers. Very simply, book-copies are what we ordinarily think of as books. They are physical, and they are individual. Books are something else: they are the abstractions that allow bibliographers to speak of two book-copies as essentially the same.[13] And it is these books, rather than their manifestations in book-copies, that are the objects of bibliographical descriptions. The purpose of bibliographical description is not to define a unique physical object (as would be the case, say, with a manuscript description), but rather to define an idea, in this case, the product of a printing press: either a standard by which all members of an edition may be judged or evaluated, or the most ideally perfect book the printer could reasonably have intended to produce. These are not quite the same thing, although in practice an example of one might be indistinguishable from an example of the other.[14]

Thus, when we see an entry in Greg's *Bibliography in English Printed Drama* or even a much less detailed entry in STC2, what we get is a description of an item (perhaps brief, perhaps lengthy), and following that description is a list of locations. The structure of the entry reflects the difference between book and book-copy. And there are many examples where none of the book-copies listed conform to the description of the book that precedes that list.[15]

Analytical bibliography thus was defined in the tradition in which McKenzie was enmeshed as fundamental to descriptive bibliography: the purpose of analytical bibliography (especially in terms of the STC project) was to produce the basis of bibliographical descriptions, which in turn would be the basis of the enumerative bibliography known as STC. Analytical bibliography is not the simple analysis of a material book (a book-copy), any more than bibliographical description is a description of one. It is an attempt to recreate or reimagine historical events based on evidence provided by material books. Its purpose is to analyze books as products of procedures at a printing press, in other words, to analyze book-copies as products of "ideal copy," understood as that abstraction in the printer's mind or the mind of the workers, as they are or have been subjected to the workings of the press. In the context of McKenzie's article, we might say analytical bibliography is not about real books (= book-copies), but about Books of the Mind.

"Printers of the Mind"

McKenzie's article is in two parts. The introductory section is a theoretical critique of method, couched in the language of mid-twentieth-century criticism. The second section is a straightforward presentation of what McKenzie defines as evidence. The validity of the second part of the study has never

been questioned, as far as I know, but it provides the assumptions that under-
lie the first theoretical critique.

> These comments are philosophic commonplaces and stated so baldly
> must seem slightly naive. Yet they do serve to point quite sharply to
> the two main directions open to bibliographical inquiry. If bibliog-
> raphers wish to persist as inductivists then they must diligently
> search out the historical facts which will alone provide a fairly ac-
> curate definition of "normality" and offer these as a corrective to
> the logical defects inherent in the method. Alternatively they may
> confess outright the partial and theoretic nature of bibliographical
> knowledge, proceed deductively, and at the same time practise a
> new and rigorous scepticism. In fact the nature of "normality" as so
> far revealed by historical evidence suggests that the "norm" com-
> prised conditions of such an irrecoverable complexity that we must
> in any case adopt the latter course. If the "scientific" proofs offered
> in some recent bibliographical analyses of older books were seen
> philosophically for the conjectures they are, we should I think be
> nearer the true spirit of scientific inquiry and the humility that al-
> ways accompanies an awareness of the possibility of fresh evidence
> and therefore of falsification. The subject would not then be circum-
> scribed by the demand for demonstrable proofs; rather it would be
> expanded in its hospitality to new ideas and in its search for fresh
> historical evidence in the service of disproof. Such a method would
> be, in the best sense, scientific. (6)[16]

His concluding paragraph, following this one, seems to argue against the
validity of any method:

> In the following section I wish to offer some varieties of fresh evi-
> dence. Its main implication is that the very fixity of the physical
> bounds within which we are asked to work is inimical to the devel-
> opment of a sound methodology—first, because if the stress is laid
> on "proof" then the small number of paradigms available to us un-
> reasonably restricts the subject; second, because in the present state
> of our knowledge the finite particulars with which we must work are
> too few and therefore permit too many alternative generalizations to
> be induced from them; third, because the conception of "normality"

as a corrective to the undisciplined proliferation of generalizations misrepresents the nature of the printing process; fourth, because induction is necessarily an inconclusive method of inquiry. The evidence is consistent with my belief that we should normally proceed in our inquiries by the hypothetico-deductive method which welcomes conjectures in the positive knowledge that productive conditions were extraordinarily complex and unpredictable, but which also insists that such conjectures be scrutinized with the greatest rigour and, if refuted, rejected.

The more I read this, the less I understand it (note, for example, how the word "positive" applies not to empirical facts, however defined, but to a type of knowledge). We cannot, he says, make laws or draw conclusions based on a limited set of facts (induction); therefore, we have to work deductively, although it is not clear to me how the hypotheses that we test through facts differ from "general laws derived by the inductive method" (4) based on a similarly limited set of facts. McKenzie concludes that when facts are available, their complexity is greater than theoretical models that can describe them. But this very conclusion seems an example of inductive reasoning. Just because one case leads to this conclusion does not mean all cases will: at least, that would not be the conclusion of a "new and rigourous scepticism."

One of the most interesting critiques of this paragraph, by one of the most interesting contemporary bibliographers, is by Blayney in *Texts of King Lear*, 35–36. The critique reveals, inadvertently, a number of further problems and assumptions. Blayney sees McKenzie as I do, or more accurately, I see him as Blayney does, opposing as alternatives the inductive approach (whereby rules are developed from details) and the deductive one (a hypothesis is tested by details). Yet no matter how many times I read this critique, I cannot determine Blayney's own position any better than I can determine how McKenzie's work fits into the schemes with which he introduces it. Of the four sentences in Blayney's summary, two begin with the adversative "But":

In the inductive approach a general rule is inferred from a finite number of observations, whereas by the hypothetico-deductive method those same observations are made the basis of a hypothesis to be tested. . . .

(I don't think these are alternatives; they say the same thing.)

But whether the hypothesis is to be used as a rule which further observations must obey, or is recognized as merely the first of several steps in a process which may ultimately discard it the process of devising it is much the same.

(These seem false alternatives to me.)

Rule or hypothesis, any theoretical framework developed as a guideline must take account of all the available primary evidence.

(By "primary evidence" McKenzie meant external evidence from Cambridge University Press records. Blayney means something else. And the word "must" is hyperbolic, since of course it is never possible to assemble "all the available primary evidence.")

But the Cambridge documents provide far more information than could possibly have been reconstructed from the CUP books alone . . .

(That is what McKenzie says, although no one has ever tested this hypothesis.)

and before the evidence can be used as a control on speculation about Okes it needs to be somewhat simplified.

(I believe this claims that evidence such as McKenzie collects can only act as a control, and even then only in "simplified" form. But this certainly involves begging whatever question might be posed.)

Reading this paragraph over and over again, with and without my comments, I am not entirely certain what Blayney claims to do in *Texts of King Lear* in relation to the alternatives posed by McKenzie's article. I think he claims to do what other analytical bibliographers have done: assemble the analytical evidence from book-copies and take into account as much external evidence as he can, decorating or ornamenting the basic evidence from these copies. I believe he also implies that his arbitrary simplification of Cambridge University Press data from the late seventeenth century is a better source of evidence for details of Okes's production in the early seventeenth century than are the nearly contemporary statements about, say, edition size from the (discredited?) records of the Stationers Company. But this is not something Blayney states directly.

Evidence, to Blayney, seems to be whatever the bibliographer chooses to see, to observe, and to collect: press variants, for example. The evidence Blayney collects and organizes is of two kinds: one consists of statements in the Stationers Register concerning Okes; the second, and more important, is from the books themselves.[17] McKenzie's facts (the records of compositors' stints at Cambridge and in Bowyer's archive) do not come from book-copies. In McKenzie's article, book-copies and their data are not part of the "complete record of facts," which consists only of press documents, seemingly unerring accounts of historical truths.[18]

Definitions of Evidence

The contrast provided by McKenzie with the work he criticizes is not, I think, one of methods. McKenzie's description of the inductive method at the beginning of the essay reads very much like his description of the hypothetico-deductive method described later.

> Nor is it simply that there is no logical way of arriving at general truths from the examination of sampled cases. To observe at all is to bestow meaning of some kind on the thing observed; to gather particular pieces of evidence is to seek those relevant to some preconceived notion of their utility. But the main point is that any general laws derived by the inductive method remain highly vulnerable to fresh evidence. Where the known particulars are few, this risk will be greatest. (3–4)

A law constructed from induction that will be "vulnerable" to new evidence does not seem to me much different from a deduced hypothesis to be tested against that same evidence.

What McKenzie contrasts is not two methods, but definitions of what constitutes evidence. If we were to define types of evidence in terms common in mid-twentieth-century criticism as internal and external, McKenzie and those he targets would likely agree that the evidence from book-copies is internal, the evidence from the printing-house records is external. Where they

disagree is how that distinction relates to what they would call primary and
secondary evidence.

> Wherever full primary evidence has become available it has re-
> vealed a geometry of such complexity that even an expert in cyber-
> netics, primed with all the facts, would have little chance of
> discerning it. (60, from the section "Plus ça change, plus c'est la
> même chose")

The "full primary evidence" here rules out any of the "limited demonstra-
tions" that could be made by analytical bibliography; primary evidence here
seems not to be the evidence from books (physical book-copies),[19] but rather
the evidence from records of book-production. Yet this identification of primary evidence is a function of method, not something inherent in the evidence
itself: there is no such thing as primary evidence per se; primary evidence is a
reflection of the methods used to manipulate or record it.[20]

If McKenzie limits primary evidence to the press records summarized in
his appendices, then his criticisms of analytical bibliography are little better
than tautologies.[21] If all primary evidence is external evidence, then analytical bibliography produces secondary evidence; the evidence from the book-
copies, as organized by the analytical bibliographer, somewhat paradoxically
becomes secondary, in that it constitutes statements about the primary evidence. Yet the analytical bibliographer could argue (and in the 1960s could
do so with conviction) that it hardly matters what the external evidence has
to say: analytical bibliographers are concerned with internal evidence, which
for them is primary evidence, and the kinds of statements assembled by
McKenzie, of whatever date, constitute secondary evidence, since records of
payment to compositors are statements about what compositors do. We have
no basis for knowing whether those statements are of ultimate validity,[22]
whereas the facts of book-copies are irrefutable. If the patterns found in those
copies are analogous to historical events, so much the better. But there is no
sense that they have to be.

Conclusion: "Lawyers find out still litigious men"

To the bibliographers considered here, praise of facts seems almost an act
of piety:

It is therefore the basic function of a descriptive bibliography to present all the evidence about a book which can be determined by analytical bibliography applied to a material object. (Bowers, *Principles*, 34)

The essential task of the bibliographer is to establish the facts of transmission for a particular text, and he will use *all* relevant evidence to determine the bibliographical truth. . . . Book listing may be degressive as it wishes, bibliography never. (McKenzie, "Printers of the Mind," 61)

Any investigation must necessarily begin by allowing the Quarto evidence to speak for itself. (Blayney, *Texts of King Lear*, 8)

This seems a reiteration of the dictum of Henry Bradshaw in the late nineteenth century, without Bradshaw's qualification concerning the extent of "facts":

As for the originality, I, of course, never laid claim to any new facts. My only point is my method, which I always insist on in anything in bibliography—arrange your facts rigorously and get them plainly before you, and let them speak for themselves, which they will always do.[23]

To claim that bibliography cannot be degressive is to suggest that evidence must not be limited, circumscribed, or falsified through restrictive organization of any kind. The history of modern bibliography, however, shows that the more we gather, the less we glean. Charlton Hinman's 1963 *The Printing and Proof-Reading of the First Folio of Shakespeare* is often taken as the model of detailed work in analytical bibliography.[24] Yet Hinman did not give a full account of press-variation in the seventy copies of the First Folio at the Folger; he in fact fully collated fewer than fifty of them, although, despite his own clear statements, he is often credited for doing more than this.[25] What he does claim explicitly is that full examination of these and other copies would not provide useful information. To compile "all the evidence," then, for the most thorough practitioner of analytical bibliography in English, was pointless. Bibliographers since Hinman have preferred the myth that he did provide that complete record of Folger First Folios to the more daunting task of completing the work themselves.

McKenzie did not reformulate the discipline of bibliography as Bland claims, nor did he undermine analytical bibliography, since this presumably seminal article attacked, however convincingly, only an ancillary set of assumptions that had little to do with analytical bibliographical methods or methodology. Neither the set of facts manipulated by analytical bibliographers nor the facts manipulated by McKenzie provide in and of themselves "what it was" or "how it was" historically, unless we beg the question by claiming what we happen to record as facts are of absolute historical validity.[26]

Analytical bibliographers were not deterred by McKenzie's article, because it only attacked the assumption of uninterrupted work at presses, single presses, uniform edition sizes, and similarly dubious bibliographical notions. All this could easily have been refuted (or at least dismissed) through logical reflection. That "average" does not translate into "normal," and that workers were inefficient—these notions need no documentation to prove, and they do not affect what analytical bibliographers do or conclude. Other assumptions criticized by McKenzie seem to reappear in his own article in much more powerful form; note how the notion of uniformity, criticized when applied to the workings of several contemporary presses, is unproblematic when applied, with a suitably moral tone, to the entire history of printing: "the integrity of the subject can be preserved and a sound methodology evolved only if we stress the *similarity* of conditions in all periods" (53).[27] McKenzie seems to finesse this issue, rather than resolving it, by resorting to paradox in his conclusion: all presses are alike in being different (63).

To me, "Printers of the Mind" raises a number of questions on method, but these do not bear on the validity of particular methods. They concern rather purely practical matters: (1) is this particular bibliographical activity what we want to do? (2) is it useful for other purposes? (3) is the history we get at of any interest?

As far as compositorial analysis goes, the answer to all those questions, at least to me, is no. The habits of a compositor (whether to spell *die* or *dye*) are not interesting to me (question 1) nor are they ingrained enough to reveal anything else of interest (question 2); there seems no hard evidence that a compositor who spells *dye* is inclined to produce a set of definable substantive errors in addition to that one and that tabulating these tendencies will get us closer to what an author wrote.[28] Knowing what a compositor did perhaps does not really help us in what we want to do. I cannot think of a single case where a significant Shakespeare word or phrase is better documented because we have determined compositorial stints.

Finally (question 3) is the history in and of itself of any interest: it seems to me we already know that spelling conventions are in flux, that individuals have different conventions, and that those conventions can change. I am not two different persons because at times I dutifully spell unaccented syllables ending in *l* followed by *-ing* with two *l*s and sometimes one. Or that I sometimes give dates with the numeral first, or that I sometimes spell my name out in full and sometimes give only initials. Nor are these implied selves of any interest to me or to anyone other than those diligent copyeditors I have been blessed with having.

I'm not sure even the most ardent practitioner of analytical bibliography would disagree with any of this, although McKenzie seems to demand that his presumed opponents have the moral and methodological purity to feel otherwise. Maybe they (or we) should. But it is unwise to accept the strictures placed on your ethics or methods by those who disagree with them, or who, in certain contexts, simply pretend to do so.

Excursus: Note on Origins and Objects

There is a certain insularity in English bibliography that describes "New Bibliography" as *sui generis*: before, there was darkness, then came the light—systematic, enumerative, analytical—all generated by a group of English-speaking bibliographical luminaries. But there is precedent for all their work, particularly in the study of incunables, in which the New Bibliographers were not much interested. Among the more notable examples are the early incunable catalogues by Michel Maittaire (1719), and in the early nineteenth century those by Panzer and by Hain.[29] English examples include Joseph Ames's *Typographical Antiquities* of 1749, revised by William Herbert and T. F. Dibdin; Dibdin's Spencer Catalogue; the descriptive bibliography of William Blades on Caxton, still basic to Caxton studies; even the booksellers' catalogue of William Lowndes.[30] Examples of what came to be known as analytical bibliography are easily found in the work on early German and Dutch printing by Paul Schwenke, Karl Dziazko, and Gottfried Zedler, and it is interesting that the assumptions behind this work have nothing to do with textual criticism, a central purpose of Anglo-American analytical bibliography.[31] These scholars are rarely mentioned by New Bibliographers and their followers. This is in part because much of their work had to do with the origins of printing (English bibliographers had no stake in the claim to priority on this question) and nothing to do with the establishment of canonical texts or textual criticism, a primary concern for Anglo-American bibliographers. It is also in part because they had the temerity to write in languages many modern bibliographers find inconvenient.[32]

The distinguishing characteristic of the New Bibliography is not, as often implied, its approach, but rather its objects: seventeenth-century English books and the literary texts they contain. And these objects and conditions of their production may not be as easily generalized as the language of English bibliography implies and as McKenzie himself advocates.

PART II

On the Making of Lists

Herman R. Mead's *Incunabula in the Huntington Library* and the Notion of "Typographical Value"

The Huntington Library catalogue of fifteenth-century books was produced by Herman R. Mead in 1937.[1] The catalogue and collection were to be organized according to the Proctor system, also the basis for a number of contemporary incunable catalogues; items are organized under country, town, printer, and date of printing within each printer, and the order of entries in the catalogue is determined by the "sequence of Proctor numbers."[2] Each entry in the Mead catalogue has two numbers. The first, in the left margin, is the Mead number: each book receives a number in sequence, so that the last number in the catalogue is the same number as the total number of incunables in the collection. The second, in the right margin, is the Proctor number, that is, the number Proctor assigned to the same book in the British Museum collection.

For the bulk of the collection, the principles of the catalogue are clear and unproblematic, and they are stated in a concise two-page Preface by Mead. But the Huntington, like other libraries with large incunable holdings, contains a number of fragments—loose fragments filed as separate items, endpapers and pastedowns in bindings of other books in the collection, and loose leaves contained in published leaf-books and collections. Few library catalogues would treat such fragments as "books"; that is, they would not be given separate catalogue numbers.[3] But precise principles to deal with such items are difficult to define.

> Fragments (single leaves, or a few leaves)—usually in the Haebler series—are not given separate serial numbers, but appear under the

preceding serial number, followed by a plus sign; and no Proctor number is given in the right-hand column, except in the few cases in which the fragment is actually shelved with the other incunabula. Fragments are not included unless they add something of typographical value to the entries under a particular printer; and they are not included in the index by authors, for their presence there would be merely misleading to one looking for a text of a work. (Mead, *Incunabula*, vii)

The "Haebler series" consists of three collections of 280 incunable leaves published by Konrad Haebler in 1927–1928: *German Incunabula*; *Italian Incunabula*; and *West-European Incunabula*.[4] Mead also included reference to fifty-five leaves contained in the contemporary collection of W. L. Schreiber.[5] As far as I can determine, all other additions to Mead's catalogue are to individual leaves or to leaves found as binding material in other books at the Huntington.

No modern cataloguer would even consider giving the individual leaves in a collection such as Haebler's or in a leaf-book a separate entry in a catalogue. That Mead would do so bears directly on fundamental questions of what a book actually is, and the nature and function of the repositories (libraries) that house such things. Questions about the development and impact of early printing, about the spread of literacy, and so forth depend on quantitative statements about, say, "numbers of books printed" during a particular period, and depend also on our intellectual systems of organizing them.

The purpose of the present chapter is first to investigate what Mead meant by "typographical value" and how that was defined in a practical sense, that is, what principles of inclusion Mead followed when dealing with the fragments in the collection. I will then consider what these inclusions imply about the nature of the Huntington catalogue and collection as it was conceived by those who developed it. Mead clearly did not think of the Huntington holdings as mere "book-copies" (that is, valuable or curious items in a museum); rather, they were "type specimens" bearing witness to the history of printing.

Early History of the Collection

The early history of the development of the incunable collection and the cataloguing decisions regarding it are recorded in large part in a series of memoranda and often laconic annual reports by Mead.[6] The earliest groups of incunables came to the Huntington as parts of the major sales from which the general collection was built: Snyder (1907), Poor (1908), Church (1911), Hoe and Huth (1911–20), Dunn (1913–17), Pembroke (1914). The majority of incunables came to the library in the 1920s, beginning with the Phillipps sale in 1923 (750 items).[7] Some 3,500 more were acquired in 1924–1925, the bulk of them in two sales from Otto Vollbehr of 400 and 1,800 volumes;[8] by 1927, an institutional decision had been made not to increase this collection further.[9] Little time was spent specifically on the collection before these major purchases. And as late as 1925, fifteenth-century books were still "arranged on the shelves according to Hain numbers" (that is, alphabetically by author).[10] At some point, a decision was made to rearrange these books and recatalogue them according to the Proctor system. In 1927, "Progress is being made towards arranging the Incunabula by place and printer according to Proctor numbers."[11] By 1931, this system was a *fait accompli*, despite objections voiced by the Huntington Director of Research: "Mr Davies and I are still unconvinced of the superiority of your method of presenting lists in Incunabu[la]; that is, of the so-called Proctor method . . . your material is already arranged according to that system."[12]

For the published catalogue, Mead at first envisioned "a checklist on the style of Voulliéme's Berlin list."[13] But the model for Mead changed to that of Proctor. Voulliéme arranges entries by country, and under country by town (alphabetically). Proctor arranges by country and town according to the first appearance of printing in the region. What Mead takes from Voulliéme is not the system of organization, but the form of the entry. A typical entry in Voulliéme is the following (item no. 1; H refers to Hain, Pr. to Proctor):

12.März 1468 Bonaventura: Meditationes de vita Jesu Christi. 2°. H *3557. Pr. 1520.

Mead's entry for this particular book is very similar (Mead no. 941):

12 Mar. 1468 *Pseudo-Bonaventura. Meditationes vitae Christi. 2°. H 3557; GW 4739; BMC 2:315 (Winans) 1520.[14]

But Voulliéme also includes some minimal copy-specific information, for example, "Tabula fehlt," "Defekt," "Bl. 88 fehlt." None of this is found in Mead. The only copy-specific information supplied by Mead is (1) when the book is bound with another catalogued incunable, and (2) a note on provenance, but only when the book comes from a major named collection. Mead notes that the decision not to "spend time" tracing provenance was made by Farrand and Davies.[15] Furthermore, Mead refused to include such information in the case of the so-called Vollbehr "collection," since "Dr. Vollbehr's status is decidedly that of a commercial agent."[16] In this sense, the history the Huntington librarians were interested in was the history of books, not the history of book-copies.

More and more during this period, the Huntington collection was seen not simply as a collection of books (texts by authors), but rather as a record of typographical history. The "gaps" to be filled were defined specifically as typographical.[17] And one apparently acceptable way of filling such gaps was through facsimiles, something stated explicitly by Mead, but never put into practice: "For some items, a facsimile reproduction will serve our purposes in a very satisfactory way."[18] The Huntington had copies of Woolley facsimiles, the publications of the Type Facsimile Society, the facsimiles of the Gesellschaft für Typenkunde des XV. Jahrhunderts and of Konrad Burger, as well as those in the more limited catalogue of English printing by E. Gordon Duff; despite this, there was no systematic effort to incorporate these facsimiles or even to reference them in the main checklist.[19]

The Mead Catalogue

What Mead meant by "typographical value" is best indicated by the catalogue itself. There are two types of items included as what I will call "additions" (items with a plus sign in the catalogue): separate fragments, either loose or occasionally binding fragments found in other books; and items contained in published collections such as Haebler's.

Individual leaves are not always easy to identify, and this is particularly true of service books (the category of book where individual leaves are most likely to be retained). As far as I know, Mead left no systematic record of the fragments he knew existed. And not all those that must have been known to Mead are catalogued in the main Huntington catalogue. There is thus no way of knowing what fragments Mead consciously omitted, that is, those that added nothing of typographical value to the Mead catalogue. For the leaves included in collections, the case is different. Mead included reference to fragments in two major collections of leaf-books, those of Haebler and that of Schreiber. These together include some 335 examples, and the majority of Mead's additions come from them.

Although Mead does not define "typographical value," what that seems to have meant for him was "typefonts not represented in the Huntington collection," that is to say, items that would fill the "few gaps in typography" noted in Mead's reports on Incunabula while his checklist was being planned.[20]

Determining which of these leaves actually shows a typefont not in the Huntington collection is not, however, entirely straightforward. One could, of course, simply look at all the books of each printer to see whether the example is there. But Mead apparently adopted another method, at least for some of the books, based on the organizing principles of the Proctor catalogue.

Proctor identified the typefonts for each printer and assigned a numerical series for them under each printer (that is, Sorg 1, Sorg 2, Sorg 3, etc.); these same numbers identifying the various types used by each printer are also found in the Haebler leaves (they should correspond to Proctor's numbers, and in most cases do). Proctor's descriptions of these types is brief, and never quite sufficient to identify them unless one has clear and unambiguous examples at hand, for example, the entry under Eggestein (*Index*, 41):

> Type 1, earliest type.—Type 2, large text type (Burger pl. 92, text).—
> Type 3, smaller type with fantastic capitals (Burger pl. 92,
> commentary.—Type 4, another small type; the capitals have some
> resemblance to those of Mainz, press 3, type 3. . . .

Proctor provides measurements "for most of the Roman types" (*Index*, 13), but even here his method of measurement ("from the top of the short letters in line 1 to the bottom of the short letters in line 20," 13) does not correspond to that of later bibliographers and is not always reliable.

Nonetheless, the use of the same typefont numbers by Proctor and Haebler provides an apparent way of determining whether the typefont in a leaf from the Haebler collections is represented in the books in the Huntington. The procedure (which is a bit more onerous to describe than to perform) is as follows. The first step, of course, is to determine whether the book represented by the leaf is actually in the collection. The introductions to the Haebler and Schreiber volumes in the Huntington have been annotated; each listed book that is contained in the collection is marked in those introductions with a penciled H. These leaves can be quickly eliminated since they already are represented in the Huntington collection.

The next step is to determine whether the typefont identified by Proctor is included in other books by that printer in the Huntington. Mead assigned every Huntington incunable a Proctor number; this is either the number assigned by Proctor or, when the book is not included in Proctor's *Index*, a Proctor number with a decimal, indicating where Proctor might have catalogued the book had that book been in the British Museum collection. Thus, a

Huntington book assigned a Proctor number with a decimal is a "book not listed in Proctor"; a Huntington book assigned a regular Proctor number is a "book in Proctor with type identification in Proctor."

To determine whether the Huntington has an example of, say, Higman 5, 8 (the two types represented in Haebler, *West-European Incunabula*, plate 35), you begin with those books by Higman in the Huntington with undecimaled Proctor numbers: Pr 8126, Pr 8128, Pr 8133, Pr 8137, Pr 8140. You check the types listed for these books in Proctor's catalogue. And indeed 5 and 8 are listed. Thus, the leaf in Haebler is of no typographical value, since the Huntington contains examples of the typefonts in other books by Higman. To go farther than this would require examination of the books themselves, and the results below suggest that Mead did not take this step. Suppose now the type numbers represented in the Haebler plate do not appear in any book in the Huntington with a regular Proctor number. This is the case with Haebler, *West-European Incunabula*, Plate 36, of Higman 12, 13, and 14. You could then check those Huntington books by Higman catalogued with decimaled Proctor numbers, that is, those books by Higman in the Huntington whose types were not analyzed by Proctor. Under Higman, there are three of these: Pr 8131.5; Pr 8131.7; Pr 8140.5. You could either analyze the type and match it with Proctor's descriptions or, more simply, attempt to match it visually with the example in Haebler. This is a skeletal version of the procedure I followed in my attempt to reconstruct Mead's procedure. I do not believe any more efficient method was available to Mead in the 1930s; nor do I think a half-century of incunable study has provided means for a more efficient method today. (Had one been available, I would certainly have availed myself of it!) But applying such a procedure consistently produces some peculiar results, which bear on both the nature of the Huntington collection as conceived by Mead and his process of cataloguing it.

The Haebler Series

I begin with the leaves from Haebler's *West-European Incunabula*. Mead includes reference to 15 of the 60 Haebler plates: 12 from France; 1 from Spain, and 2 from England (none from the Netherlands). For convenience, I will deal with the French books first. Of the twelve plates included by Mead, use of the Proctor catalogue alone (following the method outlined above) suggests that the types in these plates are not represented in the collection. That is to say, the Huntington books with regular Proctor numbers do not, according to Proctor, contain examples of the typefont identified in Haebler. But what about those books whose types are not identified by Proctor?

For most of these printers, the Huntington has books that are not included in Proctor. I simply checked these against the Haebler plates included in Mead to determine whether there was any evidence that Mead had actually referred to them. These are the results:

Plate 15, Huss, 13, 14. Mead identifies the printers as Maréchal and Chaussard. The types, however the printer is identified, are all represented in Pr 8632.7 (*Libri Salomonis*).

Plate 17, Balsarin 1, 4. Not represented in the Huntington.

Plate 19, Carcain 1, 2, 7. I only can find two of the three types in the leaf included in the Huntington copy of Haebler, and both of those are found in Pr 8590.2 (*Destructiones*).

Plate 23, de Vingle (1), 6, 7. As far as I can determine, these types are not represented in the Huntington.

Plate 29 (listed by Haebler as Matthias Huss; by Mead as Davost). Only example of Davost printing in the Huntington.

Plate 31, Martineau. No non-Proctor books by this printer in the Huntington.

Plate 36, Higman 12, 13, 14. These types are not listed in Proctor, whose lists stop at #11. None of the Huntington books not in Proctor (Pr 8131.5; 8131.7; 8140.5) have the particular types in this plate.

Plate 37, Bocard 3, 6, 7, 8. It is not obvious from Proctor that these types are represented in the Huntington; but all four of them are in fact included in books at the Huntington, although not in any single book. The text type (72mm) is in Pr 8170.2 (Philelphus), and the heading type is on its title page. The gloss and display type are in Pr 8165.5 (*Rhetorica Divina*). It should be noted that what Haebler means by these numbers is not entirely clear, nor are the four types clearly identified in the corresponding numbers in Proctor. None of Proctor's descriptions define the text type (72mm), nor is that text type clearly identified in Haebler's *Typenrepertorium der Wiegendruck* (2: 287).

Plate 40, Pigouchet 6, 7. Both types are included in Pr 8210.5 (Philippus de Monte Calerio).

Plate 45, Bouyer & Bouchet 11. The type is not included in any Huntington book.

Plate 46, Jean le Bourgeois. No examples of this printer in the
   Huntington.
Plate 47, Mayer 1, 3. These types are not represented in the Hun-
   tington.

Thus, of the twelve examples included by Mead (those listed above), three
contain types that are indeed represented by books in the Huntington collection. But this could only be determined by referring to the books themselves,
not by the use of Proctor.

For the non-French books included by Mead from Haebler's *West-
European Incunabula*, the results are less clear; for Mead 5186+, (Biel), the
types are not in the Huntington. Plate 60 shows de Worde 3, 5, types that are
obviously in the Huntington from Proctor. Mead 5380+ (Pynson) is in Proctor, but the types are not identified. For English books, however, the easiest
way to determine whether the types are represented in the collection is
through the indexes in Duff, *Fifteenth-Century English Books* (Duff numbers
are included in the Mead catalogue). A glance at the entry in Duff shows that
these types are indeed represented by books in the Huntington. The inclusion of the de Worde leaf must be a mistake. The inclusion of the Pynson leaf
seems to be the result of following the procedures used in the French books.

Thus, if we consider only those leaves included by Mead from Haebler's
West-European Incunabula, it appears that Mead followed a simple rule: when
it is not obvious from Proctor that the Huntington has a typefont, include the
leaf. But we should also consider the Haebler leaves excluded by Mead. And
when we do, it appears that this principle was not followed with precision.
There are 45 plates from *West-European Incunabula* omitted by Mead, and 28
of these come from books found in the Huntington collection. Of the remaining 17, all those from the Netherlands show typefonts that are said by Proctor
to be represented in other Huntington books. Of the 9 others (from France),
it is obvious from Proctor that the Huntington has the typefont in 6 cases, but
in one the typefont does not seem to be represented (Syber 2, 5, seen in Plate
14; there is no example of Syber 5 in the Huntington). In another (Plate 41
showing Baligault 3, 4, 5), Baligault 3 does not seem to be in the Huntington,
unless one accepts Proctor's note that this = Bocard 4 (Proctor, *Index*, 591).
From the consistency with which the principle of inclusion is applied, however, the exclusion of the Syber reference may have been an oversight.

Now to identify these types and match those descriptions with Haebler's
facsimiles, Haebler's *Typenrepertorium*, and Proctor is by no means straightfor-

ward, as the examples under Bocard suggest. But it would not be difficult for someone with easy access to the Huntington stacks to determine whether or not these books had the types in the Haebler leaves (provided that those stacks were organized as they are now, with the incunables arranged by Proctor number within each format). It seems clear from these examples that, at least for Haebler's *West-European Incunabula*, Mead did not refer to the physical books in any systematic way when making his decisions. Rather he worked from a copy of Proctor, the very basis of the catalogue system he was producing.

The additions in the Italian section of Mead's catalogue tell a similar story. Of the seven additions, six are from Haebler's *Italian Incunabula*, a collection that contains 110 leaves. For the excluded leaves, I again eliminated books found in the Huntington collection (one can do this through the penciled notes in the introductory pamphlet in Haebler, or through the Hain concordance in the Mead catalogue, 361–80). The Huntington collection is extremely rich in Italian incunables, and this accounts for most of Haebler's examples.

Four of the six plates included by Mead contain types not in the Huntington. But two (Plates 30 and 41) are problematic.

> Plate 4. Britannicus. Pr 2975; only example of this printer in the Huntington.
>
> Plate 8, Cenninus. Mead 3560; not in Proctor. Only example of this printer in the Huntington.
>
> Plate 30, Han and Chardella. (Lactantius, 1474) The book is in Proctor (Pr 3660) listed as having type 6, a type represented in the Huntington by Virgil, Pr 3358. I can see no rationale for including reference to this plate.
>
> Plate 41, de Spira 2 (Caracciolis). Using Proctor alone, one cannot be certain that the Huntington has the type. But the type is certainly found in Pr 4039.6 (Duns Scotus) and Pr 4037.5 (Tudeschis).
>
> Plate 64, de Tortis 3, 4, 5. These types are not included in Proctor books at the Huntington; nor are they found in books with decimaled Proctor numbers.
>
> Plate 87, Saracenus 6. Proctor lists only five types for Saracenus, all in the Huntington. The type here does not match that in the remaining Huntington book not listed in Proctor.

Again, with the exception of Plate 30, Mead's procedure seems to be that followed in *West-European Incunabula*. Of the Haebler plates omitted, the vast majority are books included in the Huntington. All but one of the others clearly show types represented in the Huntington (a fact that can be determined by Proctor). The sole exception is Plate 55, Rubeus 3, 5. It is not clear from Haebler and Proctor that the Huntington has any examples of Rubeus 3 (101 mm by Proctor measurement; all Huntington books are listed and their types identified in Proctor, with the exception of Pr 4245, which does not have this type).

Thus, of the six Haebler plates included, two are included because no other examples of type from these presses are in the collection. Two others are included because the particular types do not seem to be represented in the Huntington (something that is suggested by Proctor, but confirmed by looking at the books themselves). But two others, by the same criteria that led to inclusion of the last two, should have been excluded. Furthermore, another is omitted that should have been included, if the principles implied by Mead's use of Haebler's *West-European Incunabula* were applied. I assume that these two exceptions are simple mistakes.

For Haebler's *German Incunabula*, the results are similar. Mead included reference to six of the 120 Haebler plates. In each case, it appears from Proctor that the Huntington does not have the type. But checking the physical books shows that the Huntington does indeed have the types found in Plate 49 (Knoblochtzer 5, 6; found in Pr 3139.6 [Chaimis]). Plates 14 and 15 show Ratdolt 19, 20. The Huntington has what Proctor describes as Ratdolt 19 in Pr 1914; I am uncertain about Ratdolt 20.

For leaves from Haebler omitted by Mead, the vast majority are books already in the Huntington. Of the remaining twelve, in eleven cases it is obvious from Proctor that the Huntington has the type. The only problematic case is Plate 37 (Froben 4, 5, 12); the Huntington has 4 and 5, but it is not clear from Proctor or from Pr 7756.5 that the Huntington has 12, unless Proctor's identification of this as = Amerbach 5 is correct (*Index*, 553).

Again, the principles followed by Mead for Haebler's *West-European Incunabula* and *Italian Incunabula* seem to apply. For the most part, the inclusion of a leaf was determined by whether the analysis by Proctor/Haebler/Mead suggested the type was in the Huntington.

Schreiber Series

In addition to the Haebler leaves, Mead included reference in the German section to a number of leaves included in Schreiber's *Woodcuts from Books of the*

XV. Century. Here, the problems were somewhat greater, in that Schreiber, interested as he was only in woodcuts, did not provide type identifications. In the cases where the book in Schreiber was represented in the British Museum, its type is identified in the Proctor catalogue, and the procedure that appears to have been used by Mead for the Haebler plates could be used here. In other cases, to determine whether the Huntington collection has the type would require physical examination of the books. Mead's reliance on type identifications of Haebler and Proctor becomes clear in looking at these books.

Mead does not seem to have followed a consistent procedure in dealing with the Schreiber plates. Again, we can eliminate those books in Schreiber that are in the Huntington (all identified with a penciled H in the Huntington copy of Schreiber). For the others, I will start with books in Proctor, that is to say, those books in which the materials clearly used by Mead would provide a quick identification of the type. There are six of these books. In four, it is obvious from Proctor that the Huntington has the type (they are omitted from Mead's catalogue). The other two (Plates 6, 7) are included in Mead, a decision that seems based solely on the information available in Proctor. Checking the books shows that in one case, the Huntington does indeed have the type. (Mead included reference to two Berger books, Pr 1916 and Pr 1917, in Schreiber Plates 6 and 7. The Huntington has the typefont shown in Plate 6 in Pr 1917.5 [*Klagspiegel*]. It does not have the type in Plate 7.) Again, Mead seems not to have checked the actual books, and this is the same procedure as that implied in the case of the Haebler leaves.

For books not in the British Library and thus whose types are not identified by Proctor, the results are not at all clear. There are sixteen of these, yet however one organizes the material, the decision to include or exclude them seems almost random. Four of these plates are included by Mead (Plates 39 and 40 are from the same book); the Huntington has the type in one case (Plate 27, Schott), and this might be determined by reference to Proctor, since all five types identified by Proctor are in the Huntington; in another (Plate 14, Schobsser) it does not have the type.

Of the twelve remaining plates omitted, the Huntington has among its books with regular Proctor numbers all the types listed for the particular printers in seven cases. In five cases, some of the types defined by Proctor for each printer are not represented by books with regular Proctor numbers. If examination of the physical books showed that the Huntington had representations of these types, we could assume that Mead had checked them, and that he made his decisions accordingly. But the results are again inconsistent.

For Fyner (Schreiber, Plate 18), the Huntington does in fact have the text type and display type (in Pr 2825.6 and 2825.2), and this plate is rightly omitted. The same is true for Schoensperger (Schreiber, Plates 12 and 13); the Huntington does in fact have all types represented. But for Baemler (Schreiber, Plates 2, 3), the Huntington has only the type in Plate 3 (in Pr 1621.5); it does not have the type in Schreiber, Plate 2.

When the Schreiber leaf was from a book listed in Proctor, Mead followed the principles used for Haebler leaves; he excluded the leaf when the type identifications in Proctor for books also in the Huntington showed that the type was already represented in the Huntington, and he included the leaf when none of the Huntington books with regular Proctor numbers were said by Proctor to contain this type. Yet for books not in Proctor, and thus with no authoritative type-identification, no clear principle is discernible.

Independent Fragments

The last major source of catalogue additions is in loose leaves independently filed, or leaves included as binding material in other books. Mead includes twelve examples of such loose leaves, pastedowns, or endpapers, most from German printers. Of the three non-German examples, the Huntington has examples of the type in one case (Mead 4874+, Alexander of Ville Dieu). In this case, the leaf is of sufficient bibliographical value to deserve entry, whatever typefont it contains, since most examples of Dutch prototypography in all libraries exist only as fragments. In another case, Mead 5269+, the leaf is the only example in the Huntington of printing by Theodoric Rood. In the third (Mead 3092+, Pincius), I cannot determine whether the Huntington has the type, and Proctor himself notes the "unusual difficulties" of the types of this printer (*Index*, 348).

For the nine German examples, the figures are comparable. In five cases, use of Proctor would reveal that the Huntington had the type; "typographical value," in these cases, is not simply "the presence of the typefont in the Huntington collection." In one other (Mead 1574+), one would have to refer to the books themselves to discover that the type was in the Huntington. In only three cases of the nine, does the Huntington have no other examples of the type.

The principles here are obviously impossible to articulate, and each case is unique. Mead included in the catalogue the leaf from the *Canon Missae*

(Mead 1+) and the leaf from Alexander of Ville Dieu (Mead 4874+) because these would be of typographical value no matter how many examples were in the library. Other inclusions strike me as problematic: Mead 1574+ (Brandis) and Mead 636+ (Koelhoff). As incunables go, these are run-of-the-mill. And in the case of Koelhoff, it is obvious even from Proctor that the Huntington has the typefont. Clearly, typographical value for these fragments is something quite different from the typographical value of leaves in leaf-book collections. And I assume Mead's inclination was to include reference to any fragment found as an endpaper in another incunable or as a clearly identified and independently catalogued fragment. There is no reference to incunable endleaves found in sixteenth-century bindings, and there are many examples of incunable fragments contained as endleaves in other incunables (in a brief survey, we found more than two dozen of these just in the folio section of the Huntington incunable collection). Some of these were clearly known to Mead, although it does not seem from our survey of these fragments that any systematic attempt was made to list or identify them. The most that can be said is that there is no clear evidence that any binding fragment known to Mead and clearly identified by him was omitted from the final catalogue.

Conclusion

The principles Mead used varied as the sources of his material varied, and his catalogue seems to be an attempt to work out its own principles of construction. For the German section of the catalogue, the areas in which the Huntington collection was strongest, Mead seems to have followed a simple rule: "I may not be able to define typographical value, but I know it when I see it." The sources of additions are diverse (nine from loose leaves and binding material; eleven from Haebler and Schreiber), as are the apparent bases of decision-making. It is only in the later portions of the catalogue, when specific principles are implied by the additional entries, that problems arise. In the Italian section and in the French and Belgian collections, "typographical value" comes to mean "a typefont not represented by Huntington books that bear regular Proctor numbers." The number of fragments included is in part a reflection of the nature of the Huntington collection. The collection surely better represents Italian in relation to Haebler than it represents French in relation to Haebler, and thus more Haebler plates are included in the French section. The greater number of binding fragments found in German books is

also a result of the nature of the collection: the van Ess incunables are mostly
German and many are in original bindings; a good portion of the Italian
books are from Vollbehr, and a large number of these have been rebound.
Vollbehr broke up many composite volumes into separate volumes, apparently to ensure the maximum number of saleable items in his inventory. I
assume that in the process he also removed any interesting fragments that
might have been used as binding material; in our survey of Huntington incunables, Vollbehr books yielded very little in the way of such material.

The inclusion of these various fragments by implication redefines the objects of the collection. The objects to which the catalogue as finally constructed
refers are not necessarily book-copies: they are rather examples of typefonts and
evidence of the history of printing history. The status of the fragments is to
some extent parallel to the status of duplicates in the early history of the library.
The early decision at the Huntington to develop its collection in part through
the de-accessioning of duplicates[21] has two implications for the materials here:
first, incunable fragments from editions already in the library are by definition
"of no typographical value" in terms of one of the basic organizing principles of
the collection. But second, given the nature of the Mead catalogue, fragments
that duplicate typefonts in the collection are equally redundant.

Mead's history of early books and printing is the history of printing as
conceived by Proctor; and even though Mead placed books within the Proctor order, something that surely involved type identification, the above study
suggests that he made no attempt in the case of the fragments to work out
type identifications from the physical books in the collection. Proctor's history of printing is a development of Henry Bradshaw's notion of a natural
history of typefonts,[22] whereby the history and identity of individual printing establishments is based on the workable assumption that, with some
exceptions, an identifiable typefont means an identifiable printer. These are
idealized printers, the printers of enumerative bibliography, not the printers
of analytical bibliography (whose variant copies are full of errors). Mead's
own version of Proctor's history is one step farther removed from the typographical evidence that supports it. And this may in part explain Mead's
ambivalent attitude toward provenance, for which he supplied notes under
many individual entries. These notes on provenance, and the few notes on
composite volumes (*Sammelbände*), are the only copy-specific information in
Mead. Mead's decision not to include a brief provenance index among his
excellent and detailed indexes shows that such copy-specific information remained secondary to his main concern.

From a practical standpoint, the inclusion of references to loose fragments makes perfect sense: the user of the Huntington collection would want to know whether the library has multiple examples of, say, Netherlands prototypography, without having to search the main card catalogue under "Donatus," "Alexander," "Pontanus," or without resorting to the powerful but erratic oral history of the library. But when it comes to Haebler leaves or Schreiber leaves, items the researcher already knows are in the collection (or should know are there), the situation is different. Without specific notes identifying what the typographical value of particular Haebler leaves is, users of the published catalogue are left to guess. They would not know why they are being referred to a particular Haebler leaf in most cases, *unless* they were to follow the rather tedious and laborious procedure I have followed above. But even this procedure reveals exceptions. Mead's reference to particular examples in Haebler and Schreiber thus provides no usable information, and one would do just as well to have a global reference to the Haebler plates marked simply: "list of Haebler leaves containing typefonts not in other books in the Huntington." Even now, the reader only has my word for it that the rules are consistently applied anywhere in the catalogue! In addition, the absence of an explicit rationale provides future cataloguers no clear guidelines on what fragments are to be included, just as the catalogue itself provides no clear guidelines on how future acquisitions of any kind are to be dealt with, something noted by Mead's earliest reviewers.[23]

Had Mead included, as Proctor does, a reference to the types used in each book, the typographical value of each additional entry would have been instantly apparent. Such a procedure would have revealed much more: it would have made explicit the principles of cataloguing, and it would have exposed any obvious errors (for example, the inclusion of plates in leaf-books with types already represented in the Huntington).[24] As Proctor-based catalogues, these catalogues and the decisions made by the earliest cataloguers were based finally on the natural history of typefonts as imagined by Bradshaw. But the evidence resists this history: types are difficult to identify; even books cannot be defined. And catalogues finally have competing purposes; like Proctor's own catalogue, they are indexes, but indexes both of a repository of evidence and of the assumptions about history that serve to organize that evidence both intellectually and materially.

Appendix: Checklist of Fragments Included in Mead

Mead	Proctor	Printer	Source (refs. to Haebler series and Schreiber)	Type id (Proctor)	Is type in other HEHL books?	Is HEHL presence established by ref. to Proctor?
Germany						
1+	640	Schoeffer	leaf	1, 2	no	no
1++	66	Schoeffer	leaf	3	yes	yes
14+	95	Schoeffer	leaf	5	yes	yes
213+	—	Schott	Schr. 27	—	yes	—
484+	794	Pfeyl	Hb GI 16	—	no	—
636+	1047	Koelhoff	in Pr 9234	7, 9	yes	yes
757+	1202	Guldenschaff	leaf	1	yes	yes
1109+	—	Froschaur	in Pr 1866.5	—	no	—
1126+	—	Schobsser	Schr 14	—	no	—
1136+	—	Ratdolt	Hb GI 14	*		
1138+	1895	Ratdolt	Hb GI 15	*		
1143+	1916	Berger	Schr 6	1	yes	no
1143++	1917	Berger	Schr 7	2	no	no
1144+	1929	Zeissenmair	leaf	1, 2	no	no
1528+	2542	Zainer	Hb GI 108	5, 7	no	no
1574+	—	Brandis	in Pr 4440	1, 2	yes	no
1631+	—	Koch	Schr 39, 40	—	no	—
1668+	—	Petri	leaves	1, 2?	yes	yes
1785+	—	Printer of Brev. Misnense	Hb GI 51	—	no	no
1796+	5145	Knoblochtzer	Hb GI 49	5, 6	yes	no (5)

Italy

Han	3360	Hb ItI 30	6	yes	yes
de Spira	4052	Hb ItI 41	2	yes	no
de Tortis	4629	Hb ItI 64	3, 4, 5	yes	no
Saracenus	—	Hb ItI 87	—	no	no
Pincius	—	in Pr 4302		?	—
Cenninus	—	Hb ItI 8	8	no **	no
Britannicus	6975	Hb ItI 4	4	no **	no

France

Martineau	7921	Hb WEI 31	1, 2	no	no (2)
Higman	8139	Hb WEI 36	9, 10, 11	no	no
Bocard	—	Hb WEI 37	3, 6, 7, 8	yes	no
Pigouchet	8201	Hb WEI 40	5, 7	yes	no (7)
Balsarin	8580	Hb WEI 17	1, 4	no	no (4)
Carcain	—	Hb WEI 19	1	yes	no
Maréchal	8629A	Hb WEI 15	5, 6	yes	no
de Vingle	8649–8651	Hb WEI 23	1, 2	no	no
Davost	—	Hb WEI 29		no **	no
Mayer	—	Hb WEI 47		no	no
Bourgeois	8770	Hb WEI 46	—	no **	no

Netherlands

Printer of Speculum	—	leaf	—	yes	yes

England

De Worde	9707	Hb WEI 60	3, 5	yes	yes
Rood	—	leaf		no **	no **
Pynson	9812	Hb WEI 58	not id'd in Proctor	yes	no

*Proctor identifies the types of Pr 1895 as 7, 9, 12, 19; Haebler as 19, 20. The 113G is not in the Huntington.

** Only example of printer in HEHL.

CHAPTER 5

Catchtitles in English Books to 1550

A little-noted feature of early sixteenth-century English books is what Victor Scholderer refers to, in reference to fifteenth-century Italian books, as the "catch-title."[1] Catchtitles are abbreviated forms of the book title printed on the direction line, that is, the line used for printed signatures and catchwords just below the text block. They appear generally on the first page of a quire, indicating the book or volume that quire belongs to. A typical example from Whittinton's grammar is shown in Figure 4 ("Syntaxis VV." on the direction line of the recto).

In early English books, their form is various. In some books (Yearbooks and Statutes), they are nearly identical to running heads. For example, in STC 9664, the catchtitle "Henrici.vi." is nearly identical to the running head on the recto "Henrici sexti"; this is the second half of the phrase read across the running heads of the open page, "Michaelis undecimo, Henrici sexti." In others, they are highly abbreviated, and could serve no imaginable function for the reader; these were clearly for the printer (for example, the abbreviations "Sar." for books of hours, Salisbury use, or "Imyta" for *Imitacio Christi*). They are a regular feature of certain classes of books such as Yearbooks and the many Whittinton grammars, but during the 1520s they appear in all genres of books. The conventions for printing them vary: for some books, they appear on the same rectos as those that contain signature marks; that is, in a quarto, they appear on the first three of four leaves. For books collated as folios or folios in half-sheets, they are commonly on the first folio of each bifolium; for quartos in 8s, they commonly appear on the first and third leaves of an eight-leaf quire. And in some books (fewer in number), they appear only on the first leaf of a quire, or, for a book with a title page of some sort, the second or third leaf of the initial quire. I have not recorded these

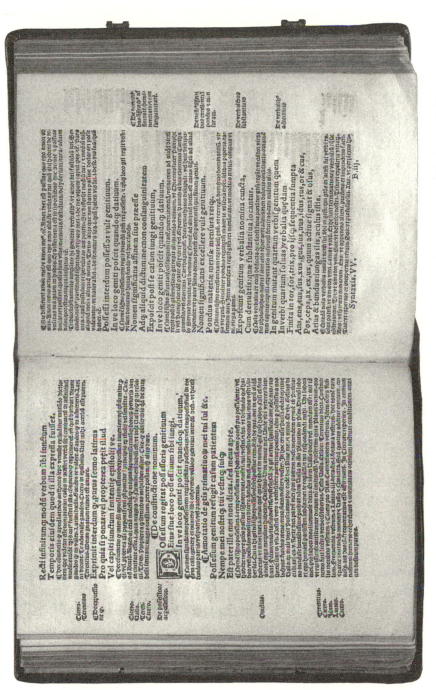

Figure 4. Catchtitle, from Whittinton, *Syntaxis* (1530) STC 25552. HEHL RB 61716. Photo courtesy of the Henry E. Huntington Library, San Marino, California.

differences in detail, since they are almost always a direct and predictable function of physical structure.

Catchtitles are clearly related to book structure and indications of book structure. The two features of structure that interest me here are (1) presence of catchwords and (2) foliation. What is the relation between these two extra-textual features of a book, and what can we find out about them by "arranging our facts" in the most obvious way? What are the limitations of our sources of evidence (databases rather than books), and what obstacles do these sources place in our way? My summary conclusions are in the two tables at the end of the chapter. Table 1 shows the simple occurrence of catchtitles year by year, along with the appearance of catchwords and foliation. Table 2 attempts to plot the specific relation of catchtitles to these other features.

Note on Terminology: Catchtitles, *Normen*, Signature-Titles

Catchtitles are different from the more familiar catchwords. A catchword is a word printed at the end of a page, leaf, or quire, repeating the initial word of the following page, leaf, or quire. Catchwords have a history, of course, their function changing from medieval manuscripts to, say, eighteenth-century printed books.[2] A catchtitle, by contrast, appears not on the last page of a unit but on the first page, and refers not to text within the book (that is, it is not useful for joining parts of a book in proper sequence, either for a printer or for a reader) but rather to the title of the book: it can only function to associate particular physical units such as sheets or quires with the whole book containing those units.

As far as I can determine, there is no set term for this feature of books. Konrad Haebler calls them "Normen" and claims they are frequent in Venice incunables, but does not say which ones.[3] They appear to be a regular feature of modern German printed books, appearing on the first leaf of each quire, and the technical term for these is again "Normen." I wasn't aware of seeing them until I began to look for them. They are regular features of books printed in the early twentieth century by the Oxford University Press, although the conventions regarding their form vary; and now that I am aware of them, I find them in books of all periods.[4] They don't seem to be mentioned in William Savage's 1841 *Dictionary*, although I would of course have to know Savage's term for them in order to find it.[5] Greg's term for these seems to be "signature-title," although few of the books in his bibliography of early drama where he defines the term actually contain them. McKerrow, referring to Greg, mentions them in his *Introduction to Bibliography for Literary Students*.[6] McKerrow's index lists these as "volume or part-signatures," but his discussion on page 81 shows that he is not really comfortable with (or maybe familiar with) what Greg calls signature-titles and the Germans call *Normen*, nor does he have a name for them. He conflates these marks with a number of marks, including press-figures. But what Greg calls signature-titles are clearly not part-titles or volume-titles; they refer to the title of the entire book, not to any structural or textual part of the book.

The term "catchtitle" is misleading, and other terms such as "foot-titles" (never to my knowledge used) might be more strictly accurate. Catchtitles do not "catch" anything in the way that catchwords do, since the same form appears throughout the book (can they be thought to "catch" the quires together?). I retain the term in deference to Scholderer and because introducing a new term only makes an already obscure matter even more obscure. Any English reader who confronts the term will quickly figure out what it refers to: a reference to a title in what is called the direction line. The same might be said for Greg's term "signature-title," although McKerrow's own confusion speaks against its use. Any term presents the same problem: as the scattered and unsystematic use of catchtitles in early Italian books suggests, and as my own survey of what appears to be the more systematic use of them in English printing shows more clearly, the function of these varied from book to book. Even if we have no idea what a catchtitle does or should do, we probably can recognize one when we see it.

Method and Qualifications

Catchtitles are not regularly noted in bibliographies, and one reason for that may be the lack of a conventional bibliographical term for them. The only way to search for them in some cases is the obvious and tedious way: you must look at the books themselves or at reasonably reliable images of those books. If the goal, as here, is to survey every English book to 1550, there is really no feasible way to do this by looking at the physical books. Even given extraordinary generosity on the part of library staff, there are few if any libraries in America that have the resources for this, and at any library with close to the numbers of books required, those books are not conveniently enough located to make the survey worth the pressure on staff and materials.[7] I used as the basis for my own searches the images in EEBO, despite the obvious limitations of this database.[8] I sorted these in the simplest of ways, year by year, using the date assigned by EEBO (a date I would probably also have had to use had I based this survey on physical books). I used as the definition of what constitutes a book the simplest one: "entry in EEBO," a much different definition from that implied if one were to look at every book on the STC shelves of a library. This means that each edition and each issue as defined in EEBO is given an entry, even though in some cases, these are clearly part of the same printing project and may even be the same printed sheets.[9] There are numerous instances where we know that EEBO classifications are strictly speaking incorrect (even though they do not misrepresent book history in any serious way), but there seems no reason to eliminate those while including the dozens of cases we know nothing about. I have thus not second-guessed the dating of these books, except in some obvious cases of mistranscription (1583 books sneaking into the database as 1538). It is possible that a number of such cases appeared. I caught those I did simply because they so quickly revealed themselves as anomalies.

I also accepted EEBO's assignment of place, and excluded as much as possible books printed on the Continent. Doubtless several Continental books leaked into my figures, due to lapses in my attention. But interesting or anomalous ones usually brought a second glance, and thus were easily eliminated. Also, I made no attempt to record any book or entry that provided no evidence, nor have I bothered to estimate their numbers, since I saw no reason to believe this would affect the distribution of the "facts" I was looking for. This meant excluding all broadsheets, all fragments that gave no indication of foliation or catchwords, and a few books whose photographed copies were too badly trimmed to provide usable information.

Tables 1 and 2

Tables 1 and 1a (incunables) show the distribution of books in four categories:

(1) those with catchwords and foliation (cw, fol)
(2) those with catchwords and no foliation (cw, ~fol)
(3) those with no catchwords, but with foliation (~cw, fol)
(4) those with neither catchwords nor foliation (~cw, ~fol)

The last column indicates those with catchtitles. Because so few books during this period are paginated (a total of 11 among several thousand), I have simply included them among the general figures (see note below). Table 2 shows the distribution of catchtitles among the same four categories of books.

The tables show two things: first, the steady and systematic rise in the use of catchtitles and their precipitous decline following 1533. This decline in the use of catchtitles seems related (correlated?) to the use of catchwords, which by 1540 are clearly the norm in English printing. Early sixteenth-century books thus show a more systematic use of such catchtitles than do the scattered examples recorded in other classes of books (for example, incunables recorded in BMC).[10] But this may be more a function of bibliographies than of the books these bibliographies refer to.

The tables do not show the genre of books in which catchtitles appear. In the earliest books in these tables, catchtitles appear or seem to appear in books of all genres. By the 1520s, it is obvious that two classes of books are conventionally printed with catchtitles and that the numbers of these books dominate. The first of these is constituted by the various editions and sections of Whittinton's Latin grammar. Almost none of these contain either foliation or catchwords, and nearly all contain catchtitles of some sort. In 1533, Whittinton's grammar is replaced as the King's grammar, and following that year no version of the Whittinton grammar is printed.[11] That alone is enough to account for the sudden decline in the use of catchtitles in English printing. The second class of books is Yearbooks: these present particular problems in dating and attribution (detailed in STC2), although those problems do not seriously affect this table.[12] It is this class of books that retains the (now obsolete) catchtitle, accounting for most of those cases in the late 1540s. It is thus impossible to isolate bibliographical facts or conventions from the conditions that produced them.

These general classes of books (grammars and Yearbooks) present further problems from a bibliographical point of view. Yearbooks are produced continually and in series: printers likely did not consider them as units that correspond neatly to what an enumerative bibliographer considers a book (a book = item in EEBO or ESTC). Whittinton's grammar is similar: neither printer nor user is likely to have considered, say, "Declinationes Nominum" and "De Heteroclitis Nominibus" or any of the other STC titles as different books; they were, rather, parts of the same grammar. Like the Yearbooks, these parts were identical in appearance, and likely sold (and later collected) together.[13] Through the catchtitles of the Whittinton, a printer could tell which book (or book part) any sheet of this grammar belonged to at a glance (for example, STC 25549 "Syntaxis.vv." or STC 25563 "Praeta.et.supi.Verborum" [1523]).[14] Catchtitles on these sheets would have been most appropriate for projects ("the-printing-of-the-Whittinton-grammar") that were carried on over a long period of time while other books were being printed simultaneously. The situation would thus be similar to that of fifteenth-century Donatus grammars.[15] But with the Whittinton, it might be more routine for a printer or bookseller to put together books (and book-copies) from parts that a bibliographer would consider belonging to different editions. This may explain in part the absence of foliation and the persistence of catchtitles in these books.

EEBO Searches

Useful though it may be, little about EEBO qualifies it as a definitive bibliographical source. The images are mediocre by modern standards and often misidentified; the descriptions have not been proofread to the standards of ESTC. Even simple searches such as those I conducted can be erratic. For my year-by-year searches, I simply typed in the date in both the FROM and TO boxes then clicked on "Organize by Title" and "Show 40 results per page."[16]

Usually this produced coherent results. But not always. EEBO has assigned one date for each book in its search field, even when the precise date can only be estimated. This convention of dating is perfectly suited for year-by-year searches such as I conducted here (although of course it means that the results cannot be too finely tuned). Yet several times my search produced lists of books that included date-ranges, the very thing the organization of EEBO seems designed to avoid. Thus, a search for a given year would list any books dated by a date-range within which that year fell: a search for 1519, for example, might include books dated 1500–1549 or 1517–1523. Five minutes later, the identical search might yield only books with the single assigned date. And certain books that are assigned such date-ranges, rather than specific dates, could not be expunged no matter what type of search I performed. Thomas Moulton's *Myrrour or glasses of helthe*, STC 18221a, with which I grew very familiar, is unaccountably assigned the date-range 1500–1546, and consequently showed up in every year search between and including those dates.

Whenever I found myself faced with a number of these books or an inordinately high number of books for a certain year, I conducted exactly the same search through the same client EEBO until these date-ranged books disappeared; to my knowledge, there was no difference, even in the order of keystrokes, that led to these different results. I am certain there is an explanation for this, but I doubt I would understand it even if it were clearly presented to me. When I was aware of a book-entry appearing more than once because it was assigned a range rather than a single date, I tried to eliminate the redundant entries, but I am sure I did not succeed in every case.

EEBO searches like this are time-consuming: I estimate I could look at perhaps fifty books an hour, working very rapidly. Looking for specific features such as catchtitles slows this down; trying to determine the pattern of those catchtitles (by quire? by folio? by recto?) slows things down even more. The relation of the evidence in EEBO to actual book structure is not always apparent from the images alone, and I eventually ignored structure nearly entirely. It is hardly feasible or useful to record book structure from EEBO images when that structure is already recorded directly in ESTC from the books; the relationship of catchtitles to structure was sufficiently clear after looking at a few dozen examples that this was not worthwhile recording in detail. Any attempt to record structure on the basis of the images would have been gruelingly slow and would have introduced far more errors than any results would justify.

The statements of book structure in EEBO are unfortunately not reliable enough to be used without reference to the images. ESTC entries tend to be better, but there was, I found, no way of predicting whether an error found in EEBO would appear also in ESTC without checking each entry against images of the book. Cataloguing rules for ESTC and EEBO now require a statement of pagination or foliation, and it should be possible to determine a book's leaf structure simply by reading the formula; the following hypothetical examples should adequately express these rules:

276 pages = a book paginated in arabic with 276 pages
[276] p. = a book with 276 pages that is neither paginated nor
    foliated
cxiii leaves = a book foliated in roman with 113 leaves

But EEBO descriptions do not follow these rules. For EEBO descriptions, I estimated an error rate of roughly 5–10 percent. Of these, many I cross-checked in ESTC revealed the same error. These are trivial errors, of course, and no one looking at the book would be misled. For example, in many

cases, far more than 10 percent for early books, EEBO might describe a
book's structure with a formula such as "[50] leaves"; the correct expression
by their own rules would be "[100] p." Brackets are often left out. Trivial as
these are, they would likely affect any attempt to search either database directly for, say, paginated books, and it is hard to say how easily and efficiently
obvious errors could be then weeded out. I can only guess that the error rate
of such searches would likely be close to the rate I have doubtless had doing it
the long way. It may well be possible to design a Boolean search for ESTC to
produce as reliable statistics as I have here, but ESTC bibliographers have
told me it is not feasible for civilians to search these databases this way.

Conclusions

The exercise here is precisely that, an exercise. I was presented with a problem
and went about solving it the only way I knew how. There is finally no way
around certain problems other than gathering up heaps of books or their
facsimiles and recording in some way what is in them. I have doubtless made
many, many mistakes. I know I have mistyped STC numbers; I have left out
numerous books. I have misrepresented where in the book the catchtitles appear. But I have arranged the facts, as Bradshaw suggests, as rigorously as my
own personality permits, and a few things reveal themselves clearly.

First, there were a number of incidental matters: it was fairly easy, while
doing this, to note facts that had nothing to do with the initial project. So I
now know when the first English books were paginated, and also when the
first English books were printed with roman type. Such things are often
misrepresented in basic bibliographical manuals, the reason being not that
bibliographers are careless or oblivious to the facts, but rather that no one
wondering about these particular questions (they cannot be called "problems") has ever taken the time required to find out the answer in the most
obvious way, which is to look at each STC book in chronological order until
the answer is found.[17] All this leads to what I think is a basic bibliographical
paradox or principle: some bibliographical facts are not worth discovering
unless you are not looking for them, that is, unless you are researching a different question altogether.

I also sensed very early on a relation between catchtitles, catchwords, and
foliation, and that is why my tables record this. There seems an obvious relationship in terms of functions. And as I went through the calming but often

tedious business of looking at these book images, I imagined various ways that these relations could be described.

But the tables themselves would not support any of the clear formulations I imagined: they do not "speak" as Bradshaw claims they always will. And as I was imagining ways of expressing this irritating conclusion, I rediscovered another general principle that was far too familiar to me. When I am spending a lot of time searching for the right expression, the right formulation, the right transitional phrase or sentence, then there is something wrong with my thinking. When I am thinking clearly, the words simply form themselves, and sections do not need much of a revision except in terms of superficial style. Thus, I think that I don't really know what the relationship between these various features is, nor why I assumed one in the first place; and I imagine that my own confusion on this matter is analogous to the uncertainty that existed historically in the printing shop: there is an association of catchtitles with genre; they have a function for the printer in associating a particular printed heap with a particular printing project. There are further norms and histories and conventions of foliation. But the relationship, overlap, redundancy—these things were never clearly worked out by the printing community as a whole (why should the revelations and logic of one printing house apply to those of another?), and I have not worked them out sufficiently here. When the facts are called upon to speak, they often mumble inaudibly.

Finally, there is the matter of the sources of facts, in this case, the now familiar databases EEBO and ESTC. I encountered the same problems, fairly predictable ones, that I have encountered before in using these, although the bibliographical standards of ESTC are generally very high and the problems I encountered were not as serious as when attempting to use the searchable text feature of EEBO books (the Text Creation Partnership).[18] EEBO images were not created for the kind of use they get today: they were never really "ersatz" books, and the initial photographs are not up to the standards of modern photography.[19] Furthermore and more important, any attempt to quantify evidence is affected both by the attempts to standardize evidence in these databases (through the conventions of bibliographical descriptions) and the inevitable errors in this standardization. Note that this is not a criticism of either database. One of the notable features of EEBO is what in bibliographical terms might be seen as a failing: it is not as consistent or reliable as the descriptions in ESTC. To me, this is a virtue. The inconsistencies, redundancies, and misclassifications in EEBO are reflections of the same inconsistencies one finds in physical books. Book production does not proceed according to the niceties of bibliographical description, although bibliographers may well gain nothing by accepting this; the strict demarcation between editions and variants does not hold in the world of real books, and Printers of the Mind, of course, are necessarily different from printers in history. Using these databases and confronting their necessary inconsistencies can be aggravating, but that is only the negative version of what one feels when realizing how strongly real books and book-copies resist the conventional categories of thought we have created to describe them.

Table 1. Presence and Absence of Catchwords, Foliation, Catchtitles

	cw fol	*cw -fol*	*-cw fol*	*-cw -fol*	*catchtitle*
1501			1	9	
1502			4	11	
1503			1	17	
1504			3	11	
1505			2	35	2
1506			5	17	1
1507		1	1	18	4
1508			6	29	4
1509			6	33	11
1510			10	49	18
1511			8	13	6
1512			5	17	9
1513				22	7
1514			2	16	11
1515			5	29	14
1516			8	21	11
1517			10	27	26
1518		1	6	33	27
1519			4	29	21
1520			8	48	33
1521	2	10	6	33	26
1522		8	1	19	14
1523	3	3	5	32	21
1524	1	1	3	14	13
1525	1	3	5	55	39
1526	3	9	19	26	35
1527	6	5	18	30	31

Table 1. (Continued)

	cw fol	cw -fol	-cw fol	-cw -fol	catchtitle
1528	4	6	21	45	37
1529	6	4	3	28	20
1530	6	14	7	49	28
1531	20	15	6	27	28
1532	14	23	8	23	21
1533	43	14	3	24	18
1534	22	31	2	16	12
1535	24	30	1	7	6
1537	15	26	4	8	3
1538	30	40	5	9	3
1539	21	34	1	4	
1540	31	39		10	1
1541	18	17	4	7	1
1542	24	35	2	6	1
1543	30	42	0	6	
1544	29	27	1	8	4
1545	28	48	1	11	
1546	32	57	1	2	
1547	23	75	1	3	7
1548	42	156	1	10	6
1549	35	84	1	3	
1550	53	118		7	6
1551	32	52		5	2

Table 1a. Incunables

	cw fol	cw -fol	-cw fol -cw pag	-cw -fol.	catchtitle
1473–80				32	
1481–85			3	58	
1486–90			1	28	
1491–95			6 fol 2 pag.	46	
1496–1500			15 fol 1 pag	116	1 (unfol.)

Table 2. Distribution of Catchtitles Among Four Types of Books Defined in Table 1

Date	cw fol	cw -fol	-cw fol	-cw -fol
1501				1
1502				1
1503				
1504				
1505				2
1506				1
1507				4
1508			1	3
1509			1	10
1510				14
1511				5
1512			3	6
1513				7
1514			1	11
1515			1	13
1516			1	8
1517			6	20
1518			4	23
1519			3	18
1520			5	28
1521	1		2	23
1522			1	13
1523			3	18
1524			1	12
1525		1	4	33
1526	3	1	10	21
1527	1	1	8	21
1528	1	1	12	23
1529			1	19
1530			4	24
1531	7	1	5	15
1532	3	2	3	13
1533	3		1	14
1534	3	1		8
1535	1	1		2
1536	1			2
1537		1	1	
1538	1			1
1539				
1540		1		

Table 2. (Continued)

Date	cw fol	cw -fol	-cw fol	-cw -fol
1541			I	
1542		I		
1543				
1544	4			
1545				
1546				
1547	5		I	I
1548	3		2	I
1549				
1550	6			
1551		I		I

CHAPTER 6

An Editorial Propaedeutic

Bibliography as understood or defined by Anglo-American bibliographers has always been closely associated with editing, and the following chapter focuses on what appears to be the most basic function of traditional editing—organizing and evaluating extant variants (a set of facts) in such a way as to indicate an original reading, or perhaps the source of error in these extant texts. A danger common to many of the editorial projects I have dealt with is their very complexity and sophistication. The richer and more impressive the method, and the more elaborate the set of facts defined by these projects, the farther these methods get from what appears to be the basic task of any editorial project. The question I pose here concerns students or novices in this field, and what they might do to learn, practice, and improve what I believe are considered basic editorial skills.

The Words of the Sybil: The Editorial Introduction

To the uninitiated, what is called the textual apparatus of standard editions of the classics is only marginally intelligible; the often bizarrely laconic introductions seem the perfect expression of the equally mysterious principles that brought that text to be. Oxford Classical Texts, producing basic editions of classics for decades, and once in common use in college classrooms (we used them for second- and third-year Latin when I was in college) have their introductions written in Latin. The following sentence appears in the introduction to my college Catullus. Its impenetrability never struck me as strange at the time, but only because I never paid much attention to any books I was assigned and none whatsoever to their introductions.

> Hinc credo explicari tot alternantes lectiones quae in *G* et *R* reperi-
> untur; quae ut ab archetypon diuerse interpretantibus sine dubio
> ortae sunt, *η* ex archetypo non ipso semper, sed apographis eius
> depromi poterant, qualia inter 1323 et 1375 quo anno descriptus est
> *G*, exarata esse credibile est.[1]

Today, things are different: students care much more about what they are
told to read than we did. Yet I doubt many students who have ever used these
editions, today or decades ago, have the competence to construe this introductory note grammatically, much less read it or understand what it purports
to explain. Even if their Latin is good enough to wade through it, whatever
"to wade through" might mean in this context, they are hardly in a position
to deal with it critically or to be much enlightened by it. General editorial
assertions here are not supported by details; few if any examples or noteworthy readings are given, and there is no detailed presentation of how manuscript groupings came to be. Scholars capable of a critical evaluation are thus
not provided the evidence required to perform one. Those who read this introduction, if anyone does, can have no idea how this text was created or
what principles it is based on, and their teachers, if they have them, are likely
not in a position to assist them.

Users of such editions can only conclude that textual criticism is not
something ordinary readers can understood, much less deal with critically.
Those who buy more user-friendly editions, with introductions in the vernacular, are little better off. The following is from Schmidt's Everyman Edition of *Piers Plowman*, an edition often used as a school edition.

> The group g is independent of w, having XII 103 and XV 373 and
> (here with F) what seems the right reading at IX 11. It is also larger
> and more complex than w, falling into two smaller subgroups.
> These are represented respectively by the lost medieval source of the
> sixteenth-century MS G, and by y, the postulated source of YOC^{2}CB.
> Of these, y has in turn four constituents, Y, OC^2 (which form a ge-
> netic pair), C and B (the three members of which, BmBoCot, derive
> from a single immediate ancestor B).[2]

The textual tradition of *Piers Plowman* is extraordinarily complex, and
Schmidt can hardly be faulted for failing to clarify this for general readers
or for the undergraduates who might use this edition. Schmidt's summary

statement above is very similar to the far more abstruse discussion in George Kane and E. T. Donaldson's edition, addressed only to specialists. Kane's rhetoric obscures the fact that his presentation of minute detail is often quite vague:

> Neither YOC^2 nor GOC^2 is strikingly persistent, and the difference in strength of support is not very great. Nor does the respective distribution of agreements appear significant. It is however to be recalled that G has figured in variational groups of two with F, C^2, Cr, Hm and S (of which GC^2 may be genetic for part of the poem) whereas Y is a very stable manuscript. For this reason, unless both groups are random, YOC^2 seems the more probably genetic; that presumption will be supported by the texts of congruency, and it then seems that GOC^2 is a random group created by convergent variation, and more specifically in view of the character of its agreements, by coincident substitution.[3]

Even when read by sophisticated reviewers, much must be taken on faith in these cases, and much has been taken on faith. One of the most striking expressions of this is the often cited review of the Kane-Donaldson edition by Lee Patterson: "As a system, this edition validates each individual reading in terms of every other reading, which means that if some of the readings are correct, then—unless the editorial principles have in an individual instance been misapplied—they all must be correct" (69)[4] The logic is breathtaking: *because* the critical evaluation of particular detail is well-nigh impossible in Kane's edition (there is, for example, no index coordinating individual editorial corrections with the principles set out in the introduction for making a correction),[5] *therefore* critical evaluation is unnecessary and superfluous; *if* some readings are correct, *then* all of them are (the same principle, I suppose, applies to a stopped clock). It is not surprising that the rhetoric of the monumental text is conflated by some scholars with that of the monumental edition:[6] the unfortunate implication is that both are beyond ordinary human understanding.

Even garden-variety editions of relatively uncomplicated texts share in this mystification. It is difficult to imagine the function of the following, although its purpose seems to be to create the illusion shared by editor and professor that they fully understand the complex textual situation of the work. I'm sure there are better examples than this. To convince myself that my generalization above was valid, I determined simply to quote from whatever edition I could find lying around my summer home.

> The collation is A1 recto (originally blank), Meighen's title page; A1 verso, blank; A2 recto, the title page; A2 verso, blank; A3-6, unpaged, the Prologue, the Persons of the Play, the Induction; B to M in fours, pages 1 to 88 (with pp. 12, 13, 31 misnumbered as 6, 3, 13, respectively), the text of the play and the Epilogue.
>
> Though the Clarendon Press kindly granted to the University of Nebraska Press permission to modernize the text of the Herford and Simpson edition, the present text is not simply a modern spelling version of the Herford and Simpson text. Risking both a supererogation of virtue and the presumptuousness of doing over (and overdoing) what had been so magnificently done, the present editor has collated five copies of the play—two in the Folger Shakespeare Library, two in the Library of Congress, and one in the Newberry Library Chicago. For the text as well as for the annotation, the Herford and Simpson edition and an excellent modern spelling edition by E. A. Horsman in the Revels Plays have proven invaluable.[7]

This was written by a justly respected Jonson scholar, whom I much admire, and I suppose the reason I have this text at all is because of that. It is only the distance, I think, between the date of this paragraph (1964) and our reading it that makes the problems with its logic and assumptions apparent. In what way are the two most prominent recent editions "invaluable"? To whom? For what? What does it mean to have collated five copies of the many printed copies of the play? which copies? copies of the same edition? different editions? against each other? against the Herford-Simpson text? And why these five copies? Does "modernized" refer only to spelling? Or has the syntax been modernized as well? Could we see examples of this?

Digital editions have so far only compounded these tendencies. Putting more information in the hands of readers does not make that information more coherent or even usable: facts do not speak, in Bradshaw's terms, simply because there are more of them.[8] Furthermore, if the purpose of editing is to get back to an original, the number of facts can actually be a hindrance: the more variants (exemplars) we have of an author's works, the more difficult it is to see our way past them to what we are willing to call an original.

The How-To Manual

A student wanting to edit is not going to get very far by consulting a fully professional edition such as Schmidt's or Kane's, and certainly will not get even a clue as to how editing is done by consulting the Oxford Classical Texts series; and there are consequently many "how-to" manuals that claim to be pedagogical guides to editing. Some of these are perfunctory. Some are sober and quite reasonable, in fact, much more reasonable than I imagined when I began to write this chapter.[9] Others are laughably abstruse, epitomizing all the absurdities of literary scholarship in general.[10] Some confuse the ideal editor with the Ideal Citizen or Lawgiver.[11] And some seem to be written for other writers of how-to manuals rather than for those who might actually use them to edit. At their most extreme, editorial dictates lapse into self-parody, as in the many guidelines and revisions issued by the MLA Center for (or Committee on) Scholarly Editions, whose combination of arrogance, pomposity, self-contradiction, and banality is, I think, unmatched in a sometimes very competitive field. When I first heard friends speaking of their edition as earning (or aspiring to earn) a CSE "emblem," I assumed they were joking.[12]

The purposes of these manuals, even at their most helpful, seem to be quite similar: they focus primarily on the question "How to Produce an Edition," which is quite a different question from "How to Edit" or "How to Perform an Editorial Task." In other words, they avoid the basic task and purpose of editing and concentrate on what amounts to a side issue: formatting the results of editing rather than making editorial choices. These guides thus tell would-be editors how to get *an* answer, and how to present that answer in an intelligible, coherent, or approved manner. But they do not give much guidance in how to go about getting the *right* answer, which I assume is an essential purpose of all editing.

The Relation of Editorial Conjecture to Factuality

The present chapter addresses this aspect of editions, that is, getting the right answer. I focus not on the production of editions (of whatever complexity) but rather on what I think is the basic work that constitutes editions. Most editing produces its text, or multiple and variant texts, by showing the relationship between various real or hypothetical texts and witnesses and subsequently evaluating what those relationships mean; for example, the editor must distinguish between scribal errors, authorial revisions, pure accidents of transmission. The rejection of Lachmannian stemmatics or Housmanian divination does not change this: whether an editor replaces a genetic grouping with cladistic analysis (insofar as I understand this), or the authorial text with the "social text," that editor is still talking about historical events, perhaps even in the most naive sense of that phrase, and attempting to reconstruct them.[13] In other words, at the heart of editing is the assumption that extant texts can be described in terms of what happened, or how they came to be. The editorial arrangement of variants represents the history of those variants: one text was copied from another; two extant texts are to be grouped together because certain events in history (which may not be finally determinable) occurred that linked them in essential ways. Textual details that have no bearing on these questions (Greg's accidentals) are not editorial facts at all.[14]

Editing decisions, because they concern a history external to the editing process, should thus be judged not because they conform to the logic of editing (whatever that is), but rather because they produce results that reflect what happened historically. This is what distinguishes editing from most other forms of literary criticism. Editors do not justify what they do simply because their systems are consistent, systematic, or elegant, or because their arguments are persuasive, powerful, or simply belligerent. Editing is not mathematics; it is more akin to counting.

A second problem I address is an extension of the first. Although we can speak intelligibly of schools of editors, there seems no accepted method or program of training in its basic procedures. You can learn to produce an edition, or to transcribe a text according to certain editorial protocols, or to manipulate a computer program.[15] You can doubtless teach these things as well. You can also teach students how to ventriloquize a mentor's voice, or to construct a literary-critical reading of any given text according to the guidelines of a particular school such that it will be recognizable as a product of that school. But how to determine, say, what an author wrote, or the precise relationship between two versions of a text and, more important, how to be reasonably certain you are correct—that remains a mystery.

What I want to do here is suggest a way, based on what editors claim to do, that will make them better at what they claim to do. My exercise distinguishes the process of editing from edition-making, two aspects of editing that in all how-to manuals I have seen are conflated. This exercise targets what editors purportedly do before they become engaged in the more arcane task of edition-making; it is designed to make them better, not at writing the kind of introductory statements quoted above (these have already achieved such levels of sophistication that editors hardly need improvement in these skills), but at performing the activities those statements claim to justify.

This is a version, a basic and elementary one, of the much more sophisticated challenge issued almost twenty years ago by Peter Robinson, during the early development of cladistic analysis in relation to Chaucer's *Canterbury Tales*. The case involved 44 late manuscript versions of the Old Norse "Grougaldr" and "Fjolsvinnsmal" (approximately 1,500 words). The question posed by Robinson to textual critics was what method (or program) would produce results most consistent with "what is known." Success was determined by the ability of various programs to identify particular groups of manuscripts known to be related by descent, and to distinguish significant readings (or characteristic ones) from random readings of no textual significance.

There are two problems I see with Robinson's experiment, the first being the sheer complexity of the exercise: there is no way anyone other than an experienced textual critic or programmer could possibly hope to answer this challenge, and no way anyone other than an Old Norse scholar and linguist could critique the results (I certainly don't pretend to do that). A second problem is that while "much" about these manuscript relationships may be known from external evidence, this does not mean that "all" is known about these relationships. Including texts whose precise relation to others was not known from external evidence meant that results could only be judged in terms of what was consistent with other textual-critical methods, and not in terms of "what was known" (as Robinson certainly implied, but did not I think state directly).[16] Limiting the evidence to variants whose precise relationship was known by external evidence might make the results far less interesting and impressive perhaps, but the results would speak more directly to the exact question Robinson and O'Hara claimed to be posing. The basic question concerning the truth or validity of an editorial method is not how self-consistent a method is, or how closely the results of a new method resemble those of an old one, but rather how close any of these are to the external facts or truths they claim to reveal.

A Practical Exercise

Purpose

The following exercise is absurdly simple, easily reproducible, and could be used to complement any of the present instruction books in editing. It addresses the problems noted above in the most direct manner I can think of:

(1) It provides a clear test of editorial skills and procedures, and allows individual editors to demonstrate their skills; results are quantifiable, and there is no question about the difference between a correct editorial choice and a wrong one. In this exercise, a good editor should make mincemeat of a mere amateur; great editors will edit circles around good ones.

(2) It allows editors to practice their skills, and because it provides the unambiguous feedback that cannot be had in ordinary editorial situations, it allows editors to improve those skills. Amateur editors can become good ones; good editors can become great ones.

(3) It provides a tool with which editing procedures can be taught.

So far as I know, none of these obvious desiderata have ever been articulated in introductory guides to editing, nor alluded to in the preliminaries of published editions.

Materials

A group of students, contemporary readers, and literate colleagues.

Procedure

I copied what I believe is a poem (in reconstructing this exercise, any literary work, historical or contemporary, would do; for notes on the effect of the literary quality of this work, see Concluding Remarks below). I handed out photocopies of my handwritten copy to a select group of readers and asked them to transcribe it. I instructed them to identify themselves, to note clearly the date of their own copying, and to identify the source they copied. (As the exercise proceeded, this posed far more problems than I expected, as there is an almost ineradicable tendency among literate copyists to misconstrue their instructions and to copy out the attributive details they see in their copy as if these were their own; professional scribes and typesetters of course do the same thing.) I then collected their transcriptions. A week later I handed a selection of the transcriptions, including the initial one, back to them in random order. I gave out transcriptions to other readers, then transcriptions of transcriptions. I varied my instructions, trying to find an infallible way of recording which scribe was transcribing which copy. I gathered up my transcriptions and gave them to others to copy. I copied some myself. I let the project go. I returned to it, handing out copies of copies to other copyists with the same instructions. Each time, I attempted in good faith to record who did the transcription, when they did it, and what the source of their transcription was.

Having produced "many" of these copies over the last two years, I made out a detailed chart noting the filiations of each copy, that is, I constructed a stemma showing the precise historical relations among the extant copies. (Note that such a stemma is not comparable to the stemmata of ordinary editions: those stemmata are necessarily conjectural; mine is an account of what happened.) I then selected a few copies at random. I have transcribed these below, although I cannot guarantee that my transcriptions are error-free, nor that more errors will not appear when this text goes to press. I know what percentage of the actual copies those I have transcribed here constitute, but obviously, I cannot at this point divulge that information. I assume a combination of logical and critical thinking supported by one of many textual-critical methods could fairly easily determine that.

I am now done with my part of this experiment, and anyone can easily construct a comparable version along the lines suggested here. What I am interested in is how well traditional editorial schools and procedures do in determining the history of these versions. I want you to reconstruct the filiation of the examples transcribed at the end of this chapter, or at least give a coherent account of their relations, and see, finally, how that compares with the real filiation of these texts that I have recorded in my stemma. Are any of these texts copied directly from other ones? Can you reconstruct for me the archetype for all of these? Can you reconstruct the hyperarchetype for any group of them, and if so, how does that compare with the real hyperarchetype in my files? Can you find coherent and transcribable versions of the text? Are all groups blurred through obvious contamination?

As an example of what we might do and what some of the problems might be, consider a simplified version of what I set out in the Appendix: here are three versions of a well-known text copied by a group of the same scribes I use in my more extensive exercise:

A

That thou haft herit is not all my griefe,
And yet it may be said I lou'd her deerely,
That fhe hath thee is of my wayling cheese,
A loffe in lout that touches me more neerly.

B

That thou has herit is not all my griefe,
And yet it may be said I lou'd her deerly,
That she haist thee is of my wayling cheese,
A loffe in loue that touches me more nearely.

C

That thou hast her it is not all my grief,
And yet it may be said I lou'd her deerl,
That she hast thee is of my wayling cheefe,
A losse in loue that touches me more nearly.

If I were editing these, I might start by noting groups of what seem to me to be clear errors. On the basis of "herit," "loffe," and "cheese," it appears that AB form a group against C. They are from the same exemplar, or one is copied from the other (I don't know so far which one is the original).

That is logical, but it is not correct. My notes tell me that A and B are in fact independent copies of the same source. C is copied from B; thus C and B form a branch against A. I don't know how to explain this; I just know that it is true.[17]

Now I remove from the exercise version B, and provide instead version D, a version my notes tell me is a direct copy of B:

D

That thou has her it is not all my grief,
And yet it may be said I loved her deerly
That she has thee is of my wayling cheefe,
A losse in love that touches me more nearly.

With only the three texts C, D, and A, now it appears C and D (from B) form a group against A. Here, we are fortunate in knowing that this is correct. I am a bit disturbed to find that in a casual example I drew up simply to use as an example, a partial sample of copies (3 of 4) produced a more accurate stemma than a complete one (3 of 3).

This exercise has to do with historical states of affairs, and this is not quite the same as what editorial procedures do, although the language of editing and the direct claims often contradict that. Editing procedures, particularly more recent ones, focus on the evidence ("facts") defined as groupings of individual variants, or more broadly, of the versions that contain those variants. Even Kane's analysis of *Piers Plowman*, which did not have the benefit of computer programs, works in this manner, organizing manuscripts into groups based on individual variants, which then become what Kane describes as "persistent groups" (this is somewhat different from describing them as genetic groups). But even though variants are abstractions (they are texts) and thus in some sense contemporary with the editor who studies them, the manuscripts or printed versions in which they exist are material and historical (that individual genes cannot be separated from the real and finite beings that contain those genes is, I assume, analogous). To organize the variants in terms of their "carriers" is to imply a relationship among those physical sources, and this implication is no different from that implied by the stemmata of textual criticism, whether those are taken as literal, or as allegories representing abstract textual relations.

Before I began dealing with specific examples (those recalcitrant versions of the Shakespeare sonnet above), I thought this exercise would pose no problems for editors of today. In no other textual situation is the cultural background of copying and transmission so well known and familiar to the editors who will unravel it. My scribes are twenty-first-century students, not professionals and amateurs living centuries ago. We also know that these examples are produced in historical circumstances far simpler than those that would ever exist in the real world of literary texts and editing histories, and these circumstances are roughly the ones we ourselves work in all the time. Furthermore, these circumstances are fairly homogeneous: no one is transcribing a copy for personal use; no one is making a fair-copy for a printing house; they are all following the same set of instructions. And while none of these was written with the sole purpose of exactly transcribing its copy-text, none was written deliberately to cause error or confusion. I'm not sure the same thing could be said about any other editorial situation.

Note that this exercise does not demand that an editor provide explanations of principles or techniques, or provide the basis for any decision. There are doubtless cases of eyeskip, *lectiones difficiliores*, smoothing, contamination, convergence, homeoteleuton. But they are not the point here, and they don't need to be identified. These concepts have little or nothing to do with the actual practice of editing; they have to do only with editorial theory: they are ex post facto explanations, chosen to justify an editorial decision; they do not serve as the basis for those decisions, and in that sense, they could be considered a smokescreen to obscure what should be the real work of editing—finding the right answer. The point of this exercise is not to practice explaining an editorial decision or to understand the language of editorial theory; it is to practice and improve editing skills. You don't need to explain how rack-and-pinion steering works in order to park your car.

The most important difference between this exercise and every other editorial situation I have encountered is that the correct answer is known; thus editorial conjectures that do not provide that correct answer are unarguably wrong and the methods that produce them suspect. They are wrong however elegant they may be, however irrefutable the theory behind them, and however sound the logic that argues in their favor.[18]

Using this and similar materials, anyone of reasonable intelligence should be able to acquire the skills necessary for the tasks that editors claim to do. Or at least anyone can improve what editors regard as the most basic of editorial skills. (Note that this is not the same as becoming what modern scholars consider a "skilled" editor or, in one of its more amusing variants, a "gifted editor"; these things have no more to do with whether editorial decisions are correct than does the phrase "gifted poet" have anything to do with whether a poetic statement is true.) You just keep working until you get that right answer and until you begin getting right answers consistently. When you make a mistake, then adjust your thinking. When you are right, do the same thing again. Editing is like everything else we do. No one will ever agree on what the adjustments to your thinking should be, but anyone can tell a good result from a bad one, just as they can in many other types of human endeavor—painting a landscape, driving a golf ball.

Limitations

I am focused only on one small aspect of editing, getting the right answer. And editions certainly have purposes greater than this one. They serve as convenient compendia of literary-historical material (for example, Skeat's late nineteenth-century edition of Chaucer); we understand through complex editing projects such as those for Langland the practical implications of various abstract critical terms, such as Paul Zumthor's notion of textual *mouvance*. None of that is at issue here.[19]

There are additional limitations here, of course. The further I proceed, the less confidence I have in my own ability to keep these facts straight, or even to record them. In addition, this and any exercise derived from it deal only with the unsettled scribal conventions of contemporary, literate readers, who are amateur scribes and in some cases have little experience with actually writing longhand. This may be such a far cry from professional scribes of the medieval period or from printers of the hand-press period that there is no relation between them. But if the procedures and habits of medieval scribes are different from those of modern scribes, such that scholarly descriptions of one are not applicable to the other, it would be most interesting to hear editors advance that claim or concede that. If error is singular, and not universal, then the situation of the medieval transcription is singular, utterly and dismally historical, and as a product of human minds and consciousnesses completely unlike our own, thoroughly, I would think, irrecoverable.[20]

The Editing Process: Preliminary Steps and Impasse

I could leave this exercise here. But since I have asked professional or prospective editors to take this exercise on, it is fitting that I take a shot at it myself, or at least make some first steps. The following discussion is based on the transcriptions I have provided in the Appendix to this chapter. I can see certain editorial statements that could be made here, the beginnings of a set of facts that might well be set out rigorously:

(1) In line 2, *canton* is certainly an error, although I'm not sure from these examples what the correct reading is or whether the correct reading was in the original (O′). Therefore, those texts that have it or the variant *cauton* are likely related.

(2) *Shakespeare* is obviously correct. The only relationships to be found would be between those that transcribe it unintelligibly. *Shalehase* might be regarded as a substantive error if it appeared in other texts; all the others are accidentals.

(3) Underlined words (likely original, although it is difficult to see errors as related). Verse form: It is obvious that this is in verse. But nothing can be said about the relationship of those that transcribe it otherwise, unless the line length is identical (which it is not).

This part of the exercise is straightforward. There are obvious relations among the variant details of these texts, and to tabulate them is not difficult. The few examples above distinguish significant variants (Greg's "substantives"), certain meaningless ones (Greg's "accidentals"), and certain extremely significant ones that might be called "sub-accidentals" (formal features of line length, underlining). To set them out systematically or rigorously seems difficult (I have given an example of each category of error above). But to set them out in such a way that the conclusions one could draw from them are true—that seems impossible.

I am able, I think, to construct a passably coherent and intelligible original. But some details are difficult. I have no idea what the original is for line 2, even though I know I transcribed the original myself not long ago. It might be "caution," or "count on." I'm not sure what the point would be of trying to determine O′ from the unintelligible variants here, since any one of them could arise from the other.[21]

By making a few choices, and assuming arbitrarily that the original I am trying to reconstruct is coherent (that is, I am trying to reconstruct an authorial original, not O′, the textual source of all variants), I am able to do more or less what nineteenth-century eclectic editors did. What I am not able to do is what I want to test: to construct the stemma or organize groups of readings that would get to this original in any systematic or scientific way. And the more evidence I get, the less clear things become: that is, the more texts I have before me, the more variants I need to explain or to explain away through whatever textual-critical language is at my disposal (coincident error, for example). Increasing the evidence does not get me closer to the original (if reconstructing the original is my goal), and it does not clarify the relationship between versions (if reconstructing the reception of the original is the goal).

Archetype and Hyperarchetype, Texts and "Variant-carriers"

In now traditional textual criticism, variants are grouped by family and a conjectured hyperarchetypal source placed at their origin. As one works up the stemma, eventually one comes to a group (usually a pair) of conjectured hyperarchetypes from which one (theoretically) can reconstruct the archetype (O').[22] No edition I have ever seen has provided a complete transcription of these hyperarchetypes, nor should that be necessary for textual criticism to work.[23] The only true texts and the only things that editors feel obliged to transcribe are the extant witnesses and the conjectured O' (or perhaps the original). But this points out how the process of editing is opposed to the real historical situation that is its object. My hyperarchetypes are not "variant-carriers"; they are texts contained in a folder ready to hand. The more real witnesses I have, the more of these sources I have to conjecture in order to explain their relationships, and the less these logical conjectures (variant-carriers) have to do with the real texts in my files.

Concluding Remarks: Great Texts Versus Run-of-the-Mill Texts; Great Editors Versus Bad Ones

Editing theories and procedures have not been designed to deal with situations like the one I have presented; they were never designed to deal with cases where their results were testable, and they depend, in some sense, on the absence of confirmation or even the possibility of confirmation (truth is excluded by the very definition of the editorial enterprise). The historical situations they faced were at times of their own creation. Certain types of editing (Kane's, derived from Housman) demand that the source text be authored by a "great" or "powerful" poet (like Lucretius, Langland, or, somewhat less understandably, Manilius). This assumption is necessary to distinguish errors made by scribes, who are not intellectually or artistically equal to the poet, from a text that is possibly from the poet's own hand. The original text in my exercise is obviously not by a poet who would be considered great or strong;

certain of my students (not all of them) are certainly the intellectual equals of the poet whose text is transmitted here. Therefore, the Kane-Housman theory of editing and all the amusing rhetoric that goes with it (and may well be its foundation) has no place, and obviously will not work. To test those methods, it might be argued, would require using as a base some unknown text by Shakespeare, or obscure but powerful work by, say, a Romantic poet.

That consideration, or concession, then, leads to a series of even greater absurdities. But I do not see how these are logically avoidable. I will state them in the most extreme sense.

If an editorial exercise such as this will only work in the case of a particular group of poets or authors, then logically it could be used as a means of distinguishing that group. What I have designed as a mere editorial tool might then be put in the service of greater things: not in evaluating competing editorial schools (my original intent) but in evaluating literary works themselves. If a particular editorial procedure works with great or strong poets, and fails with weak ones, it ought to be a relatively simple matter to use those textual-critical methods as tools for testing the strength or greatness of different poets or different poetic works. All that is needed is a set of transcriptions of a given poet's work; any transcriptions, even contemporary ones, will do. The poets on whose works the "Great Poet" editorial procedures work and provide the correct answers—those poets are obviously superior or stronger than those whose poems are recoverable only through other editorial procedures.

I had thought this chapter might act to challenge certain editorial principles by forcing them to consider real-world problems with real-world solutions. But if all I have finally accomplished is the development of a method to distinguish great poets from ordinary poets, I consider the time I have devoted to "getting my facts before me" well spent.

Appendix. Transcriptions

I

Fletcher Arise! Usurers share thy bags,
They canton thy vast wit to build small plays
He comes! His Volume breaks through clouds and dust

Down, little wits! ye must refund ye must
Nor comes he private, here's great Beaumont too;
How could one single world encompass two?
For these Co-heirs had equal power to tech
All that all wits both can and cannot reach.
Shakespare was early up and went so dust
as for those dawning heirs he knew was best
But, when the sun shone forth you too thought fit
To wear just robes and leave off trunkhole wit.

2

Fletcher Arise! Usurpers share thy bags,
They canton thy vast wit to build small plays
He comes! His volume breaks through
clouds and dust
Down, little wits! Ye must refund ye must
Now comes he private, here's great Beaumont too;
How could one single elephant
world encompass two?
For these Co-heirs had equal power to
teach All that all wits both can and
cannot reach. Shakespeare was early
up and went so dust as for those
dawning heirs he knew was best
But, when the sun shone forth
You too thought fit to wear just robes
and leave off trunkhole W.T.

3

Flecher, arise! Usupers share thy bays
They *canton* thy vast wit to build small plays: He
comes! His volume breaks through clouds and dust;
Dawn, little wits! Ye must refind, ye must
Nor comes he private, here's great Boumont too;
How could one single world ecompass two?
For how co-heers had equal power to teach all

that all wits bath can, and cannot reach.
Shahesheare can early at, and went to dreamt
As far these *dawning* heavy to know who about;
but, when the sun shown forth, *you two* thought
to wear just robes, and leave off *trunkhole* wit.

4

Flethcer, arise! Usurpers share thy bays, they
can't they vast wit to build small plap: no
comes! His *volume* he alas through
and lands and dust; dawn, little wits! Yo
must refind, ye must. Nor come he private,
here's front Boumant, too; How could no
single world ecompass two? For how
Co-heirs had equal power to bud all
that all wits both can, and cannot
reach. *Shalehase* even every art, and
went so dreamt. As for these *dawning*
heavy to know was about. But, when
the sun shown forth, you two thought
it to war just robes, and leave
off trunelle wit.

5

Fletcher, arise! Usurhers share thy Bags,
They *canton* they vast wit to build small Plays.
He comes! his Volume break, through clouds and Darts
Down, little wits! ye must refund, ye must
    Nor comes he private, hi's great Beaimont too;
How could one single world encompass two?
For chore CO-heiss had equal Power to teach
All thou all wits bath can, and cannot, teach,
Shakesphere won early up, and went so crest
So for those *dawning* hows he knew was bexs
But, when the SunShine forth, *You Two* thought fit
To wear just Robs, and leave off *Trunk-hol* Wit

6

Fletcher, anse! Usurpers shore thy Prey,
They *canton* thy vast wit to build small Plays.
He comes! his Volume breaks through clouds and dust;
Dawn, little wits! ye must spend, ye must.
Now comes he private, here's great Beamont too;
How could one single world encompass two?
For they co-hector, had equal Power to teach
Al that all wits both can, adn cannot tough.
Shakespeare was early up, and urn! to dust
as for those dawning have to know best;
Bud, when the sun shone forth, You Two thought fit
to wear jus Robes, and leave oof Turnk-hole wit.

              (3.2 from 2.2 signed Geoffrey Plauger by scribe J.K.)

PART III

Ironies of History and Representation: Theme and Variation

Playing Bibliography

Most of the scholars I know settled into their fields by accident. As a would-be medievalist, I found myself, through no doing of my own, in Los Angeles. Medieval resources there, primary and secondary, could not compete with those of New York or large European libraries, but materials in book history and bibliography were abundant. I could claim almost convincingly that I decided to redirect my interests from the abstractions of criticism and literary texts to the more solid and now readily available material objects known as books. But things were actually much simpler. I saw no compelling reason to compete with other young academics on a level playing field, and going into book history, rather than continuing in medieval studies, seemed a way to tip that field in my favor. Examining these books for the first time, I was especially intrigued by the ironic relation I thought I might have to the standard image of a bibliographer/book historian/librarian (roles more or less conflated in my mind). I am surely not really a bibliographer, having come to this field late, and perhaps I will never be one, although I might perform the functions of one. There is nothing unique in that particular alienation—all scholars must feel this. We are not like the others; or perhaps worse, we are. I am not really a book historian or a bibliographer. I just play at being one.

Only a few decades ago, bibliography was regarded as an introductory field, a requirement in many doctoral programs, something along the lines of Old English. The restructuring of English Departments changed all that, transforming Old English into a curiosity and bibliography into an abstruse specialty: most American scholars who remember these courses are just entering retirement. Whether this is regarded as a boon or a tragedy, bibliography has yet to establish or reestablish itself in the curriculum as an autonomous field, subject only to its own rules and conventions, and ruled over and supported by deans and administrators and even heads of libraries or technical services departments. You rarely find job descriptions for "Book Historian," "Bibliographer." In a library, bibliographical skills are of course recognized, but the central positions involve something else: administering, cataloguing, curating. In a university, anything a bibliographer or book historian might do would be categorized as a sub-specialty of the kind tolerated (or ignored) in literature departments or as cross-disciplinary, combining history, literature, technology, and many things about which bibliographers might well know nothing.

This in and of itself does not distinguish academic bibliographers from any of their colleagues. Instructors in literature departments are quite used to teaching things they don't know much about, and that is where most bibliographers find themselves today. Playing bibliography thus should be little different from playing Shakespeare or playing medieval. And perhaps my privileging this field as having special difficulties and complexities is only a version of the way we tend to look at our own specialties; what we study is obviously much more complex, problematic, and difficult than any of the surrounding areas of which we have only a superficial knowledge.[1] It is difficult, nonetheless, for a bibliographer or book historian to concede that. Instructors can hand out to a group of students what they will all agree for the moment to call the "same" poem by Shakespeare. But providing these students with the "same" book, one that can be examined and studied in a bibliographical sense, that is more problematic. Except in certain rarefied settings that reinforce the conditions of bibliography (a special collections reading room, for example)—settings where students already know enough to be permitted to be there—bibliography cannot be taught in the ways many of us learned it. No one taught this field to me, or had the opportunity to do so in an institutional setting, and I have never attempted to teach it to anyone else.

That is why, until recently, playing bibliography always seemed self-contradictory to me. The easiest way to play bibliography seriously, I thought, was not to support the grand theories and abstractions that are the presumed foundation of this field, but rather to challenge them. Bibliographers are human and make mistakes; anyone with an eye to detail will have no trouble ferreting these out. Furthermore, the fit between fact and description is never perfect, and in book history, "facts" are usually easier to define than in other fields. Individual books (or book-copies as I now scrupulously call them) are always full of things professional bibliographers will agree to consider facts, evidence, and anomalies. Many of these are exemplary and illustrate basic principles articulated in the fields of book history and bibliography; but many others sit very uneasily with these larger abstractions. The things I was supposed to find in these books, I had great difficulty seeing at first. And that might be, I thought, a great boon. An introductory student can see things a practiced professional will miss. Somewhat more unsettling was the consequence of this: the realization that the more I studied these books, the less visible these anomalous and interesting details might become.

Most bibliographers, real and would-be, have Eureka moments, those times when we feel that we should run screaming through the rare book room announcing our grand discoveries. Yet surely we know that no one in that setting cares about what we do or think; more likely, they are shocked and chagrined to realize that we don't really care about what *they* do. Perhaps there is no bibliographical community after all; that too is simply an abstraction that we pretend has real existence when it is convenient. And those moments of discovery?—nothing but bibliographical theater to be shushed by a librarian.

III.1. Book History and Book Histories:
On the Making of Lists

The Princess thought that, of all sublunary things, knowledge was
the best. She desired first to learn all sciences, and then proposed to
found a college of learned women, in which she would preside,
that, by conversing with the old and educating the young, she
might divide her time between the acquisition and communication
of wisdom, and raise up for the next age models of prudence and
piety.

—Samuel Johnson, *Rasselas*, Conclusion

Most of us have at some point been commissioned or required to compose
a "Survey of Scholarship," perhaps as a free-standing monograph, perhaps as
an introduction to a scholarly article, or even in the opening meetings of a
class. On the one hand, the allure is irresistible: that perfectly designed lecture or schema, making sudden sense of the conflicting, contradictory, and
too often repetitive voices in a scholarly field. On the other hand, the very
thought can lead to despair: there seems no way to accomplish this without
giving a superficial and uncritical view of everything being surveyed. Even in
a survey of such introductions (entitled "Introduction to Introductions," and
not intended in any way to be a critical evaluation of these introductions), I
could not seem to single out the most important, significant, or basic works
in the field, nor could I draw the obvious relations between them, despite my
familiarity and comfort with the totalizing charts and displays that were
quite the rage in the late 1970s. My own displays simply lacked conviction;

they were like the editorial stemmata I discuss in Chapter 6, and they obscured and misrepresented more evidence than they revealed.

The creation of a list (a "reading list") is a familiar academic exercise: it is a traditional task assigned to dissertation students or to ambitious undergraduates, and as teachers and scholars, we often find ourselves doing the same thing. List-making gives us the illusion that we are working, and implies that academic work or scholarly work in general is incremental; it is just a matter of, say, marshalling the evidence to suggest or support whatever thesis we come up with, or in most cases doing these two things in reverse order. But for many of us, this comforting task, having been performed a few times, no longer functions as it once did. The once satisfying illusion seems to have lost its power, and the resultant list deteriorates into something else: not a coherent body of information, but rather a bunch of titles. Critical work A never quite balances or coordinates with critical work B. Critical work C doesn't really fit either. Mastering the lists and the critical introductions to such lists, or even creating them—this does not provide a foundation for primary research in a field. It is just a way of passing tests.

In my aborted introduction to introductions, I nonetheless began with just such a list. I would get my facts, as facts might be in this case, plainly before me, and with luck, they would speak to me. Among the obvious categories and entries were the following:

The Annales School (Febvre/Martin, the *Histoire de l'édition français*)
Abstract Cultural History (Eisenstein, Johns)
Anglo-American Bibliography (Bowers, Greg, McKerrow)
Textual-Critical History (McGann)
Critiques of any of these (McKitterick)
General Histories (McMurtrie, *Dolphin* 3)
Relation to Computer Studies (Peter Robinson and the Chaucer Project)
Printing History (Steinberg, Pettegree)
Popular History (*Smithsonian Book of Books*)
Encyclopedic Histories (*Glossary of the Book*; Carter, *ABC of Book-Collecting*)

Such a list at least responds to the basic history of Anglo-American bibliography; it suggests the close relation between editing and bibliography (Greg,

McGann), the similar relationship between a dilettantish, belletristic look at books and the relation of bibliography to the book trade (*Dolphin* 3, even to some extent Carter's *ABC of Book-Collecting*), the relationship between studies on bibliographical detail and larger cultural issues or history (Eisenstein, Johns, Pettegree).

There are no studies in this list based exclusively on detail: press-variants, imposition procedures, type-manufacture, although many of them, of course, incorporate such detail into their discussions. Detail is generally treated, even in a basic study such as McKerrow's *Introduction*, as in the service of something else, although when individual scholars study such detail and become obsessed with it, this is not necessarily the case.

I thought that this problem might be solved simply by extending this list and including studies of illustration, paper, specific printing houses, economics, typography. I could include as well exemplary bibliographies, for example, the great analytical bibliography by Hinman on the First Folio, enumerative bibliographies such as the STC, descriptive bibliographies such as Greg's on Restoration Drama, Blayney's study of Okes, or detailed catalogues such as BMC. I could also include article-length studies. Even though few are as comprehensive as McKenzie's "Printers of the Mind," these have been a staple of Anglo-American bibliography, due in large part to the commitment of the present and former editors of two American journals: *PBSA* and *Studies in Bibliography*.

So I revised my list, by dividing my subject as I am told medieval preachers used to do. I added a section on typography and typefounding, basic studies on descriptive bibliography and cataloguing; although my list never attained the astonishing heights of the thousands of works cited in Tanselle, I was well on my way. I encouraged readers just to sit down and contemplate a library catalogue, for example, Consuelo Dutschke's *Guide to Medieval and Renaissance Manuscripts in the Huntington Library*. I tried to expand the category of Anglo-American bibliography (analytical bibliography); I added Neil Ker's book on pastedowns, even though the first time I saw it recommended I thought I was the victim of an abstruse joke, and I don't know how I could convince introductory students otherwise.[1]

Yet however I design this list, as long as I am concerned with primary-source research (in whatever sense), the list continues to reflect my own myopic and gerrymandered view of things. Whatever is outside my interests is just "not part of the subject."[2] I understand nothing of spectrographic analysis (if that is even the right term for it), economics, business, statistics, brain waves, politics. So books and even definitive articles on these subjects rarely appear in my lists, however detailed and elaborate, or even in my notes. I can hardly justify providing a reference when I have no idea of its utility. Nor can I spend a month reading up on fields just to enable me to cite them more fluently or place them in a bloated and finally unusable bibliography.

> The Prince desired a little kingdom in which he might administer justice in his own person and see all the parts of government with his own eyes; but he could never fix the limits of his dominion, and was always adding to the number of his subjects. (*Rasselas*, chap. 49)

On the Makers of Lists

Many of the introductory books in bibliography and book history have conceded in their very choice of subjects that a comprehensive view is not possible; the boundaries of this field have not been well enough defined even to permit challenge.[3] The two most extensive introductory works that attempt such comprehensive coverage are now almost twenty years old: D. C. Greetham's *Textual Scholarship* and G. Thomas Tanselle's two syllabi, *Introduction to Bibliography* (for a week-long course offered by the Rare Book School in Virginia) and *Introduction to Scholarly Editing* (designed for a semester-long course at Columbia). The "Selected Bibliography" in Greetham is over a hundred pages long; Tanselle's is over 350 pages. I will focus on Greetham's *Introduction* simply because its text makes the narrative that holds all these works together explicit.[4]

It is no criticism of this book to point out that the task Greetham sets is impossible, and the problems in this book are an inevitable consequence. Greetham's *Introduction* seems to be two things, a summation of Anglo-American bibliography, or what Greetham, quoting Tanselle, calls "the single great enterprise" of the historical investigation of texts.[5] In that sense, its chapter headings represent the conventional branches of the field as seen by American scholars who work in it, progressing toward Greetham's own more focused interests in textual and editorial studies. Chap. 1—Enumerative and Systematic Bibliography; 2—Bibliography of Manuscript Books; 3—Bibliography of Printed Books; 4—Descriptive Bibliography; 5—Paleography; 6—Typography, followed by chapters on textual criticism. It remains primarily an introductory manual, not a survey of a field or a polemic along the lines of Febvre and Martin's *Coming of the Book*, and that is how it is packaged, marketed, and reviewed.[6] No other "manual" I know covers quite the same ground, or covers what American bibliographers might consider their field so comprehensively.

There are many problems with this book. There is an uneasy relationship between the treatments of two types of subjects: those that reflect Greetham's own interests in textual studies, and those, like typography, that do not. Some of the chapters are thus nothing more than cut-and-paste jobs of basic sources. The list of illustrations notes that all the illustrations for the Typography chapter are there by permission of Harvard University Press. What is not stated directly is that most of them are simply copied from Updike's basic *Printing Types*, which serves also as a source for many of the words and phrases in the text; others are reproduced from S. H. Steinberg's *Five Hundred Years of Printing* (there is, as far as I can see, no reference to this, other than in the list of illustrations indicating permission from the press). In the Paleography chapter, again, all illustrations are second-hand, many taken from obvious and often quite dated sources, for example, E. Maude Thompson's *An Introduction to Greek and Latin Palaeography* of 1912. I don't recognize and have made no attempt to trace other illustrations; I will assume generously that these are original (that is, they were commissioned for this book, rather than taken from another one) but it is possible I am simply less familiar with the topics and thus less familiar with the reprinted illustrations.

These borrowings ought to have been acknowledged more directly, but using these materials is not in and of itself a flaw; Greetham is doing exactly what he claims to be doing—summarizing a field—and an English writer cannot deal with the history of typography, for example, without relying to a large extent on the still definitive work in the field. The words of our sources sneak into our own work, and at times, ours sneak into theirs.[7]

What concerns me here is the section on pages 419–526 entitled remarkably "Selected Bibliography."

> There is no attempt to cover the bibliography of the entire field of textual scholarship, but only to suggest further readings to the student. . . . Items with a good introductory coverage, or with other features likely to be of value to the beginner, are marked with an asterisk (*). (429)

Because many items appear more than once in this bibliography, I have made no serious attempt to count them, but I believe there are over 3,000 entries (fewer than appear in Tanselle's *Syllabus*).

First and foremost, there is hardly any reason a beginner should read or consult these books, even those cited with an asterisk, which are claimed to be more basic. Readers are referred in one unwieldy list to even more unwieldy ones: the STC, Walford's "Guide to Reference Material," whatever that is, "Year's Work in English Studies," Howard-Hill's excellent *Index to British Literary Bibliography*, completely useless for beginning work. Unless they have much more intellectual stamina than I had starting out in this field, beginners will likely find Bowers's *Principles of Bibliographical Description* a bit rough going, and clearly will get nothing other than an uncritical view of Briquet's *Filigranes* (they are not told to look at the much more reliable but even more unmanageable *Wasserzeichen* by Piccard, begun in 1961). Nor do I see how Gabbard's *Ulysses* edition is going to be useful to anyone who does not already have a clear idea of the textual-critical controversies at its base. It is difficult to give a sense of the nature of this through mere description (see Figure 5).

List-making, taken here to an extreme, is a problem now built in to many pedagogical projects (undergraduate term-papers, graduate school papers, dissertation projects, graduate examinations). These lists are a remnant of now obsolete twentieth-century technology; decades ago, coming up with hundreds of titles was a much more interesting exercise than it is today. Anyone going through the American higher education system when Prof. Greetham did and when I did is familiar with the impetus here: make a book list, the longer the better.

But a principle I sketched out in my chapter on editing returns: lists and sets of facts, however extensive and comprehensive, do not speak in any coherent way, nor is any rigorous setting forth of those facts entirely convincing. Even more alarmingly, the more facts one has at one's disposal (that is, the more diligent one's research is), the farther one is from the illusion of truth a much smaller set of facts might have suggested.

When I was first in graduate school, I was assigned to a professor who smoked or chewed a lot of cigars. For reasons that had as much to do with my personality as his, we didn't get along, and any illusions I had about the happy community of scholars in academic institutions were quickly shattered. As his first assignment, he required that I produce in the next week a

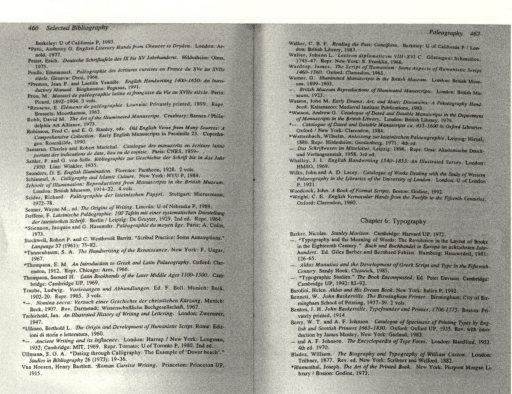

Figure 5. Greetham, *Textual Scholarship*, bibliography.

200-item bibliography on the subject I had chosen (or rather he had chosen for me): Old English riddles. It would settle my hash, he must have thought, and pay me back for that retort I had made a day earlier in answer to his baseless threat to question me on Melville's short fiction, a quip that, as a first-year graduate student of extraordinary naïveté, I thought especially learned and witty. Although I had no idea how to proceed, and had never even heard of the MLA let alone its then annually produced Bibliography, I came up with this list, much to his annoyance, even reading several of the tedious late nineteenth-century German articles and dissertations that were entries on it, and the many notes, some in English, all treating these riddles with a grim seriousness I then assumed everything in English literature deserved. Even bad teachers can teach you something: I learned then all I needed to know about list-making, and most of what I have relearned since. Perhaps this is why "getting my facts before me" has never come easy to me.

Conclusion: From Expertise to Experts

I conclude with a genre of studies I deliberately left off all my lists, a genre of works that is becoming one of the most common in contemporary scholarship: the commissioned collection. In all the humanities fields I know, there is a proliferation of these overviews and histories, works that cover an entire field, or at least the field as recognized by the Research Assessment Exercise (now incredibly and laughably renamed, I read, "The Research Excellence Framework"): The Cambridge History of the Book, the Oxford History of the Book.[8] Some of these I am told are the product of the English examination tradition. They are surveys intended to provide answers to exam questions, whether in high school, university, or graduate school; professionals can use the more advanced variants as a source for learned footnotes (they of course can use Tanselle's Syllabi or Greetham's *Textual Scholarship* the same way). Some provide a version of "coverage," in the sense that they define a field: their footnote apparatus cites the relevant scholarship in the field, and their list of contributors, the relevant and chosen authorities in the field.[9] Others are less comprehensive, and few individuals other than their contributors and reviewers own them: you find them at your library or maybe you received an author's copy. In both cases, the tables of contents are peopled by those you would expect and burdened by references to articles you think you should have read. They are on subjects you think you should master, but secretly you think the whole thing might turn out to be a gigantic fraud.

It is as if the History of Books in the Last Century led in these works only to its self-validation, at the very moment the book itself seems to have announced its extinction. Here is a comprehensive history where the authors, blessedly, need not themselves be comprehensive; it is the professional version of the freshman essayist: just tell me what to write and I will write it. Or perhaps, just take what I write and give me an A. The following is from the introduction to one such volume:

> The aim of this volume was ... to publish the work of scholars whose approaches to books, words and texts are engaging, innovative and always rigorous. ... All the writers here demonstrate

convincingly the importance of scholarship on the material text in its context.[10]

It is easy enough to dismiss such works with phrases like the following: "Quality is here associated not with works but with authors—persons of quality all, who, for these essays at any rate, were happily spared the indignity of submitting them over the transom."[11] The history of books proceeds; only now, it no longer is subject to peer review.

I have two responses. First, I would rather have the erratically docu-mented and wild enthusiasms of Febvre and Martin than the steely cold and mind-numbing footnotes of the New Professionals in this field. At least their Annales-style coherencies and polemics offer a critical handhold, something to talk about. Second, it is just such coherences I have spent most of my time arguing against, at least, when I am writing in any context other than the article or note (genres where I can do more or less as I please, as long as my footnotes are in order). And my history—the history that I argue for, the history that I construct in my own books—likely looks a lot more like those disorganized, bloated, and crushing "Institutional Histories of . . ." or "Essays On . . ." than I want to admit.

Imlac and the astronomer were contented to be driven along the stream of life without directing their course to any particular port.

III.2. Meditation on the Composing Stick

The composing stick is an essential piece of equipment in traditional printing. It is the basis for most of what Moxon says about the "Compositor," who in turn is the basis for much of modern bibliographical discussion, both in analytical bibliography and in the textual criticism related to it.

> Though every *Compositer* by Custom is to provide himself a *Composing-stick*, yet our *Master-Printer* ought to furnish his House with these Tools also, and such a number of them as is suitable to the size of his House; Because we will suppose our *Master-Printer* intends to keep some Apprentices, and they, unless by contract or courtesie, are not used to provide themselves *Composing-sticks*; And besides, when several *Compositers* work upon the same Book, their Measures are all set alike, and their *Titles* by reason of *Notes* or *Quotations* broader than their common Measure, So that a *Composing-stick* is kept on purpose for the *Titles*, which must therefore be common to all the *Compositers* that work upon that Work; And no one of them is obliged to provide a *Composing-stick* in common for them all. (*Mechanick Exercises*, sec. 9, par. 4)

Moxon is here interested in human beings and their organization in a printing house, and he is straining to describe this in terms of physical equipment and book appearance. If I understand this passage correctly (the things I am concerned with here are secondary in Moxon's mind), by "Titles" Moxon means running heads, which would be wider than the text block (the "common measure") due to marginal notes and quotations. This feature of layout then has its analogue both in the social relation of workers (master printer and compositor) and in the material tools of the press: the composing stick set for the running heads is "common to all compositors" and is supplied by the master printer. And each compositor has an individual composing stick set to the "common measure" (a different sense of "common") of text.[1]

You can clarify Moxon's meaning either by looking at the illustration or (for the modern printer) by referring to a twentieth-century version of this, and rearranging or rewriting Moxon's words to conform to it. The "sliding measures" correspond to text and marginal notes; also implied in Moxon's Plate 24 are the units of composition—three to five lines of text (Moxon, *Mechanick Exercises*, Pls. 2 and 24, and sec. 3, par. 4).[2]

Associated with the composing stick, perhaps its raison d'être, is the galley (both are shown in Plate 2). The galley is mentioned by Moxon in sec. 5:

> Our *Master Printer* is also to provide *Galleys* of different sizes. That the *Compositer* may be suited with small ones when he *Composes* small *Pages*, and with great ones for great *Pages*.

These are not described in detail; I assume this is because they are simple enough that the illustration alone is sufficient, or because Moxon is so familiar with them he has difficulty imagining anyone who is not. The galley and the composing stick are part of the same operation: the compositor sets type in the composing stick, places it in the galley, and from there composes pages on the stone, arranged then into formes (see series of illustrations through Plate 28). Note that galley composition seems to be page by page (Plate 25, and sec. 22, par. 6)

In nineteenth-century manuals of printing, these descriptions are unchanged. Or at least, the descriptions of nineteenth-century descriptions suggest they are unchanged. Hansard uses for his first illustration the illustration in Moxon. His description obviously owes much to Moxon:

> [A composing-stick] is the only instrument or tool with which a compositor has to provide himself at the outset; and which, with due care, will last him the whole of his life. To make this little instrument quite perfect requires a great deal of mathematical nicety.[3]

The relations between these two texts could be due to traditions in the print shop, or they could be due to traditions in descriptions of them (see above, Chapter 2). The instruments shown in Rummonds's illustration on the same

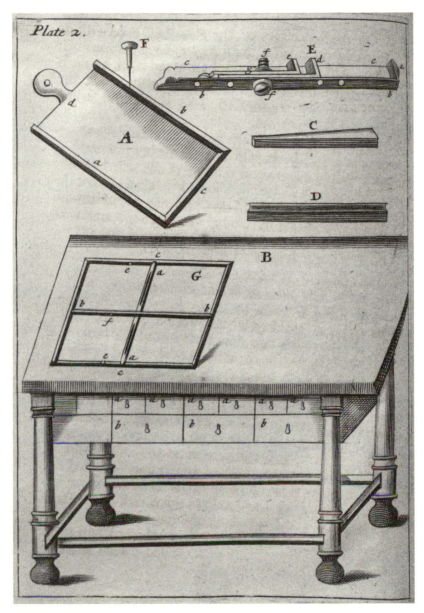

Figure 6. Composing stick and galley, from Moxon, *Mechanick Exercises*, Pl.2. Photo courtesy of the William Andrews Clark Memorial Library, University of California, Los Angeles.

page are from MacKellar, 11th ed. 1878, p. 305; they are all variations of Moxon's design. The bodkin, pictured in Rummonds, Fig. 7.29, 1: 229, is also the same as that depicted in Moxon.

The illustrations are obviously derivative. And perhaps one could argue that the illustrators, professional specialists, could not have the same familiarity with the operations of printing as did the writers of the manuals. Rummonds's Fig. 7.48 (*Nineteenth-Century Printing Practices*, 1: 258), from Jacobi 1890, 62, seems to be a freehand version of Moxon, Plate 24 B ("*The manner of* Emptying *a* Stick *of Letter*"). The hand positions are different, but otherwise the illustrations are almost identical. Why would even a knowledgeable illustrator have referred to real or imagined operations of compositing when there was a model illustration ready to hand?[4]

According to many bibliographers, a printer in the nineteenth century could walk into Caxton's shop and feel perfectly at home; thus if printing historians want to know what things were like in the fifteenth century, they only need to go to a modern hand-printing shop, with its iron press (modeled after early nineteenth-century presses), or wooden press (modeled after the illustrations of the seventeenth-century press in Moxon). Casual statements like this eliminate many of the problems in real printing history, for example, the lack of evidence for fifteenth-century printing, our sense of alienation from the past, the clear lines of continuity in our histories, and the obscurity of those lines in history. To our uncertainty concerning the past, material tools and their modern descriptions can be brought to bear as evidence: hand-molds, composing sticks, knocking up our balls. We can read about these things in Gaskell, Moxon, the *Encyclopédie*, or any of the manuals and dictionaries summarized and anthologized in the collection of Rummonds.[5] But we will not find material evidence of these things from the first two centuries of printing or even statements about them. When evidence is found in modern printing, what linguists would call a back-formation; these materials do not constitute that seamless continuous history our scholarly narratives provide. Willing or wishing these material things to fill up the vacancy in our histories is different from willing them into real existence.

The Construction of Verse and Initial Capitals

A well-known peculiarity of early Aldine books is the manner of setting initial capitals: lines of verse (whether in italic or roman) are set with a space

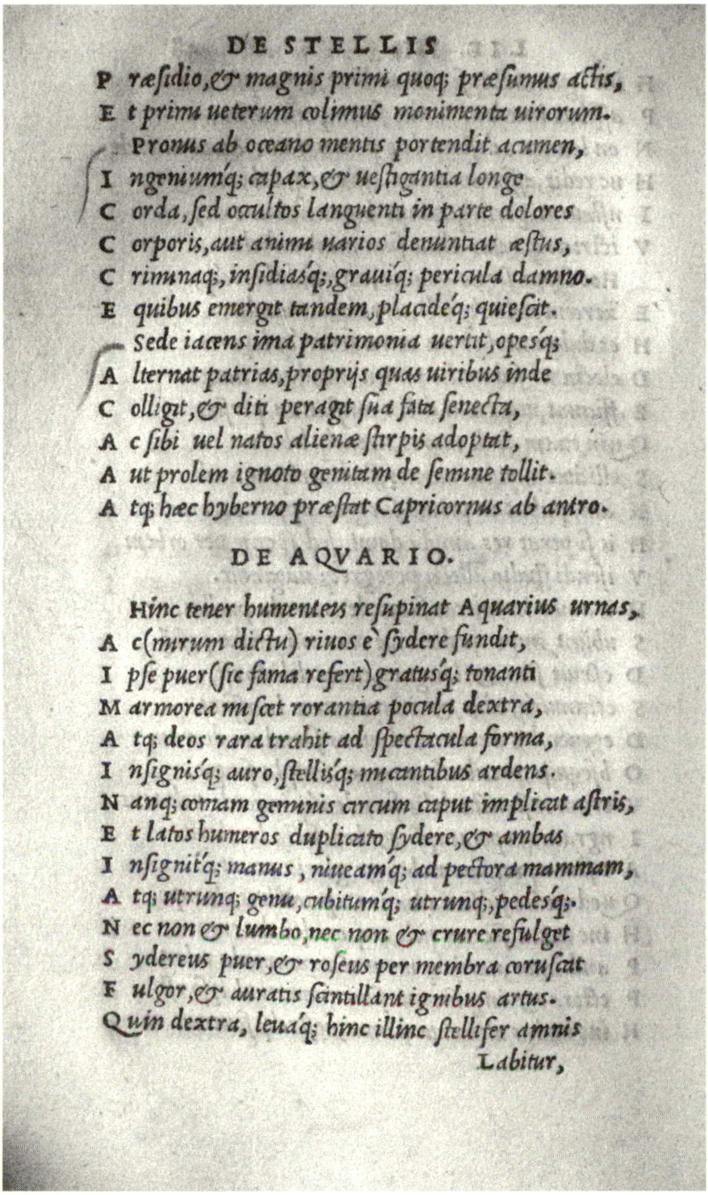

DE STELLIS

P ræsidio, & magnis primi quoq; præsumus actis,
E t primi ueterum colimus monimenta uirorum.
Pronus ab oceano mentis portendit acumen,
I ngeniumq; capax, & uestigantia longe
C orda, sed occultos languenti in parte dolores
C orporis, aut animi uarios denuntiat æstus,
C riminaq;, insidiasq;, grauiq; pericula damno.
E quibus emergit tandem, placideq; quiescit.
Sede iacens ima patrimonia uertit, opesq;
A lternat patrias, proprijs quas uiribus inde
C olligit, & diti peragit sua fata senecta,
A c sibi uel natos alienæ stirpis adoptat,
A ut prolem ignoto genitam de semine tollit.
A tq; hæc hyberno præstat Capricornus ab antro.

DE AQVARIO.

Hinc tener humenteis resupinat Aquarius urnas,
A c(mirum dictu) riuos e sydere fundit,
I pse puer(sic fama refert)gratusq; tonanti
M armorea miscet rorantia pocula dextra,
A tq; deos rara trahit ad spectacula forma,
I nsignisq; auro, stellisq; micantibus ardens.
N anq; comam geminis circum caput implicat astris,
E t latos humeros duplicato sydere, & ambas
I nsignitq; manus, niueamq; ad pectora mammam,
A tq; utrunq; genu, cubitumq;, utrunq;, pedesq;.
N ec non & lumbo, nec non & crure resulget
S ydereus puer, & roseus per membra coruscat
F ulgor, & auratis scintillant ignibus artus.
Quin dextra, leuaq; hinc illinc stellifer amnis
Labitur,

Figure 7. Pontanus, *Opera* (Venice: in aedibus . . . Aldi Manutii, 1533) Photo
courtesy of the George J. Mitchell Department of Special Collections & Archives,
Bowdoin College Library, Brunswick, Maine.

between the row of initial capitals and the following lines of verse; the vertical line formed by the second letter of each verse (that is, the left edge of what could be called the text block) is often perfectly straight, as if set with a rule.

Under the conventions implied by most printed verse, this peculiarity is nonfunctional, or the effect counter-functional in that the ordinary conventions of reading the line are opposed (a space ordinarily means a word-break). What could be called the "zero degree of typography" is obvious from the page illustrated here: these conventions are seen in the opening line of the paragraph unit and in any of the many words capitalized in the text. The proper way to set words with least impediment for the reader is defined as providing no spacing between the upper-case roman and the following word (as in the words "Capricornus" and "Aquarius," lines 15 and 17).[6]

Furthermore, at least in this page, there seems to be no certainty regarding the proper way to space words and punctuation: commas are sometimes set with spaces on either side, sometimes with no space whatsoever, and indifferently with space preceding or space following. The proper handling of parentheses is uncertain and the parentheses themselves are clearly upright (roman style), not slanted (italic style). If this were prose, an obvious or at least a reasonable explanation for this might involve the requirement of right justification. But it is verse, and there seems no rationale. Some of the lines with extra space are longer lines. There is no apparent adjustment of lines to make the right margin more uniform.

The Aldine illustrated above is not early. Aldine italics had been in use for some time, and there would be no way what appear to us to be obvious aesthetic errors could be excused as a product of early experiments in typesetting. The same conventions, or variants of them, can be seen in the earliest Aldine books (Juvenal and Virgil, 1501). It is just "the way things are," and perhaps Aldus felt things would last this way forever.

The usual explanation for these conventions involves an appeal to aesthetics:

> au contraire de la graphie gothique qui agrippait l'oeil dans ses brisures, dentelures, tel un roncier d'ogives, le bel italique de Griffo invite par son inclinasion et ses courbes à glisser vers la droite, et ainsi de ligne en ligne. Une merveille. . . . Ce petit livre [the 1501 Juvenal] au format de poche est un chef-d'oeuvre de clarté avec ses marges importantes, ses initiales détachées et la belle lisibilité de ses italiques aériennes.[7]

Yet such appeals to aesthetics are circular in reasoning: this is a book by Aldus, and Aldus produced beautiful books; anything in this book is therefore a component of Aldus's attempt to produce beautiful books.[8]

The reason I once imagined for this feature of typesetting is a simple one: the Aldine book is a reflection or version of the manuscript page. In a manuscript page, the construction of initial capitals on a verse line is a matter of page format and ruling. Pages are pricked; the text block is set out, and an extra line is placed down the side, creating a space for initial capitals. Examples are easy to find.[9]

When I first encountered or imagined this problem, I thought there would be three ways of reproducing the look of such a manuscript page in a printed book: (1) the most obvious, writing line by line, (2) the construction of the text block, then a return to fill in the larger initials (essentially doing what a rubricator would do to construct the initials of a paragraph unit), and finally (3), the writing of the initials first in a single vertical column, followed by filling in the following lines of text.

Why not (3), I thought? A convenient way of solving the problem, say, of eyeskip in verse. And one that also seemed to obviate the use of that device characteristic of traditional printing, but for which no evidence can be found in early printing, the composing stick? The compositor lays the initial capitals on the forme, which follow the sequence of capitals on the copy-text, then fills in the following text line by line.

Some Aldines, such as that pictured above, support this notion. Others (the 1501 Juvenal) do not. To obtain the straight line seen in the example above, the two blocks could be set separately, first the initial capitals, then the text block. This might be analogous to the way that marginal notes were constructed in a printed page before the invention of the sliding composing stick. In this case, the result would be a flush left margin on the text block (so the 1501 Virgil). The late Aldine here, the Pontanus, alas, must have been set line for line (see lines 18–19, and the single *Qu* sort in the last line). Perhaps this is an attempt to achieve the effect of the 1501 Virgil (two parallel vertical lines, the first the left edge of the capitals, the second, the left edge of the following text block), through whatever techniques were used to produce the Juvenal.

My imagined method had the advantage (aesthetic?) of eliminating what seems an obvious flaw of Aldine italics: the lack of upper-case, and the unsettling contrast of the mixing of "ductus" in the upper-case letters or even in such nonliteral marks as parentheses. Upper-case letters are highlighted, set apart from the italics of the text, and the contrast of the two types is thus less noticeable. It also seemed to have the advantage of efficiency; and because that supported the general argument, I ignored the fact that modern notions of workmanlike efficiency do not necessarily apply to early printers.

Having come to this conclusion, I began to look through the varying column justification in these books, especially those that showed an obvious attempt to keep the aesthetic of the Virgil (left flush for the first letter following the capital); I could find no pattern of variation that suggested the setting of these lines in three- or five-line units. Wouldn't that be the case if the independent unit set by the typesetter were the three- to five-line unit set in the composing stick? Perhaps one imagined conclusion supported another.

The Aldine page, a staple of most histories of early printing, is incompatible, I thought, with the composing stick, a device described and defined in those same histories. Initial capitals were set as were marginal notes, independent of the text block.[10] At some point between the early sixteenth century and the Moxon's *Mechanick Exercises* of 1683, the composing stick was introduced and developed to its perfected form, that is, the form in which it remained unchanged from the seventeenth through the nineteenth century, as evidenced by printing manuals throughout that period.

Or so I claimed.

What a shame that, now less committed to this explanation, I could find no corroborating evidence for it and plenty of evidence against it: the 1501 Juvenal, for example; the obvious attempt in the Pontanus to reproduce the aesthetic of the Virgil with the techniques of typesetting of the Juvenal. Even the clear and unambiguous writing of manuscripts in this form line for line (it is easy enough to determine the sequence of writing from the ink). I had wished to demonstrate that the feature was a function of typesetting or scribal techniques: the history of Aldines sketched here suggests that it was seen as purely aesthetic. I am arguing for technique over aesthetics, and I am returned to aesthetics.

So I fall back on another thesis, one I have advanced here and elsewhere involving another discontinuity in history, itself a reflection, analogue, or perhaps an intellectual allegory of the actual gaps in our knowledge of history. We simply do not know how type was set in the fifteenth and sixteenth centuries.

The Huntington Proof-Sheets

The Huntington Library has proof-sheets of ps-Donatus, *Rudimenta Grammatices* (Ulm: J. Zainer, 1478–82); these were once sandwiched together and used as the board for a binding. They consist of ten paper bifolia, some over-printed, of an apparent edition evidenced elsewhere in a similar set of fragments in the Pierpont Morgan Library. These cannot be collated as a set, even though they have obviously been together as a set since they were printed (they are printer's waste, not binder's waste). That is, they were never part of a printed book and never left the printing shop before going to the binder.[11]

When I first examined these sets of fragments, it seemed that bifolia from HEHL collated more logically with the fragments from Pierpont Morgan Library than with each other. The distinction found in catalogues (HEHL = edition 1; PML = edition 2) was thus misleading. If there were two (or more) editions, these editions do not correspond to the sets of fragments in their present locations. I still accept this negative conclusion (that modern location does not reflect the original edition): the positive version (that certain of these fragments can be assembled from different locations into an historical edition) seems a stretch to me now.

So I took a different approach: what we see in these pages does not necessarily correspond to the final page of any historical edition. Perhaps the instability in pages is a sign of the use of something approaching a mid-twentieth-century galley sheet. The text-block in the galley proof bore no necessary relation to the text-block of the pages; text was corrected in long galley proofs, which were then "made-up" into pages. An hypothesis like this would be perfect for organizing the evidence of these fragments: diverse pages, with a problematic relation to the pages of the final text. The Huntington proof-sheets constitute not parts of books; they are rather preliminaries for books, and thus cannot really be catalogued according to the rules of descriptive bibliography (which presuppose the existence of a "book" even if completely idealized).

But that entails another appeal to modern printing practices: the taking of proofs from galleys. It also entails reintroducing something equivalent to the galley tray, which my earlier speculations tried to argue out of existence. Even Moxon describes taking proofs from made-up pages, and these pages it seems are close to what the final pages will be (see *Mechanick Exercises*, sec. 22, par. 7–8, pp. 233, 238). But the pages in the Donatus fragments, whatever they are, are proofed not in formes but as pages (the page-impressions on the conjugate bifolium have no relation to each other, and in some cases are printed upside down). And if the formes are not set up as the formes of the final edition would appear, it is also reasonable (or not unreasonable) to wonder whether the proofed pages are also not set as the pages in the final edition.

These fragments thus are not galley proofs in the modern sense (the primary "being" of a galley is that it contains more than a page). Nor are they proofs as described by Moxon, which seem to be taken in units of the forme, and thus of course can be bound up with the final book. These are single-page units, but the page does not necessarily correspond to the page of the final edition, about which we conveniently know nothing more than is in these very pages. Such units do not support either of the key instruments in printing. The instability of pages I am claiming suggests a method of composition that does not involve galleys or the composing stick, but one whereby the unit of the page dominates, even though the nature of that unit is not the same as the page that ends up in print.

The example is ready to hand: it supports whatever argument I wish it to make. And I am still troubled by the following set of questions, gleaned from a longer list of questions whose answers are incorporated into the discussion above:

(1) In medieval verse, is it possible to demonstrate that an initial row of capitals was constructed prior to copying out the lines of verse?

(2) Are there printed books where line units and blocks move in relation to each other in units of three or five blocks?

(3) Are there cases of eyeskip in medieval verse with the layout similar to the Aldine seen in Figure 7.

I have shown elsewhere how these myths of continuity affect our notion of fifteenth-century printing.[12] Here, the real and potential checks on pure speculation, due to the availability of evidence and the sophisticated research tools we now have, seem to function paradoxically to make the earliest period of printing even less accessible than it was when free from such constraints.

III.3. The Red and the Black

I am sitting in a rare book room . . .

*   *   *

With that, I am pretending to concede that I have given up methodological strictures and shifted to the personal. In fact, that concession is a gambit. I am conceding this in order to enforce the argument I have made all along: that bibliographical arguments must be made in the context of particular problems, particular settings, and finally particular researchers with their own unique and mysterious histories and personalities. I am sitting in a rare book library, and I am about to discover that one more example of my grand musing is erroneous.

This time it is the Museum of Fine Arts, Boston, my first visit. I am here to look at a book I have never seen, its copy of Boccaccio's *De Casibus virorum illustrium* (Bruges: Colard Mansion, 1476). This is a famous book as these things go, rare in every sense of the word, since some copies have large, hand-painted miniatures at the beginning of each of the main sections, and others have had these pages reset to allow space for even larger copper engravings. This copy is the only one with all extant copper engravings. I have seen a copy in one other library, and checked most of the available facsimiles; I have notes on others based on published descriptions and communications from generous librarians. I will write an amusing chapter, "Note on a Note by Seymour De Ricci," which has virtues quite other than those I imagined when I started it.[1]

This book exists in various settings, another indication that books at this period (at least, the high-end books produced by Mansion) had a bibliographically inconvenient relation to book-copies, as do many texts embodied in manuscripts.[2] Some of the leaves in some copies have red guide rules framing the text block and lines within the block, much like the decorative ruling found in some expensive eighteenth-century books and nineteenth-century imitations of them. These rules are, I think, the late transformation of the formatting lines used to lay out pages in medieval manuscripts.[3] They provide an interesting case of the transformation of a functioning technique into an ornamental one, but that is not the reason I am discussing them here.

In the Huntington copy, one sheet and one sheet only has these red rules. All other leaves are unruled. What could be simpler than finding among the extant copies a second copy with red ruling on all but that single sheet, the single ruled sheet of the Huntington copy, and to consider then what terms like *integrity* or *belonging* might mean in this context? These leaves did not get exchanged due to an accident of provenance: these are not, that is, signs of the manipulations of books by the book trade. Rather, these books came to be in their present, apparently disordered state at press; leaves are included in what seem to us the wrong books not because of what should be considered an error at press but rather because bibliographical notions such as *ideal copy* cause us to understand the integrity of particular book-copies in a somewhat different way from how this might have been understood by printers.

This is a routine analysis of a routine bibliographical situation. Bibliographers know that sheets that seem morally destined to be bound together according to some rational bibliographical principle in practice get mixed up at press in various systematic and unsystematic ways. The only interest in the case here is aesthetic: instead of a run-of-the-mill book, a rare and luxurious book is involved. Even when a printer planned two coherent and autonomous variant editions, it was difficult to keep them straight.[4] The number of sheets in the two impressions might not match; and consequently, some sheets proper to variant A necessarily had to be bound in with a copy of variant B, that is, the wrong copy. Examples of this can be found wherever rare books are found.[5] There are obviously a number of unstated assumptions in our notions of book-copy integrity concerning the institution of printing and the continuity of book construction from the days of Gutenberg to some vaguely defined moment in the early nineteenth century. But anyone who can even follow the above discussion knows this already.

I shift in embarrassment, waiting for the book. There is probably nothing here; driving to Boston and dealing with parking—how pointless. Yet I assure myself that it is impossible to look at a book of such complexity without coming up with something interesting. And I soldier on.

The Museum of Fine Arts copy is ruled with red throughout, with the exception of a single sheet. All seems well. But alas, the ruled and unruled sheets in the two copies at the Huntington and the Museum of Fine Arts do not match in any coherent way.[6] Maybe, I think weakly, I could argue that these two copies indicate that there were once many others, several with mismatched single sheets like these, and that it would only take one or two more to make exactly the same point I could have made had they matched more coherently. But even this argument, if tenable, requires a series of straw-man assumptions: first, a McKenzian Printer of the Mind employing perfectly regular procedures whereby each sheet is printed in exactly the same number as every other sheet, and second, a sudden lapse in distributing these sheets to the right copies, the simplest of procedures. The first assumption is so preposterous that there is no need of the second one positing an exception to it. No printing historian believes such things, so why refute such an argument? What was I thinking?

Red/Black

When I first began to study early printing I decided to take advantage of the Huntington's collection of fifteenth-century books, the second-largest collection in the country. The best way into such a collection in my view is simply to call up all the books, one by one or cartload by cartload, whatever the library policies will permit. Something will always turn up. Sadly, libraries, rationally but paradoxically, do not and cannot encourage research procedures like this, the kind of methods that actually result in scholarly discovery and progress. Those who wish to use the resources of a rare book room are better advised to present themselves as already conversant in what they expect to find: the true scholar, by Reader Services Department standards, is looking for mere confirmation. This institutional quirk, innocent enough, has perhaps been internalized by junior and senior scholars alike. If the library policies seem designed to have you confirm things you already know or suspect, it is not surprising that for many scholars the purpose of primary research is to do the same thing.

So instead of telling the librarians the truth (bring me the books, and after a few hundred of them, I may have some idea what I should have looked for in the first one), I designed a study that would enable me to see these books, by posing as one of such expertise I hardly needed to glance at them. I had seen examples of color printing in Haebler's leaf-books—probably my first serious source of incunabula—and thought it would be an interesting exercise to test various things I had seen written concerning the techniques of early two-color printing.[7] I would simply look at all available books printed in two colors in the fifteenth century. Step one would be to determine a method for identifying those books. It would be unsporting, I thought, to start with Mead no.1 and move on to Mead no. 5291, and the rare book custodians would quickly be on to me. Maybe I could select the books that should be printed in two colors, without predetermining my results. I chose liturgical books, early Bibles, and legal books. There were roughly, I thought, a thousand of these in the Huntington, and I estimated they constituted about 90 percent of the examples of fifteenth-century two-color printing in the collection. And perhaps they did. It wouldn't be difficult to test this figure—90 percent—but I'm not sure what the point would be. This elegantly designed research project then gave me a chance to look at hundreds of books that weren't within the bounds of my study, those random heaps of books that make true research possible.

Using a photographer's loupe (or a linen counter), it is quite easy to determine the order of colors in multicolored books. At least, it once seemed to be easy. You simply look to see whether the red ink lies over the black ink or vice versa. If, say, black lies over red, then red was printed first. All printing manuals going back to the seventeenth century and the bibliographical manuals based on them describe the standard method as follows.[8] First, the entire forme is set in type, and the frisket cut in such a way as to mask all text but the words to be printed in red. The forme is then inked in red and printed off. The frisket-mask is then removed, and the typesorts printed in red removed and replaced with quads. The whole heap is then printed off in black, following ordinary printing procedures. Ink is not free, and I suppose after a few impressions the printer could be illiberal with the amount of red ink used, since so much of it would end up on the frisket (such red-printed frisket masks do exist).[9] But this would be a practical problem for printers, not an intractable one for analytical bibliographers.

A little reflection shows that a printer cannot just recut the frisket to print the second color. No forme printed under this technique can have both red and black islands (one color surrounded by the other on the same forme). Reflection will also show why "red first" is the norm: there is less red than black, and consequently less chance of a black island, which under a strict application of this method is unprintable.[10]

Few techniques of printing or any other trade are so perfect as to hide their procedures completely. Here, mistakes often occur in the placement of the masking frisket (or more precisely, the placement of the forme in relation to that frisket). Any slight error will mean that portions of type intended to be later printed in black will show traces of red (the frisket was off a bit and did not completely mask the type to be later printed in black). Sometimes this type inadvertently printed in red will "shadow" the correctly printed black type, as the two impressions (for red and for black) were not perfectly registered. But you will never find the reverse, since when the second color is applied, the type already printed in the first color will have been removed.

Briefly:

(1) Some text, printed in black and intended to be printed in black,
    will have what appears to be a red shadow at the edge (the
    frisket was mis-set and an edge of some of these sorts was thus
    inadvertently inked in red: i.e., the edges of these sorts were
    printed twice).
(2) No text, ever, in any circumstance, intended to be printed in
    red and black by the standard method will have a black shadow
    on letters printed in red, since these sorts were removed before
    black ink was applied.

I looked at each of the thousand or so incunables I thought might be printed in red and developed a shorthand way of referring to this, using old-fashioned 3x5 cards to record my results. Yes, with the exception of the earliest examples, red was ordinarily printed first, and for each card in my notes, I simply wrote "Red first," without specifying the evidence, or even the pages on which I found it. I was "getting my facts before me," I thought, and things were going well. Organizing the cards would be a simple matter; the facts would speak, as Bradshaw assures us, and the narrative of the development of printing techniques would more or less write itself, which it did.[11]

The Museum of Fine Arts is not a rare book library, and Mansion's Boccaccio is here not as an example of early printing, but rather because of the copper engravings that make it a work of art. Nonetheless, I have brought my bibliographer's loupe to the Museum and the curators have generously allowed me to use it.[12] I am wondering about the red rules on each page in the book, and when I look at them through the loupe as I had trained myself to do all those days at the Huntington, I notice what I had seen hundreds of times in other incunables: red first. I should add a large exclamation point, because this is absolutely not what one would expect in this case. The red is not the red of print, but that of the hand-drawn lines framing the text. Red first. "RF" I would have written on my fact-recording card. Incredibly, the red rules seem to have been drawn onto the sheets not after printing, which would have been an easy thing to do, but before the text was printed, necessitating an entire process of registration (placing the text within the tight red border) that could easily have been avoided. I recall taking some pride in this discovery: the observed facts were inconsistent with our normal assumptions of printing efficiency, and I had apparently been open to recognizing a fact that contradicted what I "knew" before confronting it.

Now this was interesting. It meant that the addition of luxurious red rules distinguishing certain exemplars of this edition from the regular exemplars was determined *before* printing, not after the sheets were run off; it was analogous to the difference in this same book between the pages printed with copper-plate engravings and those intended for hand-drawn miniatures. The pages with the copper-plate engravings require a different setting of type from those intended to be finished with miniatures, and these settings must be determined before printing. Such pre-planning of the edition seems consistent with the fact that certain ruled sheets appeared in some copies where they did not belong: paper too was prepared prior to printing of the edition, not after the print run was completed (that is, not as in eighteenth-century luxurious editions whereby the decorative ruling was put in last). The Mansion Boccaccio was thus a perfect example of a "transitional volume," produced by combining techniques associated with manuscripts and those associated with printing: hand-painted miniatures in some copies, engravings in others. As in manuscripts, the red ruling preceded the creation of the words, just as the penciled or dry-point rulings preceded the writing of the manuscript page, even though it no longer had the function borders had in manuscript production.

I was happy. These abstruse bibliographical facts and their narratives began to make sense; they came together in a logical and persuasive way. I explained this to the librarian, whose name I have forgotten. He was one of the few researchers I had met who instantly understood the consequences, and rather than smile politely, he said somewhat skeptically: "Let's have a look under the binocular scope." We moved from the reading room to the lab.

When we viewed the page under the binocular scope, the banality of the operations at press that produced it was obvious. And that banality destroyed all the elegant theorizing of the preceding paragraphs. The blown-up image clearly showed *black first*. Of course. Anyone thinking twice about this problem, even in the fifteenth century, would have predicted that or known it. It is exactly what I myself "knew" before examining the page under the loupe. The text was printed; the red rules were drawn in by hand afterward, just as they were hand-drawn in luxurious copies of eighteenth-century folios. Seen under my loupe, however, the red ink lying over the black simply does not show clearly; it is obscured by the intensity of the black, and perhaps, due to the oil-based nature of the black ink surface, the red ink never gripped the paper to begin with.

I didn't worry about the aborted note I had thought to write: there is always a note that can be written despite the recalcitrance of the evidence. I thought rather about my now completely useless 3×5 notecards recording "RF" ("red first") in the thousand incunables I had examined at the Huntington; the perfectly coherent history of printing procedures I had written ten years earlier, one that conformed to every methodological procedure I have come to argue against since, whereby the narrative history takes precedence over the facts. I had been reasonably diligent in those days, checking most of the books again after I had surveyed them the first time, and rewriting my notecards according to a standardized protocol. Yet once I began to see the pattern of history in these books, I found nothing but confirmation. Thus, I no longer distinguished what was decisive evidence of red-first printing (traces of red shadowing sections of text intended to be printed in black) from what I considered confirming evidence (cases of black ink seemingly printed over the red). I simply recorded each of these quite different situations as an observed fact "RF," red first. I find on my cards no notes saying how I concluded that or what made me conclude that or on what page I found it or how subtle the evidence was. And now, I confront the Boccaccio by Mansion, printed just as one would guess, whose anomalies are visible to any scholar not blinded by theories of what that history should be.

I am now ready to return to that study of two-color printing. I will do it all over again, I think. And this time, I vow determinedly, I will do it right. But then, it is likely I will only follow whatever bibliographical predispositions I am not aware I have internalized since constructing that same study years ago.

III.4. Fragments

Bowdoin College Library has what I call a run-of-the-mill early sixteenth-century psalter in a cheap contemporary binding.[1] Bound in as an end-paper is an equally routine sheet of another nearly contemporary psalter or breviary.

There is nothing unusual about this. Loose sheets or leaves of books are routinely used as pastedowns or binding material, whether originally printer's waste (that is, proofsheets or unused sheets) or binder's waste (leaves from books that have been in circulation).[2] Binder's waste, that is, leaves with evidence of having been used or read, are less likely to appear as visible flyleaves or endpapers. I don't recall ever having found an endpaper with interesting contemporary annotations (that is, written in before it became an endpaper for another book), or even signs of heavy use, although I am certain they exist. All the annotations on the pastedown in the book here—ownership, herbal recipe—were added after the leaves were incorporated into this book-copy.

The endpaper and its inclusion here raise a number of questions, not the least of which is broached in the preceding paragraph. Immediately upon confronting that endpaper and thinking about it, I attempt to come up with some general principle regarding it: binder's waste/printer's waste, aesthetic rules involving endpapers of all kinds.[3] And I consider this despite my claim to distrust all general principles, and despite my usual emphasis on the way in which actual books and book-copies defy the very principles required to understand them and talk about them.

What is important about fragments such as this one is that they reflect not so much on the history of books in general (how could one possibly make

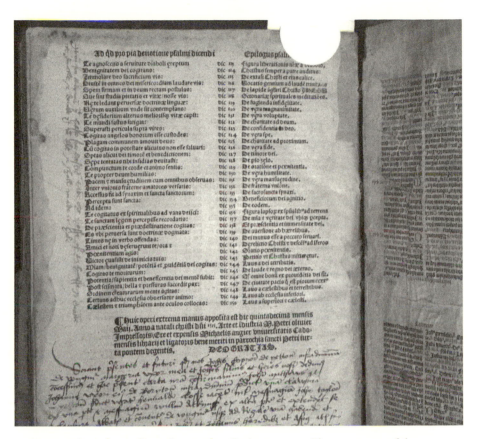

Figure 8. Pastedown, from *Quincuplum Psalterium*, 1515. Photo courtesy of the George J. Mitchell Department of Special Collections & Archives, Bowdoin College Library, Brunswick, Maine.

a comprehensive study of endpapers?), but rather on the relation between chronological history (that is, events that occurred over time) and the perception of that history by the modern bibliographer. A book fragment is difficult to abstract into the realm of bibliographical categories such as editions, issues, states. When a leaf from a book is used for something else (an endpaper), that instance of use remains stubbornly singular as well: the leaf is no longer part of a book; it is rather a feature of a unique copy. The fragment, or bit of binding material, might be a witness to or index of certain abstract things such as bibliographical states and editions or the conventions of a bindery, but it is rarely a perfect exemplar of them.

Fragments such as this turn up whenever you deal with large numbers of rare books, and in that sense, there is nothing particularly rare or noteworthy about them in and of themselves. How one speaks of them or classifies them bibliographically or intellectually is what matters, and among the more interesting I have run into from this standpoint are the following:

1. A leaf from a verse grammar printed by Theodoric Rood, the earliest piece of English printing at UCLA's Special Collections. I assume the book was bought more for the endpaper and the early English binding than for the text.
2. Fragments of a Carolingian MS of Bede's *Homilies*, contained in an early binding at the Huntington.
3. Fragments of Donatus, *Ars Minor*, the earliest example of Netherlands printing at the Huntington.
4. Also at the Huntington, what appears to be a partial page (red impression of a page intended to be printed in two colors) of an unrecorded edition of a legal text by de Tudeschis, *Panormitanus* included in several copies of Ratdolt's 1484 Ptolemy.

These are disconnected. I am able to group them here for what will seem to be completely arbitrary reasons. They could be held together more generally by the notion of "early," and without that notion, I would never have bothered with them; for most historians of early books, a binding fragment from, say, a nineteenth-century newspaper is defined, somewhat tautologically, as of no interest. In some sense, any conclusion I could draw from this particular group of fragments would be included in the assumption I used to categorize them as a group. They are interesting not because they are representative, but rather because they can serve as allegories for something beyond themselves.

Somewhere in my files, I have a notebook recording every piece of printed binding material in the incunables at the Huntington. Originally, I had thought to survey them, writing up a small note documenting their existence and noting particularly those of typographical value or even bibliographical value; following the principles sketched out above in Chapter 4, I would record only those fragments from editions that the Huntington does not possess, or those representing typefonts not in the Huntington collection. I identified about half of them—something that is neither particularly difficult nor unamusing—but my survey never got written, because of that recalcitrant 50 percent. How can you legitimately define as a corpus of material the most convenient half of the evidence you compiled? A scholarly contribution requires either a single piece of evidence or a complete survey of a coherent corpus, and I found no usable category to describe what I had been doing: "Unrecorded fifteenth-century typefonts contained in binding material of other incunables at the Huntington Library—half of them."

Thus, this group of fragments has no noteworthy coherence as a unit or as a corpus. They are individuals, and each in its way points to a problem in determining what a book is and the relation of that book to "things we put in catalogues." They are thus signs or allegories of general bibliographical problems, not exemplars of specific bibliographical principles or rules. The most prominent question I can formulate from these concerns the "names for things." To what extent is the mere existence of these things connected with or even dependent on the bibliographer's ability to give them names, that is to say, proper entries in a catalogue?

Words and Things

The question I will address here is the same one I asked in Chapter 5 and in other cases. In its simplest, and seemingly most trivial form, that question is "what should we put in a catalogue?" I ask this not because I think these fragments are related to that question in some essential or essentialist way, but rather because it seems to provide a first step toward talking about them. In some of the above cases, the answer seems obvious, but in others, the answer is elusive. And in each case, the decision seems to create as many problems as it solves. For most of these, the problems are primarily bibliographical: the historical facts (that is, the actual events, not the expression of those facts) are clear, and there is no mystery about how these fragments came to be, how and when they were printed, and how they ended up in their present condition. We thus know as much about them as any amateur or professional would ever want to know. In these cases then, our bibliographical language does nothing to increase our knowledge or understanding, but only directs us away from the history it is intended to describe.

I will start with the Donatus fragments; these are two binding strips contained in a fifteenth-century *Sammelband* constituted by two books printed in Strasbourg: Petrus de Palude, *Sermones quadragesimales* (1488) and Bernardus de Parentinis, *Expositio officii missae* (1487).[4] The fragments have been cut from a leaf in a printed grammar book that was used and read (they are rubricated), but it is not possible to determine from the text in the fragments whether the edition they represent is recorded in any incunable catalogue. In terms of the question formulated above, this is the easiest case. Of course they should be catalogued. They are of typographical value by any standards (the type is not represented by any book at the Huntington) and they are as much a "book" (whatever that is) as are the later proofsheets from the ps-Donatus *Rudimenta Grammatices* purchased by the Huntington specifically as a book, that is to say, as an exemplar of an entry in a catalogue.[5] Yet they are not yet in the catalogue, and there are good reasons for that.

First of all is the matter of shelving.[6] One question for the Huntington cataloguers is whether these are more interesting as part of a book-copy or as a book (an indication of an edition). At present, they are within a manila envelope within the covers of the book where they were found. To remove them seems absurd, and would surely lead to an eventual "disappearance," either of the fragments or of their provenance. Without the strips in the folder, no one calling up that *Sammelband* would know why its binding had been cut and two of the five binding strips removed.[7] A similar strain between bibliographical and ontological identity (that is, books vs. book-copies) can be seen in a number of books from the van Ess collection at HEHL, where original *Sammelbände* were quite reasonably cut apart, long before they got to the Huntington, in order to make it possible to shelve the individual units of those composite volumes (the bibliographical entries identifying each unit as an edition).[8]

The Rood fragment is also easy to deal with: there are no fragments from this early English press at UCLA and this leaf is complete. Why it is not catalogued as a book is not clear to me, since many of the exemplars of books as early as this one exist only as fragments. The bookblock that happens to be bound with this endleaf (and is of course catalogued) is completely run-of-the-mill and uninteresting (at least by the standards of UCLA Special Collections). The interest is entirely in its provenance and binding material, that is, in the fragment, the early English binding, and the evidence this provides about the book trade.[9]

The Bede manuscript fragments at the Huntington are a completely different matter. They have doubtless been "discovered" a number of times in the library's history, although there is no record of this in any of the various Huntington catalogues, nor in any internal records, nor in the somewhat unreliable oral history circulated through the library. There are a number of early fragments such as these, and two (from bindings of St. Peter's in Salzburg) come from the same manuscript. The existence of these and other fragments is noted in Scott Husby's catalogue survey of early bindings at the Huntington, but their nature is rarely specified. I am dating those in Figure 9 "ninth century," which would put them among the earliest examples of manuscript at the Huntington. In Dutschke's *Guide to Medieval and Renaissance Manuscripts in the Huntington*, only one such fragment of comparable date is recorded.[10] There are doubtless other manuscript fragments hidden in the library stacks. Our survey dealt only with fifteenth-century books, but Carolingian fragments are just as likely to appear in sixteenth- and seventeenth-century books. At some point, the value of medieval manuscripts as physical antiquities compensated for their decreasing value as repositories of texts.

These should be included or at least noted in the Huntington manuscript catalogue (here meaning Dutschke's *Guide* and its continuation) because of a rule its entries suggest: by including a manuscript fragment as item HM 41785, *the Guide* implies that all fragments with some claim to chronological distinction should be included.[11] That is, manuscripts are "representatives of periods" or "examples of scribal hands" as well as "repositories of texts," and it does not matter whether they are complete books or merely fragments.

As shown in Chapter 5, the first librarians at the Huntington imagined that their fifteenth-century books might be considered exemplars of typefonts, and consequently the collection could legitimately be expanded through facsimiles. Yet the archives do not show that they ever considered producing a comparable checklist or catalogue of scripts, or, given the nature of the collection, perhaps a "catalogue of early English scripts"; such a catalogue or checklist would have been extremely useful, both for specialists and for the many amateur paleographers who pass through, although much more difficult to produce than a comparable checklist of typefonts or printed books. Some manuscript fragments clearly are of paleographical value just as some typefonts are of typographical value; others are not. And this of course needs to be defined not absolutely but rather in the context of the library in which they are housed.

The precise conditions for inclusion (what makes an item valuable or of interest) are more difficult to delineate in paleographical terms than in typographical terms. For early printing, it is at least theoretically possible to name or point to all the typefonts used in the fifteenth century: there is a finite (albeit unknown) number of these, and that number is quite manageable. For

Figure 9. Pastedown, from Nider, *Sermones*, 1479. HEHL RB 104110. Photo courtesy of the Henry E. Huntington Library, San Marino, California.

scripts and hands, the organizing units are units of nomenclature, and no example can ever perfectly exemplify a paleographical term. The B42 type used by Gutenberg in theory refers to a physical set of historical typesorts, or at least an evolving one; Carolingian script, by contrast, is a category that exists only for the modern paleographer. "Paleographical value" then is finally far less definable than "typographical value." And I suppose the rule would be that if you don't know what paleographical value is, then it wouldn't help to have it pointed out to you.

The 1484 Ptolemy is a different case. It contains on the verso of its final leaf some red-printed text that seems to represent an edition not only unrecorded at the Huntington, but unrecorded anywhere else, even though the British Library catalogue notes an essentially identical leaf in its copy of this same book. It can only be an edition of the legal text by de Tudeschis, *Panormitanus*, something the history of Ratdolt's press suggests he might well have printed, but that same history says he did not.[12] My conclusion is that it represents no edition at all, since the only evidence of the existence of such an edition is the leaf in the Ptolemy. That leaf includes rubrics printed in red and blank space where the black text was surely set; there is, however, no evidence that that imagined book was ever printed (on the conventional methods of two-color printing, see section III.3 above). To catalogue these rubrics, even as containing typographical value (which at least in the Huntington catalogue, it would not have) may well be to catalogue a nonexistent book. Or perhaps to create one, that is to say, bring a book into real existence that had only theoretical existence for the printer who began, then apparently abandoned, the project of printing it.

The Bowdoin fragment shown in Figure 8 is another story, and the questions involving it must again be formulated in the context of the collection holding it. That is, the value and interest of this fragment depend on the nature of the holdings and the very purpose of the library where it is housed. If this pastedown were found in the Huntington, it would be pointless even to make a note of something so routine. There are scores of fragments earlier than this one. The only interest the fragment has is that it is printer's waste, an uncut leaf of a quarto forme showing basic format structure. The book containing it could serve as an excellent example of the incoherence of book-copies that our bibliographical systems necessarily rationalize. What is the possible relation, say, between a legal agreement for an estate, a herbal recipe for what I believe is an oozing wound of some sort, a Bible, and a breviary?

Because this is contained in a small library, there are a number of features that become important. On the final sheet of the tripartite breviary (sign. E), preceding the new text on sign. F (parallel texts of two variant psalters) is a will in English and Latin, dated 1530. I doubt this library has any nonliterary document this early, or any example of English handwriting of this date. It also contains the curious remedy: "hoffe of a horsse grated small and drunk with ale" (shown in the top margin of the illustrated leaf), which is said to heal some kind of wound or disease I am glad does not afflict me. The text of the endpaper (a folded quarto, shown on the bottom of the illustration) has obviously never been read and may well be a proof.[13] The book, thus, becomes a repository of documents that have nothing whatsoever to do with the text included by the printer or binder.

It would be an easy matter to continue this list. The point of all of it is that there are no general principles that can apply to what seems the simplest of decisions: how to make accessible what exists in the archive. To make the decision, we need to have all the answers in advance. And we must have all examples ready to hand, since our decision regarding one of them has implications for them all.

None of the above examples would be regarded as unique in a bibliographical context: you find these whenever you begin to look for them. The Huntington Library has a *Sammelband* of Whittinton grammars in a blind-panel stamped contemporary binding (RB 61711-20; see Figure 4 above). The pastedown on one of the boards has been removed, leaving behind visible offsets of an early printed leaf. That leaf was apparently of enough value for someone to rip it from the book (the other blank pastedown is intact). I can identify the type (95G, a de Worde type). It would not be all that difficult to identify the edition. Does the Huntington thus own a copy of this edition, identified only by the offsets in this binding? And if so, is it thus possible for a single exemplar of an edition to be in two places at once? One of my own books has visible binding material, part printed, part manuscript. Do I own the books or texts they record? Or do I own them only after I have identified them? There do not seem to be any convenient principles to apply.

Jeffrey Henderson once said to me that in editing, each case and each reading is singular. At the time, I paid not too much attention to this. I recognized that he, as a classicist and an editor himself, was channeling Housman on this, or at least giving a version of Housman's famous dictum of a dog catching fleas. What strikes me about bibliography is how much that same principle or non-principle has come back to me, despite the fact that the major bibliographical achievements in Anglo-American bibliography have been the creation of abstract categories ("editions") allowing for enumerative compendia of otherwise disordered heaps of books. I have never been systematic enough to find such general principles or categories I could use to organize evidence; when I do find the abstract categories into which a book or fragment fits ("oh yes, this is an example of GW no. . . . ."), I move on to something else. By contrast, all the interesting singularities I found seemed to invoke other things: this is *not* an example of edition X, or not a pure example. Sometimes they invoke grander things and principles that in the end are far more banal than the bibliographical abstractions I thought I was transcending: the incomprehensibility of the universe, for example. Each successive case contradicts the one before, violates the principles suggested by the preceding case, or has, it seems, nothing to do with either of them.

III.5. The Nature and Function of Scholarly Illustration in a Digital World

A recent scholarly book I reviewed has a number of illustrations, twenty-eight by my count.[1] Of these, most have the requisite permissions, all written in formulaic phrases, "Reproduced with the permission of the President and Fellows of Saint John Baptist College in the University of Oxford." This must have been composed by the institution owning the image, as this is not a phrase others would come up on their own, nor one that would be formulated at press. All appear in a list of illustrations in the front matter, where eleven have such attributive notes. And that means, of course, that seventeen do not. The unattributed illustrations do not indicate a failing of scholarship. All the contributors to this volume are reputable scholars, and the press is a mainstream academic press, whose editorial standards are generally quite high. It is thus difficult to know what to make of this. Perhaps the editors gave up; perhaps the illustrations come from an unrestricted source as do some of my figures above; or perhaps, my thought here, certain of them did not need attributions because they do not function as we ordinarily think illustrations should.

The illustrations are all of early printing or documents related to early printing: articles from the *Encyclopedia Britannica* of 1911, nineteenth-century books of scholarship, and then STC books, that is, books printed in English or in England prior to 1641. In the list of illustrations and in the scattered attributions, STC books are referenced two ways: some are described with the phrase "copy of STC . . ." and others simply "STC" (for example, STC 7273). Strictly speaking, an STC number refers to an edition, that is to say, an abstraction, not a material book-copy; such things cannot be portrayed or illustrated in the same way as a material book. And that, I suppose, is the reason for the phrasing in chapter 4: "Fig. 4.2. Copy of Christine de Pizan's *The Morale Proverbes of Cristyne*, William Caxton, Westminster, 1478 (STC 7273)." This is technically correct, or would be correct if the particular copy and the particular page of that copy were identified, which they are not. If the editor or contributor does not know which copy of Christine is the basis of this illustration, there is no way to include a note of attribution, and no way, in addition, to ask for permission to reproduce it. (No library is thanked for its generosity here in allowing its images to be reproduced.)

This poses a series of questions, beyond the most glaring and basic one concerning which copy is being reproduced here. What is the difference between a book and a book-copy? or the difference between a repository for books and an enumerative catalogue of those books? What is the difference between illustrative, evidentiary, and ornamental illustration in a scholarly article?

Books Versus Book-Copies

A book-copy is the physical object housed in a library; it can be held and read, and parts of it can be used as objects of photographic reproduction. It is part of a series and a member of what is called an edition. An early printer intended to produce a certain number of identical, interchangeable objects (maybe 275, maybe 1,500). Once these objects were distributed and put into use, each became a book-copy, an individual with an individual history (that is to say, provenance). A book, by contrast, is an abstraction; it could be the abstraction indicated by the ideal-copy description of descriptive bibliography: what the printer intended to produce, or what the printer could reasonably expect to produce. It could also be simply the sum total of all the copies; this is what we likely mean when we use such phrases as "The First Folio of Shakespeare."[2] "The First Folio of Shakespeare" is not on any library shelf; copies of the First Folio are. And most important, "The First Folio" cannot be accurately illustrated in a conventional photograph. It can only be described through ideal-copy description.

But that formulation is too grandiloquent, and does not quite describe the case. A book-copy can be transformed into a book, and most literary scholars, myself included, when looking at a book-copy describe it in terms more appropriate to a book. Furthermore, a photograph of a book-copy, or any textual part of that copy, can transform that book-copy into a book by a caption. You buy a photo of the title page of The First Folio and label it: "First Folio, title page." You then include in your footnote which copy you are using, for example, "reproduced by permission of the William Andrews Clark Library, University of California, Los Angeles." You had access to the Clark copy, or an image of it; but the implication of the caption is that any other copy would have done as well; what you are interested in is the book, the edition, not the material details of this particular copy. The same is of course true if you take a photograph yourself, reproducing the binding. There will likely be flaws consequent on your amateurish use of the camera (image shape and focus errors), and because of them, your image will be an image of a particular book-copy, the physical object you are photographing. But if you label that as a book, not "Tyrwhitt's Chaucer, 1775 (personal copy)," but simply "Tyrwhitt's Chaucer, 1775," the copy becomes a book, and these technical flaws of photography are by convention to be overlooked: they are invisible or irrelevant.

If you reproduce an image from a database, say from Early English Books Online (EEBO), many of the details that define the book as a book-copy (binding, any marks of physicality) are suppressed. You are probably intending to reproduce a book; EEBO images and the copies that are their basis are readily accessible and thus more convenient to use for most scholarly purposes than others, any of which could have been chosen. Even though no two copies may be strictly speaking identical, they are, from the standpoint of the scholar interested in the "book," interchangeable.

Most illustrations of books used in general studies of early printing are of this nature. The intention of the scholar is to illustrate the book (that is, Caxton's first edition of the *Canterbury Tales*), and not to illustrate a particular copy of that book (one of the British Library copies). That scholar might draw from the photo collections of the Huntington, the Folger, or the British Library. But the implication, and what readers of the article assume, is that any other copy of this book would serve. I look at the illustration of Tyrwhitt's Chaucer. What I see is what I would see if I looked at any other copy of "the same thing." Time, space, material—these do not matter.

Now let us consider the illustrations in the collection cited here. Several of the illustrations, all attributed, are to manuscripts, and manuscripts are obviously unique. Others refer to annotations in printed books. Again, these illustrations are clearly to particular book-copies, since only these copies have the annotations shown in the illustration.[3] The annotations are what is at issue, not the printed book in which they happen to appear. All other illustrations, as the implications of the articles make clear, are intended to be to books, not to book-copies, despite what the captions might imply through their notes on provenance or location. None of the discussions referring to these books refers to a particular copy in a particular library.

There are no visual signs in any of these illustrations of features that define book-copies, that is, the materiality of the object illustrated. Book-copies have bindings; books do not (at least, they do not until the nineteenth century, or maybe in some cases the eighteenth). Book-copies can have annotation; books do not. Book-copies suffer damage; books do not, at least, they do not suffer damage from biblioclasts. Accordingly, none of the illustrations here shows the three-dimensionality of a physical material book. They reproduce, rather, pages of books, that is, two-dimensional surfaces. The illustration of Caxton's edition of Christine's *Morale Proverbes*, for example, is not presented as an illustration of a particular copy of this book. It is an illustration (a partial one) of the generalized book. Objects such as copies can be located; ideas, such as editions, cannot, and thus no location is given here. I assumed at first that the reference "STC" in the caption meant that the illustrations were taken directly from the EEBO collection of STC books. But this seems not to be the case. I collated the copy in this illustration with that in EEBO (from the Huntington), and they are absolutely not the same (there are obvious differences in type in lines 12 and 13). There are copies at Rylands and the Pierpont Morgan. But I cannot determine which of these copies is illustrated here.[4] I can only assume the illustration isn't original. It must come from another article or book on Christine. But here I reach an impasse. The author is clearly not trying to hide anything, or dodge this issue; the author is simply not interested in it.

Of the images in this collection, some are presented as classic photographs, that is, we see the paper on which the ink is printed. Those classic photographs with the grey background (representing the paper or vellum of the illustrated book or manuscript) announce: this is an illustration; these are the boundaries of the illustration; everything on the surrounding white background is the scholar's text. Others, however, are half-tones: the paper of the illustrated book is invisible; that is, the background on which the printed words are shown is indistinguishable from the background on which the scholar's own words are printed in the text. Even some of the images from manuscripts are printed this way, with only the pen characters visible. In these cases, the illustrated text or image floats on the page, with the same status as the contributing scholar's printed words. We know this is an illustration only because it has a caption and because it is not in the typefont used for the scholarly text. What the white or potentially white background does is de-materialize the image, transforming that image of a book-copy into the image of a book, or even more abstractly into the reproduction of a text contained in the book.

The collection is about William Caxton, or rather, the books printed by William Caxton. But the contributors have a peculiar way of citing Caxton, always in the 1928 EETS edition of Caxton's Prologues and Epilogues by W. J. B. Crotch.[5] They do this without thinking (or at least without comment), much the same way as I cite Moxon in the convenient modern edition of Davis and Carter. Crotch's edition of Caxton, however, is an editorial construction, not a facsimile in any sense of a book-copy. Caxton is treated in Crotch's edition and by those who cite this edition not as a printer but as an author, and his texts are now textual abstractions, that is, things that can be reproduced on a keyboard, as his material books cannot. And this suggests an answer to what these illustrations mean or are. In most cases, they are neither illustrations of particular copies, nor are they illustrations of the generalized book or edition. They are even more abstract: they are illustrations of texts, just as their authors' quotations of Caxton are quotations of texts. Caxton is not a printer, but rather a writer, an author, whose words are reproduced in his books which in turn can be quoted in other books. There is no particularity to any of the images of Caxton's books or other early printed books. When the editor himself provides an illustration of a page printed by Machlinia (*Caxton's Trace*, fig. 6.1), that illustration is merely the page (the source) of the text quoted by the modern scholar. It is the source of the text in which the scholar is primarily interested; it is neither a book nor a physical book-copy, and this illustration (fig. 6.1), like many other illustrations in the volume, seems a pure ornament, not part of the evidence presented, nor in any way advancing the argument that is perfectly well presented in the author's text.

The most generous interpretation of these illustrations is that in the hands of these scholars, the illustration functions not as a piece of evidence on which the arguments of the text are based, but rather as an index. It is like the catalogue reference of an enumerative bibliography, pointing to the "thing" that is at issue. My objection to this is that the analogy ends there. It is not like the entry in a descriptive bibliography, an entry that crystallizes all the chaos of particular books under the abstraction of ideal-copy description. The illustration becomes something far less, not an illustration, but an ornament, a decorative image to a prefabricated argument that proceeds on the basis of texts, not on the basis of evidence indicated by or comprehended in that illustration.

Image Versus Icon: Classic Versus Modern Photography in the Photo Lab

Photographers used to take pictures the Old Way: flattening a book as well as possible and reproducing the image on a piece of film. There were a lot of things one could do in the development process, but most of these involved retouching, fixing or adjusting light and contrast, manipulating the size. Whatever distortion existed through the inevitable optics of the camera lens was transferred in some way to the film and to the final print. Photographers could change the size of an image, sometimes to support whatever conclusion the scholar wanted, but the basic nature of the image was determined before it got to the lab.

Modern digital photography has progressed to the point where problems such as amateurs once experienced seem naive and ridiculous. Anyone can correct the basic distortions of the camera lens. Keystoning: the conversion of a rectangle into a trapezoid, when the lens is not positioned dead center, and the shooting angle is not perfectly perpendicular to the object. Or barreling: the inevitable curving of lines away from the focal point. Photoshop or any similar program can so quickly fix these problems that they can hardly be defined as problems at all. Photoshop does this because its designers know that we prefer to "see" straight lines in space represented as straight lines on the printed page. We also prefer not to be bound by the fixed viewing point implied by the pin-hole camera lens or the classical camera lens.[6] But this routine manipulation transforms what we are seeing into something else: what was once an image of the page becomes an icon of the page, a model of the page, or, more abstractly, even a description of it (for example, "all lines in this object are evenly spaced, as represented in this illustration, even though you would never actually 'see' them that way due to the rules of perspective"). If we were dealing with architecture, we would call the first of these (the image) a "picture"; the second is what we call a "blueprint."

The Huntington Photo Lab

John Sullivan, head of the Photography Department at the Huntington Library, places the book on what was once called a book stand. It opens the book only a fraction of its complete opening. There is no danger to the spine such as there has always been when opening old books. The light is blinding, the colors perfect, even though the image will ultimately be interpreted as black-and-white. Any color adjustments can be made in terms of the color matrix: Mr. Sullivan has explained this to me on numerous occasions, but it remains a mystery. Since he is used to reproducing the maddeningly difficult hues of William Blake's illustrations, the problem of reproducing an incunable or an STC book, where the relevant details are defined (perhaps arbitrarily) as matters of black-and-white—this is child's play.

The computer can be instructed to make all the necessary adjustments. It is "known" that lines on the page are straight (line of text), that the ruler placed over the page is itself straight, and any deviations from this must be corrected. Barrelling and keystoning—the bane of amateur photographers—barely rise to the level of consciousness.

It is easy to compare the results of this process with the results obtained by a civilian photographer. The photograph above in my Figure 7 is about the best I can do, or even want to do. The camera is hand-held, the light imperfect. The image is consequently and very obviously of a particular book; there is no way I can disguise that, nor do I want to disguise that. Mr. Sullivan's images, by contrast, are works of art, often abstracted from the particular books in which they appear.[7] On his and other commercial photographs, you will not see the ripple of the pages and the distortions you see in mine. He of course knows absolutely what this means in relation to the book. But I'm not sure his viewers know this or even want to know it.

Icon Versus Image

What Mr. Sullivan produces for Huntington publications and for Huntington readers is not an image of the book. Not one of the books at the Huntington has a page that appears the way it does in most of his brilliant photographs of them. They have weight, texture, even smell. What professional photography does is transform these book-copies into books. This is not a result of what photographers want: it is the result of what scholars want.

When scholars order up prints from the Huntington or simply download them from EEBO, they are often (not always) looking for something from a book, not something from a book-copy. They are interested in the repeatable text of that page (or a repeatable image) which they then reproduce in their own articles and monographs. Thus, EEBO images do not show page texture and on individual pages rarely show bindings; the edges of the print block in Mr. Sullivan's photos are perfectly straight and the page perfectly rectilinear. These are not books one would ever find in the real world, nor even the books one would buy or sell through an auction catalogue.[8] They are those peculiar, otherworldly things (books?) discussed by scholars. They have the same relation to physical objects (book-copies) as do the notes in a catalogue entry, or the more elaborate ideal-copy descriptions in a descriptive bibliography. Furthermore, most of the images now on EEBO were produced with what is now considered primitive equipment, producing microfilm-quality images. The equivalent to this is the automatic machine now on lease at the Huntington, designed to produce serviceable images of the science collection. Left alone, and functioning perfectly, this is said to produce 3,000 pages a day, but it can only do this at the cost of many ripped leaves. The operator is simply a monitor, and the resultant images could have been produced almost a century ago. Mr. Sullivan has contempt for this machine, since the images are no better than what by his own lab's standards are the execrable microfilm images now in EEBO. But the question I am asking here does not deal with the quality of these images. I am concerned rather with the extent to which any of these illustrations reproduce the objects we claim to study and how they actually define the nature of those objects.

The EEBO images had one function when they were first produced in the microfilm series Early English Books in 1938: they were ersatz originals, something that might take the place of the original books if those books were destroyed.[9] Books, in this case, were defined not as physical objects, but as repositories of texts printed in a certain way, and the EEBO images contained nothing but accidental traces of bindings or marks of provenance. Libraries such as the Huntington purchased the microfilm collection of Early English Books because it included STC books not in its own collection.

With the advent of modern printing, the reproduction of images became relatively cheap (as little as twenty years ago, the cost of an image to be used in a scholarly article, even without permission fees, was as high as $50; now the same image might cost as little as $10, or it might be free). And with this ease of reproduction, the function of EEBO images changed: the items in EEBO were no longer ersatz books (which were now as safe as they feasibly could be), but rather, sources of cheap illustrations. They served not to recall a material book, but to illustrate largely textual problems in those books. The difference between a first-rate image such as those produced in the Huntington Photo Lab (whereby many of the traces of "bookishness"—size, weight, and perspective—are eliminated) and a third-rate one (EEBO) becomes a purely aesthetic one. In both cases, the book, the physical object, is only incidentally related to the text it contained through an accident of provenance.

Our machines have seemingly improved our access to books. But the better our investigative machinery becomes, the farther away we move from the objects we claim to investigate. We don't need books, because we have their sanitized and largely aestheticized images, which now decorate, rather than constitute, our scholarly arguments. Not only do they establish our basic discourse, they even unsettle the counterdiscourse, such as I intend my own to be here, daring it to wax nostalgic over the smells and textures of the objects as do the dilettantes we might claim to despise.

III.6. Art of the Mind

A recent Getty Museum project involves the restoration of a Roy Lichtenstein piece, reported in the *Los Angeles Times* in "Lichtenstein's Three Brush
Strokes gets a Brush Up."[1] The project is a poster-child for restoration. The
artist/restorer is James DePasquale, "a longtime Lichtenstein assistant who
manages the late artist's studio in Southampton, NY." The Getty received the
sculpture in 2005 and displayed it in 2007 "after relatively minor repairs."
Since Lichtenstein's sculpture was often repainted in his own lifetime, mor-
alistic arguments against repainting, based on some strict and unworkable
sense of the integrity of the past, hardly apply. The work, like any theater
piece (a play, a musical composition), was expected to change through history: it would deteriorate; it would be restored. History is thus not something
to be recovered; it is, rather, performance, and performance (the way the art
work appears to the public) is part of the history or being of the artwork. Yet
despite this, and despite Lichtenstein and DePasquale's obvious awareness of
these processes, the contrapuntal romantic rhetoric of the purity of origins
remains, as evidenced by the *Times* article on this piece.

A camera records DePasquale's progress every 20 seconds. "Every last
detail of the process is being documented for future reference." We hear of
perfection and completion. DePasquale had painted this sculpture in 1984:
"More than 20 years later, he could describe the original process step by
step. . . . Tests confirmed DePasquale's recollections." We don't hear anything about the details of DePasquale's "recollections" or the nature of these
tests, since they apparently uncovered nothing of interest and only confirmed
what we believe must be true.

DePasquale's language is quite different from that of the *Times* reporter
who invokes him: "It's really kind of fun." Determining where one color ends

and another begins—that is "the trickiest part." "You know the edge is some-where in there," he says. "You just sense it." The stated intentions of the re-storer are completely at odds with the rhetoric and the implied assumptions of the reporter. The *Times* piece recognizes the fact that artworks exist in history, that they change in history, then promotes the fossilization of that history through the glorification of an act of restoration.

No one questions DePasquale's good faith. When he says the sculpture will last "a real long time," he means "10 years easy, maybe more." De-Pasquale, thus, is not involved in what museums lead their customers/clients/supporters to believe is restoration; he is rather working within a living his-tory and continuing it, as well as participating in the documentation of that history. This history includes his own recollections of the processes used in the past construction of the artwork, his recreation and improvement of the process, the modern technology that reproduces or confirms this process. "If he were doing the usual restoration, applying layers of color by spray instead of brush, the job would probably last longer." DePasquale is deliberately re-storing the sculpture in such a way that it will not last; perhaps his expertise may be called on again.

I wonder whether DePasquale is involved in an ironic refutation of the forces that brought him there. Repaint a Lichtenstein? Why not simply rebuild it? Why even use the original materials? In the nineteenth century, viewers were accustomed to looking at wax and plaster models of original sculpture. Goethe was thrilled in *Italian Journey* to be able at long last to see the originals of the sculptures whose reproductions he had seen in Ger-many. Yet this attempt to re-make the sculpture according to the history of its creation has the paradoxical effect of denying that history. Despite De-Pasquale's efforts to insert his own history into this physical object, some-thing he does without qualms, his own history is effaced in the description of the process.

When you go to the Getty, a miserable place to view art, a marvelous place to view the living city of Los Angeles, you will confront many works of art that have been subjected to the same kind of treatment as the Lichten-stein. It is extremely difficult to find a Lichtenstein there, since every painting in the museum, it seems, has been transformed into a gleaming pseudo-acrylic print; it might be Lichtenstein, it might be Dali, it might be a college dorm room. It is difficult to determine what century you are in. The Getty is a museum, an ahistorical place of the imagination, where paint does not fade, where candlelight does not encrust objects with smoke, where varnish remains as clear and transparent as the day it was applied. Where plaster frames perfectly imitate the original woodcarving.

Most people interested in rare books or early books go to museums. Maybe professional art historians spend more time in museums than bibliographers do, but no one other than the rankest dilettante spends more time in libraries than we do. Whether at a museum or in the library, we try to recollect what we have seen, what we have read, and, if we are at all diligent, we try to map that onto the textbooks and catalogues that are our usual source of art history or book history and what these histories are. After a while, I cannot recollect whether I have actually seen the paintings I talk about; I know I have never read the fifteenth-century books that get most of my attention. Although I rarely buy a catalogue unless I buy it where the originals are on display, I still cannot remember, looking at that catalogue, whether I really saw what is depicted there: I cannot convert the numbers describing the dimensions of the original into sizes in the real world. And I have no idea what the original settings of those paintings might be. That description of the artwork—the image in the catalogue—no more reproduces that original than does the bibliographical formula in a rare book catalog. Of course I know exactly what the following means and would recognize the object it refers to instantly:

[18], 303 [1], 46, 49–100, [2], 69–232, [2] 79–80, [26], 98, [2], 109–156, 257–993 [i.e. 399], [1], p. (fol.)

But holding one of the book-copies it represents (Shakespeare's First Folio), that is a different matter altogether.

Original History

The caricatures of Fragonard, I once reasoned, were like place-settings. You cannot think of them the way you see them in a museum. They are occasional pieces, and you must imagine a history for them, even a fantastic one. You go to a dinner party, and find instead of place cards, your own sketched portrait telling you where to sit. Or you arrive in time for home movies, porno-movies, it turns out to be, and you are shocked to find (due to the wonders of digital technology) that you yourself are the star, performing with the very host of the party, whom you may never have met.[2] There is no way to experience this at a museum.

The analogy I am drawing here has its counterpart in all the areas I have talked about: the history of the printing shop imagined by analytical bibliography, the invention of the composing stick, the casting and manufacture of the earliest type, the process of editing. Editors have little to gain by taking up the challenge I pose in Chapter 6 and nothing to lose by ignoring it. Perhaps they know that their own rhetoric of originality and history is at best metaphorical. No editor, no historian, no bibliographer really wants to get at "what it was." "Originality" means other things. Note that even in editing, where this presumed principle is of paramount importance, originality has two diametrically opposed (moral?) meanings: when applied to the work of a scribe or copier, "originality" is bad, the source of error; when applied to the work of an author, it is good. But unfortunately, the only real evidence produced by editorial methodology is the first: authorial originality is in the nature of a conclusion based on evidence. In art restoration, the same equivocation in the word *original* applies.

Binding Materials

At the Huntington, I became interested in the deteriorating bindings of run-of-the-mill deteriorating books. No one cares much about these. Few readers bother to look at them. Eventually, the deterioration will reach the point where the book will be reported to the Conservation Department. A certain kind of damage, unlike "ordinary wear and tear" (whatever that is), is beyond the limits of acceptability (whatever they are). A reader or librarian forms this arbitrary judgment and talks to the conservators who will have to rebind the book. At the Huntington, the result will be not a faux-antique, heavily tooled binding, but rather a serviceable, sturdy, and utterly nondescript industrial binding that no one will ever mistake for an original.[3]

The conservators (or restorers) once took me through the process and pointed to the detritus of rebinding: fragments of the old binding, headbands, cords. For some reason, locked in my own romantic notions of what it is I do, I asked where these shards of history would end up, with their invaluable evidence of the binding that "once was." "And what would you like?" they asked. "A separate box perhaps? Can you suggest a catalogue number for that?" Or should these scraps from the incunable heap all have a heap of their own? Maybe diligent scholars with time to burn could sort them all out in the future and tout their discoveries ("A Lost Headband from HEHL, Mead no. 486"). Realistically, if you can't catalogue it, then by definition it does not exist. "We toss them."

I was lucky to be once with a rare book librarian in the stacks of the Huntington. He was brilliant but disorderly, lost amid the heaps of books, discoursing on particulars. We discovered a set of early printing fragments in an incunable binding, and found it quite remarkably because we had been surveying the collection looking for just this sort of thing (see above, III.4). The fragments had been cut out from the binding, in the early twentieth century I am certain, and sandwiched in cardboard inside the cover of the book, left there to be discovered seventy years it must have been in the future. The first thing my guide did was throw the cardboard away, and all I could think of, dumbly standing there, was that as that cardboard hit the wastebasket, with it went all but the most speculative of histories concerning how those fragments happened to be discovered, recognized, and placed there, unidentified by some hardworking but anonymous librarian of the 1930s, to be forgotten entirely until we chanced on them. Now there is a history worth thinking about!—the intellectual world of the bibliographers who would first ignore, then recognize, the value of such things, deface the book to remove them from the binding, and leave them there without so much as a note on their existence—all that alluring history to be teased out of the cardboard, with its evidence of who these early librarians were. Gone. Instead, the only history that seemed of interest to us was that very "originality" I am disparaging now. Hey, get a look at this, Louie. Pontanus Type! From 1460!

The same principle applies here as applies to cataloguing. It is very difficult to use a catalogue, or even a library, without internalizing to some extent the principles that brought it into being. You are examining this material because someone else determined that it was worth examining. You are recording this evidence because someone earlier decided that it would be evidence. You are looking through the author or printer list in a database because someone earlier determined that this was the way the evidence they defined and presented to you should be organized.

Like most museums, the Getty claims to have strict documentation on its restorations. This documentation can be examined. But most of what is put on public display here and elsewhere are rhetorical laudations like what is found in the *LA Times* article quoted above, or photos of happy and serious restorers at work. Such things do not document an original; they are a restorative *petitio principii*, justifying the initial assumptions by an appeal to them.

Yet the Lichtenstein restoration project discussed above is also completely entwined in my own attitude toward the Getty itself, which I cannot untangle from my attitude toward my subject. Here, in this sanitized viewpoint of a beautifully sanitized Los Angeles. A fall evening watching the sunset. A tangle of tiny rooms like my grandmother's hideous Victorian house. The loud and raucous reading room, with its open air offices for staff, which makes the Getty collections unusable for any but isolated scholars with their personalized offices. The unwieldy geometry of the bookstacks. And two unpleasant personal incidents that I will do no more than allude to.

All that, of course, is irrelevant according to the conventions of scholarship, where the full presence of the past, stripped of all the dimness and distortions of perspective, stripped of all the unstable emotions of those who have experienced a past of their own, is finally revealed. Where economics do not matter. Where the crass vulgarities and prejudices of the public, which includes all of us, are finally suppressed for good.

Coda: The Joy Of Referentiality

I am in a familiar chain of stores in Los Angeles called "Out of the Closet," and it smells like all such stores do. It must be the old upholstery of the furniture sold here, or perhaps the racks of used clothes that cycle through. I am looking for old canvases for a friend. She will scrape off the paint, gesso it, and start again, an interesting allegory in and of itself. I find exactly what I seem to be looking for on the shelf over the mismatched glasses and crockery. A frameless canvas, easel sized (24×36 is that?), landscape orientation, execrably painted.

I begin to examine the painting, since it will soon be gone, and a gaze, I suppose, is a fitting last tribute to any art work, however pedestrian. Most of the discarded canvases I find here are half-finished or badly damaged. This one is complete. But it is hideous. Thin layers of paint in impossible colors, unmixed and pure. The cheapest of acrylics, I think, perhaps some oils pressed into the texture. There are large shapes formed of oblique lines, laid on with a knife or large brush, and I realize, with some difficulty, these represent mountains. The opposing verticals must be trees. Suddenly the genre is clear to me, and I look for a signature. And there it is. Only this signature itself is clearly faked: "Bob Ross." It is fake, because no one who could paint this badly would ever admit to it.

Bob Ross's *Joy of Painting* was a staple of 1980s television. I used to watch it on a small black-and-white set with rabbit ears. Bob Ross died in 1995 at fifty-two, but you will find nothing of his death on "BobRoss.com" which has as a title "Bob Ross Incorporated." It is as if nothing happened in the past nearly two decades. It is as if his "happy trees" will live forever.

Neither the paintings produced by Mr. Ross nor the Old Master paintings and techniques he occasionally references in his shows are "really realistic." The world is not two-dimensional; the colors of the world are produced neither in a series of dried glazes nor in heavy swatches laid on with a knife or three-inch brush. He paints within the late twentieth-century aesthetic, which is marked, at least to amateurs and dilettantes, by aggressively abstract and anti-realistic work, whether we call it impressionism or modernism or surrealism; constructionism, found painting, post-modernism, or abstract expressionism. Yet I cannot be alone in imagining that with a few pats of the brush, punctuated by Mr. Ross's marvelously unlocalized but distinctive accent "Jes' draw down the paint, sumpin' like 'at . . ." we would be suddenly looking at Leonardo's Last Supper, or the Last Judgment of Michelangelo.

What distinguishes Mr. Ross's paintings from what we think of as landscapes is that the landscapes are completely detached from anything we might consider objective reality; there is not even the pretense that one might find one of these scenes "out there," nor do they meet even the basic conditions of what is traditionally considered nature. These are mountains of the mind, and landscapes of the mind, where things "live," as Mr. Ross often instructs us, exactly where we, and we alone, want them to be. How could the word "live" be so unsettling?

Anyone who has read anything about Mr. Ross or has listened to him for any extended period of time knows of his attachment to animals. The gentle Bob Ross, arch-sentimentalist, holding a baby raccoon in the photo on his website. Yet none of the landscapes I have seen him paint show an animal or even allusion to one. No abandoned nests, dens, or coyote trails through the mountains. Animals are confined to a separate series of paintings, and never intrude on his famous landscapes.[4] There is thus no "history" there, no reality that the painter alludes to, or studies, or tries to uncover. There is only the recycling of the painter's own techniques and imagination, in what appears to be an endless feedback loop. There is thus no test of this art. It cannot in any way be falsified.

Mr. Ross provides a theory of representation, perfectly intelligible to everyone, that has just as obviously no relation to anything we would consider real in any sense whatsoever. We are left with the simple Gestalt of seeing, realism without reality. The perfectly self-confirming scholarly article or presentation that miraculously silences all but the most unseemly ad hominem critique. And we see things suddenly, not as they are, but as we wish them to be.

Except for Bob.

Bob Ross. Dead at fifty-two.

NOTES

INTRODUCTION

1. Joseph A. Dane, *The Myth of Print Culture: Essays on Evidence, Textuality, and Bibliographical Method* (Toronto: University of Toronto Press, 2003), 148–54; cf. most recently Kristine Louise Haugen, *Richard Bentley: Poetry and Enlightenment* (Cambridge, Mass.: Harvard University Press, 2011), 211–29.

2. Joseph A. Dane, *What Is a Book? The Study of Early Printed Books* (Notre Dame, Ind.: Notre Dame University Press, 2012), Introduction.

3. "Unfinished Business: Incomplete Bindings Made for the Book Trade from the Fifteenth to the Nineteenth Century," William Andrews Clark Memorial Library, 30 October 2012.

4. E. Ph. Goldschmidt, *Gothic and Renaissance Bookbindings*, 2 vols. (London: Benn, 1928), 1:36.

5. E.g., Stuart Bennett, *Trade Bookbinding in the British Isles, 1660–1880* (Newcastle, Del.: Oak Knoll Press, 2004). On the general point, see Paul Fussell's note that the only reliable first-hand accounts of war were written by those (even illiterates) who had no notion of the genre of war memoir: *The Great War and Modern Memory* (Oxford: Oxford University Press, 1975), 173.

6. Robert Proctor's reimagining of the organization of fifteenth-century books is just one example; see Alfred W. Pollard's "Memoir," in *Robert Proctor: Bibliographical Essays* (London: Chiswick, 1905), esp. xxii–xxx; Martin Davies, "Robert Proctor," in William Baker and Kenneth Womack, *Nineteenth-Century British Book-Collectors and Bibliographers*, Dictionary of Literary Biography 184 (Detroit: Gale Research, 1997), 354–63.

7. David McKitterick, "Not in STC: Opportunities and Challenges in the STC," *The Library* ser. 7, 6 (2005): 178–94; Stephen Tabor, "Additions to STC," *The Library* ser. 6, 16 (1994): 109–207.

8. David McKitterick, *Print, Manuscript and the Search for Order, 1450–1830* (Cambridge: Cambridge University Press, 2003).

9. Ibid., 80, quoting Allan Stevenson on bibliographical "ideal copy" as "a will o' the wisp," 136, characterizing Anglo-American bibliography as "a blunt instrument."

10. G. W. Prothero, *A Memoir of Henry Bradshaw* (London: Kegan, Paul, 1888), 349; see Paul Needham, *The Bradshaw Method: Henry Bradshaw's Contribution to Bibliography*

(Chapel Hill, N.C.: Hanes Foundation, 1998), also McKitterick's rebuke in *MLR* 107 (2012): 590–92.

CHAPTER 1. PALEOGRAPHY VERSUS TYPOGRAPHY

1. Joseph A. Dane, *Out of Sorts: On Typography and Print Culture* (Philadelphia: University of Pennsylvania Press, 2011), 3–7.

2. Thomas Frognall Dibdin, *Typographical Antiquities, or the History of Printing in England, Scotland, and Ireland*, 4 vols. (London: Miller, 1810–19), 2: viii–ix.

3. Edward Rowe Mores, *A Dissertation upon English Typographical Founders and Founderies (1778), with a Catalogue and Specimen of the Typefoundry of John James (1782)*, ed. Harry Carter and Christopher Ricks (Oxford: Bibliographical Society, 1961), Catalogue, 20–21. The term "black" appears in W. Thorowgood's Specimen, 1824, shown in Daniel Berkeley Updike, *Printing Types: Their History, Forms, and Use; A Study in Survivals*, 2 vols. (Cambridge, Mass.: Harvard University Press, 1937), fig. 335. See also W. Turner Berry and A. F. Johnson, eds., *Catalogue of Specimens of Printing Types by English and Scottish Printers and Founders, 1665–1830* (London: Oxford University Press, 1935); Stanley Morison, *John Fell: The University Press and the "Fell" Types* (Oxford: Clarendon, 1967), "The Fell Black-Letters," 109–22 (Fell calls these "English").

4. Robert Proctor, *Index to Early Printed Books in the British Museum . . . to the year 1500* (London: Kegan Paul, 1898); Frank Isaac, *English and Scottish Printing Types, 1501–58, 1508–58*, 2 vols. (London: Oxford University Press, 1930–32); *Catalogue of Books Printed in the XVth Century Now in the British Museum*, 13 vols. (London: British Museum, 1908–) (hereafter BMC).

5. Joseph Moxon, *Mechanick Exercises on the Whole Art of Printing (1683–4)*, ed. Herbert Davis and Harry Carter, 2 vols. (Oxford: Oxford University Press, 1958), 20–21, distinguishes size ("Bodies") from "Face" (Romain, Italica, English, the threefold classification familiar in later typography). See also Joseph Moxon, *Regulae Trium Ordinum Literarum Typographicarum or the Rules of the Three Orders of Print Letters: viz: the Roman, Italick, English, Capitals and Small* (London, 1676).

6. Updike occasionally refers to these as "tribes." There are inconsistent attempts to follow classical biological hierarchy: class > order > family. Ronald B. McKerrow, *An Introduction to Bibliography for Literary Students* (Oxford: Clarendon, 1927), 288–90 follows Updike. McKerrow notes that A. W. Pollard "regards [terms] as a great nuisance" (290).

7. Proctor's Type Index is more systematic, but still imprecise; see A. F. Johnson, "The Classification of Gothic Types" (1929), in *Selected Essays on Books and Printing*, ed. Percy H. Muir (Amsterdam: Van Gendt, 1970), 1–17, esp. 10. Johnson's essay should be read against other essays in this collection, stressing the individuality of types. Stanley Morison (on gothic types), distinguishes textura, rotunda, fere-humanistica, bastarda, mixed. Within bastarda, Morison distinguishes for Germany four types: Schwabacher, Upper-Rhine, Wittenberg letter, and Fraktur. Harry Carter, *A View of Early Typography*

Up to About 1600 (Oxford: Clarendon, 1969), quite deftly avoids the problem in chap. 2, "Diversity of Letter-forms in Print": "It is evident that in considering the face of a fount of type we are in a world of art, styles, difficulty of saying what styles, inherited forms, human hands" (24). See further Paul Needham, "Palaeography and the Earliest Printing Types," in Holger Nickel and Lothar Gillner, eds., *Johannes Gutenberg: Regionale Aspekte des frühen Buchdrucks* (Berlin: Staatsbibliothek zu Berlin, 1993), 19–27.

8. There are of course exceptions. See, e.g., the two examples of Schwabacher and Fraktur (a large heading type) noted by Isaac, *English and Scottish Printing Types*, vol. 2, Type Index.

9. On early treatises see Albert Derolez, *The Palaeography of Gothic Manuscript Books from the Twelfth Through the Early Sixteenth Century* (Cambridge: Cambridge University Press, 2003), 100; S. Steinberg, "Medieval Writing Masters," *The Library* ser. 4, 22 (1941): 1–24; Stanley Morison, *Selected Essays on the History of Letter-Forms in Manuscript and Print*, ed. David McKitterick (Cambridge: Cambridge University Press, 2009), "The Art of Printing" (1949), 9-10n7, for bibliography of early treatises and specimen sheets.

10. G. I. Lieftinck, "Pour une nomenclature de l'écriture livresque de la période dite gothique: Essai s'appliquant spécialement aux manuscrits originaires des Pays-Bas médiévaux," in B. Bischoff, G. I. Lieftinck, and G. Battelli, *Nomenclature des écritures livresques du IXe au XVIe siècle: Premier colloque international de paléographie latine, Paris, 28–30 April 1953* (Paris: CNRS, 1954), 15–34. See esp. Derolez, *Palaeography of Gothic Manuscript Books*, "Nomenclature," 13ff.

11. These objective criteria were the same used for the "non-objective" classifications of early typography, although I'm not sure typographers have ever articulated them this clearly.

12. Lieftinck's appeal to his French colleagues to give up this term is surely facetious (28).

13. Derolez, *Palaeography*, 176–82. Dutschke calls this "oddly reassuring," in that "the full range of actual scripts was not obliged to submit to the system"; Consuelo W. Dutschke, review of Derolez, *Palaeography*, *Speculum* 81 (2010): 171–72.

14. See Julian Brown, "Names of Scripts: A Plea to All Medievalists," in *A Palaeographer's View: Selected Writings of Julian Brown*, ed. Janet Bately, Michelle Brown, and Jane Roberts (London: Harvey Miller, 1993), 39–46; see also "The Humanist Hands," 69–78.

15. Joseph A. Dane, "Bibliographical History Versus Bibliographical Evidence: The Plowman's Tale and Early Chaucer Editions," *Bulletin of the John Rylands University Library of Manchester* 78 (1996): 47–61.

16. See Lieftinck, "Nomenclature," Gothico-Antiqua and other "hors système" scripts, 10ff. "That [humanist script] could be accepted so rapidly, within a few decades, by a whole society, and ultimately by the whole world as the preferred script for the Latin alphabet, remains a fact of the utmost importance and testifies to the superior intrinsic qualities of the script" (Derolez, 177). So M. B. Parkes, *Their Hands Before Our Eyes: A Closer Look at Scribes* (1999) (Aldershot: Ashgate, 2008), 58.

17. See text/gloss in Lieftinck, figs. 15, 41. In fig. 30, scribe indicates distinction by shifting from textura to bastarda, on same measured line.

18. Needham, *Bradshaw Method*; Dane, *Out of Sorts*, chap. 2, and fig. 12, from Gottfried Zedler, *Die älteste Gutenbergtype, mit 13 Tafeln in Lichtdruck*, VGG, 1 (Mainz: Gutenberg Gesellschaft, 1902), Tafel XIII; for the relation of such tables to nineteenth-century biological classification, see Seth Lerer, "Caxton in the Nineteenth Century," in William Kuskin, ed., *Caxton's Trace: Studies in the History of English Printing* (Notre Dame, Ind.: University of Notre Dame Press, 2006), 325–70.

19. For example, the facsimiles of individual letters given in Michelle Brown, *A Guide to Western Historical Scripts from Antiquity to 1600* (Toronto: University of Toronto Press, 1990).

20. Moxon, *Mechanick Exercises*, secs. 12–14.

21. These distinctions seem to be followed scrupulously by Peter W. M. Blayney, *The Texts of King Lear and Their Origins*, vol. 1, *Nicholas Okes and the First Quarto* (Cambridge: Cambridge University Press, 1982), although in some scholarship, the terms seem at times interchangeable, e.g., Hendrik D. L. Vervliet, *The Palaeo-Typography of the French Renaissance: Selected Papers on Sixteenth-Century Typefaces*, 2 vols. (Leiden: Brill, 2008).

22. See Dane, *What Is a Book?*, 208–10.

23. William Blades, *Life and Typography of Caxton*, 2 vols. (London: Lilly, 1861); Robin Myers, "George Isaac Frederick Tupper, Facsimilist," *Transactions of the Cambridge Bibliographical Society* 7 (1978): 113–34.

24. The most useful and comprehensive list of Caxton editions remains Seymour De Ricci, *A Census of Caxtons* (Oxford: Bibliographical Society, 1909; reprint 2000). See Wytze Hellinga and Lotte Hellinga, *The Fifteenth-Century Printing Types of the Low Countries*, 2 vols., trans. D. A. S. Reid (Amsterdam: Hertzberger, 1966), and Lotte Hellinga's less useful "narrativization" of the evidence in *William Caxton and Early Printing in England* (London: British Library, 2010), William Kuskin, rev. *RES* 62 (2011): 805–6.

25. For the value of freehand drawings in bibliographical work, see Adrian Weiss, "Font Analysis as a Bibliographical Method: The Elizabethan Play-Quarto Printers and Compositors," *Studies in Bibliography* 43 (1990): 95–164. Weiss notes that such drawings are more useful than photographic images in identifying particular typesorts since they can better highlight the distinctive features of the sorts; this is not to say the stylized drawings better "represent" the font.

26. All other illustrations of type in vol. 2 are clearly labeled "Imitation" or "Facsimile" and the difference is obvious, even in the reduced "facsimile" edition of this book published by Burt Franklin in 1965.

27. The setting conventions for Gutenberg were completely different from those for Caxton, and required nearly double the number of letterforms. It may be that this number "ca. 290" is "what is thought appropriate for early fonts," rather than "what is actually in them." See *Out of Sorts*, 20–25.

28. These are the only sorts depicted in BMC XI as distinguishing the two fonts, although the language in BMC is ambiguous.

29. Blades notes the two fonts 2 and 2* are never mixed (2:xxxii). All books before 1479 are exclusively in 2; all after 1479 are 2*. See also paper evidence compiled by BMC XI, 86–87, confirming the same chronology.

30. If the new variant font were only partially recast, it ought to be possible to find a "rogue sort" in 2 making an appearance in 2*. See George D. Painter, *William Caxton: A Quincentenary Biography of England's First Printer* (London: Chatto & Windus, 1976), 95 n3: "The easiest dodge for distinguishing the two states is to look for the letters th, which are printed from two separate sorts in the first state, but from a single ligatured sort in the second. A defective A with three prongs instead of two at bottom left is frequent in state one, but very rare in 2*." This statement also implies that the two variant fonts share sorts.

31. "We" I think refers to Blades alone. For support, he cites Ben Franklin: "I contrived a mould, and made use of the letters we had as puncheons, struck the matrices in lead, and thus supplied, in a pretty tolerable way the deficiencies. I also engraved several things on occasion" (xxvi).

32. Blades says font 2 is "modified" to form Caxton 6, but he does not detail how he believes that was done, and this claim makes his history of 2 and 2* more difficult. If 2* used old worn sorts of 2 as punches, it is hard to imagine that the original punches were available later to cast 6 as he claims on 2: xxxv, quoted below.

33. A complete font of 4 would have 194 sorts; 4* would have 187.

34. The notion that the same individual sorts appear in both fonts seems to contradict Painter's explanation of their manufacture.

35. Consider the difference, for example, between the first two single-bowled a^2 and a^*. You simply cannot start with a pattern from a^2 and cut and trim it to produce a^*. The same is true of *da*. I have blown up and cut out models of several of these typesorts; and I cannot derive one from the other.

36. The contexts in which discussion of early typography took place in the late nineteenth and early twentieth centuries were different from those in the late twentieth century. Among the other common theories: sand casting, casting in clay, wooden punches, and an elaborate and difficult to comprehend process known as the "Abklatsch" method; the most coherent description of this process in English is James Mosley, " 'So du die chrift abformen wilst': Abklatschen, clichage, Dabbing and the Duplication of Typographical Printing Surfaces," in Peter Rück and Martin Boghardt, eds., *Rationalisierung der Buchherstellung im Mittelalter und der frühen Neuzeit* (Marburg: Institut für Historische Hilfswissenschaften, 1994), 197–204. For a brief history of less coherent explanations, see my *Out of Sorts*, 206–7 n21.

37. E.g., Konrad Haebler, *Typenrepertorium der Wiegendrucke*, 5 vols. (Leipzig, 1905–24); see contemporary critique of this assumption by Ernst Consentius, *Die Typen der Inkunabelzeit: Eine Betrachtung* (Berlin: de Gruyter, 1929).

38. See also "A type modelled on Caxton's Type 2 but cast on a smaller body is St Albans Type 2A: 122B, first used in 1480."

39. The fonts 4 and 4* are distinguishable by 20-line measurement.

40. Blades states explicitly that "not any of the letters of the first section are absolutely identical with those of the second."

41. Hellinga refers to the "distinctive sorts" of Type 2, but given the discussion and the history of discussion in Blades, it is not absolutely certain what she means, or more precisely, what this phrase should mean. Does it refer to the new sorts shown in the plates? or to the font generally?

42. The phrase "Veldener's pronouncements" probably refers to the statement in a colophon: "Jan Veldenar qui quam certa manu insculpendi, celandi, interculandi, caracterandi assit industria [= cutting, engraving, pressing, stamping]; adde et fugurandi et efficianti"; Alfred W. Pollard, *An Essay on Colophons, with Specimens and Translations* (Chicago: Caxton Club, 1905), 162. Cf. BMC XI, 335, referring to "continental punch-cutters."

43. Discussion based on Severin Corsten, *Die Anfänge des Kölner Buchdrucks* (Cologne: Greven, 1955), 1–98.

44. J. P. Gumbert, "A Proposal for a Cartesian Nomenclature," in J. P. Gumbert and M. J. M. de Haan, eds., *Essays Presented to G. I. Lieftinck*, vol. 4, *Miniatures, Scripts, Collections* (Amsterdam, 1976), 45–52; see esp. Derolez, *Paleography*, 20 n60.

45. Note that his term "isotopes" means that two scripts are plotted at the same location of his cube, but has nothing to do with any historical relation (49).

46. The names of the points are chosen "mnemonically" although Gumbert leaves it to us to guess what these names are. A—anglicana K—Karolingian? C—? H—hybrida? T—Textualis. T C H A K are "purely mnemotechnical," 47 n2, meaning that E Z (whose meaning is not defined) are not.

47. Vincent Figgins, *The Game of the Chesse, by William Caxton, Reproduced in Facsimile from a Copy in the British Museum, with a few remarks on Caxton's typographical productions* (London: John Russell Smith, 1860), "Remarks," 1–8, and a subscription sheet: "A tribute to the Memory of William Caxton."

48. So William Herbert, in his revision of Ames's *Typographical Antiquities* as quoted in Figgins, noting a "perfect resemblance" between the two editions of *Recueil* and the first edition of *Game of Chess*, "not only the page itself, but the number of lines in a page, the length, breadth, and the intervals between the lines, are alike" (4).

CHAPTER 2. "CA. 1800": WHAT'S IN A DATE?

1. Rabelais, *Gargantua, Pere de Pantagruel*, chap. 9.

2. David Aers, "A Whisper in the Ear of Early Modernists: or, Reflections on Literary Critics Writing the 'History of the Subject'" (1991), rpt. in David Aers, ed., *Culture and History (1350–1600): Essays on English Communities, Identities, and Writing* (Detroit: Wayne State University Press, 1992), 177–202; Fred C. Robinson, "Medieval, the Middle Ages," *Speculum* 54 (1984): 745–56; E. G. Stanley, "The Early Middle Ages = The Dark

Ages = The Heroic Age of England and the English," in Marie-Françoise Alamichel and Derek Brewer, eds., *The Middle Ages After the Middle Ages in the English Speaking World* (Cambridge: Brewer, 1997), 43–78; W. P. Ker, *The Dark Ages* (New York: Scribner's, 1904).

3. See, e.g., Malcolm Lowry, on the transformation of the press "from a mere machine . . . into a dynamic, self-generating force that could examine and criticize its own products"; *Nicholas Jenson and the Rise of Venetian Publishing in Renaissance Europe* (Oxford: Blackwell, 1991), 127–36. Andrew Pettegree, *The Book in the Renaissance* (New Haven, Conn.: Yale University Press, 2010): the codex form itself "encourages reflective thought," 5.

4. Sven Birkerts, *The Gutenberg Elegies: The Fate of Reading in an Electronic Age* (Boston: Faber and Faber, 1994).

5. The most egregious example of this attitude is Elizabeth Eisenstein, *The Printing Press as an Agent of Change: Communications and Cultural Transformations in Early Modern Europe*, 2 vols. (Cambridge: Cambridge University Press, 1979), e.g., 1:xi, 1:4. See my critique, particularly of her methodological statements, in *The Myth of Print Culture*, 11–15.

6. One of the most important expressions of this is McKerrow's *Introduction to Bibliography* (1927). By contrast, Douglas C. McMurtrie, *The Book: The Story of Printing and Bookmaking* (1927) (New York: Oxford University Press, 1943) suggests a continuous history, but does not deal with alternate forms of printing (stereotyping), nor with the issues that became central to Anglo-American bibliographers.

7. Dane, *What Is a Book?*, Introduction, 11–12.

8. Dane, *Out of Sorts: On Typography and Print Culture*, 34–39.

9. Ludwig Hain, *Repertorium Bibliographicum* (Stuttgart, 1826–38); Georg Wolfgang Panzer, *Annales typographici ab artis inventae origine ad annum MD . . .* , 11 vols. (Nuremberg, 1793–1803).

10. See the paradoxical definition of the hand-press period by Richard-Gabriel Rummonds, *Nineteenth-Century Printing Practices and the Iron Handpress*, 2 vols. (New Castle, Del.: Oak Knoll, 2004), 1–4; discussed below.

11. Because of the frequent use of half-sheet imposition, format for fifteenth-century books is often ambiguous and misleading. On type identification, see Chapter 1.

12. Blockbooks are included even though their structure and production defies the ordinary methods of edition making. See my "The Huntington Blockbook Apocalypse (Schreiber, IV/V), with a Note on Terminology." *Printing History* 42 (2001): 3–15. See Helmut Lehmann-Haupt, *Gutenberg and the Master of Playing Cards* (New Haven, Conn.: Yale University Press, 1966).

13. One of the few bibliographical sources to describe this that are now considered basic is Philip Gaskell, *A New Introduction to Bibliography* (New York: Oxford University Press, 1972).

14. This change has practical implications for the analytical bibliographer. While it is no more cumbersome to describe and to identify such paper than it is to describe handmade paper, it is pointless in nineteenth-century paper to look for the individuality of sheets found in earlier paper or to write their histories.

15. See the nineteenth-century manual Frederick John Farlow Wilson, *Stereotyping and Electrotyping*, Wyman's Technical Series (London: Wyman & Sons, 1880), or the early essay by Thomas Hodgson, *An Essay on the Origin and Progress of Stereotype Printing: Including a Description of the Various Processes* (Newcastle, 1820). There are also some exceptionally good images of stereotyping available simply by Googling Stereotype Printing Images, although the metaphorical uses of this word, as is the case with associated words such as "typecasting," are far more frequent than literal ones.

16. Fredson Bowers, *Principles of Bibliographical Description* (Princeton, N.J.: Princeton University Press, 1949), esp. 113–23.

17. How disruptive a change in procedures can be for ordinary bibliographical language can be seen in the trenchant and often amusing exchanges over Paul Needham's notion that one of the earliest books—the *Catholicon*—was produced by an early form of linotype, where two-line slugs are used and retained over a period of years. Paul Needham, "Johann Gutenberg and the Catholicon Press," *PBSA* 76 (1982): 395–456. See James Mosley, "Typefoundry: Documents for the History of Type and Letterform," Typefoundry.blogspot.com, 22 June 2007.

18. On these various techniques, see esp. Bamber Gascoigne, *How to Identify Prints: A Complete Guide to Manual and Mechanical Processes from Woodcut to Ink-Jet* (New York: Thames and Hudson, 1986). See further Linda Stier Morenus, "Joseph Pennell and the Art of Transfer Lithography: A Technical Study," in Jane Colbourne and Reba Fishman Snyder, eds., *Printed on Paper: The Techniques, History and Conservation of Printed Media* (Newcastle upon Tyne: Arts and Social Sciences Academic Press, 2009), 83–95.

19. A concise summary is in R. C. Alston and M. J. Jannetta, *Bibliography, Machine Readable Cataloguing, and the ESTC: A Summary History of the Eighteenth Century Short Title Catalogue* (London: British Library, 1978), and Henry L. Snyder and Michael S. Smith, eds., *The English Short-Title Catalogue: Past, Present, Future* (New York: AMS Press, 2003).

20. ProQuest: Nineteenth Century Short Title Catalogue (NSTC), www.proquest.com/pdpq/19thcen_stc.

21. Dane, *What Is a Book?*, chap. 13: "Electronic Books and Databases," 211–28.

22. Katherine F. Pantzer, Introduction, in Alfred Pollard, G. R. Redgrave, et al., *A Short-Title Catalogue of Books Printed in England, Scotland & Ireland and of English Books Printed Abroad, 1475–1640*, 2nd ed., 3 vols. (London: Bibliographical Society, 1976–91), 1: xix–xliii; W. W. Greg, *A Bibliography of the English Printed Drama to the Restoration*, 4 vols. (London: Bibliographical Society, 1939–59).

23. The present Wing catalogue (1641–1700), is listed as having "over 100,000 items," which I believe is only slightly more than the original 1972 edition, www.proquest.com.pdpq/wing.

24. Michael Maittaire, *Annales typographici ab artis inventae origine ad annum MD* (The Hague, 1719).

25. McKitterick, *Print, Manuscript and the Search for Order (1450–1830)* (2003); David Pankow, *The Printer's Manual: An Illustrated History: Classical and Unusual Texts on Printing from the Seventeenth, Eighteenth, and Nineteenth Centuries* (Rochester, N.Y.: Rochester

Institute of Technology Cary Graphic Arts Press, 2005); Richard-Gabriel Rummonds, *Printing on the Iron Handpress* (Newcastle, Del.: Oak Knoll,1998), and *Nineteenth-Century Printing Practices and the Iron Handpress* (Newcastle, Del.: Oak Knoll, 2004).

26. Pettegree, *The Book in the Renaissance*, 25–26, describes early printing exactly according to methods set out in Moxon.

27. Moxon sold more copies in the twentieth century than it ever did earlier. There is a "third edition," I see, printed in 1703; but I believe these later editions only include vol. 1, "Handy-Works, and not vol. 2 "Printing." The first reprint is by Theo L. DeVinne (line-for-line reprint, with type cast from eighteenth-century punches of Caslon) in 1896.

28. *Encyclopédie, ou dictionnaire raisonné des sciences, des arts et des métiers* (Paris, 1751–72), *Recueil de Planches sur les sciences, les arts libéraux, et les arts méchaniques*, section on Fonderie in vol. 3, pt. 1. Pierre-Simon Fournier, *Manuel typographique utile aux gens de lettres, & à ceux qui exercent les différentes parties de l'art de l'imprimerie*, 2 vols. (Paris, 1764).

29. See my reproduction in *Out of Sorts*, 28, fig. 9, http://users.telenet.be/waarde /Handmoulds: A Website about the development, shape, and use of typefounders' moulds, citing James Mosley's notes about technical errors in this illustration. See also Mosley, Typefoundry 9 April 2007 "Drawing the Typefounders Mould," on errors in standard depictions of this device. Typefoundry.blogspot.com.

30. Robert Darnton, *The Business of the Enlightenment: A Publishing History of the Encyclopédie, 1775–1800* (Cambridge, Mass.: Harvard University Press, 1979).

31. On Luckombe, see notes in McKitterick, *Print, Manuscript and the Search for Order*, 187–97.

32. For example, from a brief search of shelves at the Huntington: Charles Frederick Partington, *The Printer's Complete Guide, containing a sketch of the history and progress of printing* (London, 1825); Charles A. Macintosh, *Popular outlines of the Press, ancient and modern: or A brief sketch of the origin and progress of printing and its introduction into this country* (London, 1859); J. Munsell, *The Typographical Miscellany* (Albany, N.Y., 1850).; Henry Beadnell, printer, *The Guide to Typography, literary and practical; or The Reader's Handbook and the Compositor's vade-mecum* (London, 1859).

33. Lawrence Counselman Wroth, "Corpus Typographicum," in *Typographic Heritage: Selected Essays* (New York: The Typophiles, 1949): "The thoughtful printer of today still goes to those manuals to learn the ancient traditions of type."

34. "It will be observed that Moxon's book has been frequently referred to and in many instances quoted from," Savage, *Dictionary*, Introduction.

35. *Printing on the Iron Handpress*, xviii: "It is a sad reflection but when I first took up the handpress in 1969, there were only five handpress printers in the United States producing books on a regular basis."

CHAPTER 3. BIBLIOGRAPHERS OF THE MIND

1. D. F. McKenzie, "Printers of the Mind: Some Notes on Bibliographical Theories and Printing-House Practices," *Studies in Bibliography* 22 (1969): 1–75; several times

reprinted, e.g., *Making Meaning: "Printers of the Mind" and Other Essays*, ed. Peter D. Macdonald and Michael F. Suarez, Jr. (Amherst: University of Massachusetts Press, 2002).

2. See "Printers of the Mind," 61: "The essential task of the bibliographer is to establish the facts of transmission for a particular text"; McKenzie is paraphrasing W. W. Greg, "Bibliography—An Apology" (1932), in *Collected Papers*, ed. J. C. Maxwell (Oxford: Clarendon, 1966), 239–66: "to say that bibliography is the grammar of literary investigation may be taken as equivalent to calling bibliography the science of the transmission of literary documents" (239).

3. In August 2011, I found in the MLA bibliography 124 results for the term "compositor"; 95 of these were after 1969 (several by McKenzie). In all fairness, 1972 was a strong year for this kind of study, and many of the articles were likely written before McKenzie's was published. In addition, these figures may reflect the interests of the editor of *PBSA*, clearly not a strong McKenzian in this regard. This belies the claim by Robert Donaldson in an early review, that McKenzie "injected so much uncertainty" into analytical bibliography that it was almost not worthwhile to do it; *The Library* ser. 5, 25 (1970): 159.

4. D. C. Greetham, *Textual Scholarship: An Introduction* (1992; New York: Garland, 1994), 7. See in particular his chapter on "Describing the Text: Descriptive Bibliography," 153–68, whose very title is indicative of the problem. Descriptive bibliography does not describe texts; as defined by Fredson Bowers and other Anglo-American bibliographers, it deals rather with features of printed editions.

5. Terry Belanger, "Descriptive Bibliography," in *Book Collecting: A Modern Guide*, ed. Jean Peters (New York: Bowker, 1977), 97–115. This article is reprinted on the BSA web site www.bibsocamer.org under "Bibliography Defined." Belanger's influence, because of his work with the Rare Book School of Virginia, extends well beyond anything his publications can document, and the same may be true of McKenzie. Sidney E. Berger, in Midwest Book and Manuscript Studies Faculty, Graduate School of Library and Information Science, University of Illinois, www.lis.illinois.edu/academics/programs/mbms/MBMS_Faculty.

6. T. Howard-Hill, "Enumerative and Descriptive Bibliography," in Peter Davison, ed., *The Book Encompassed: Studies in Twentieth-Century Bibliography* (Cambridge: Cambridge University Press, 1994), 122.

7. G. Thomas Tanselle, *Bibliographical Analysis: A Historical Introduction* (Cambridge: Cambridge University Press, 2009), 3: "Bibliographical analysis . . . concentrates on using physical details to learn something about the manufacturing processes that produced a given book and its text, the historical influences underlying its physical appearance, and the responses that its design engendered (which may require some attention to what successive owners have done to individual copies)." Cf. Tanselle's *Introduction to Scholarly Editing*, Seminar Syllabus (eighteenth rev. Charlottesville, Va.: Book Arts Press, 2002), and his articles on enumerative and descriptive bibliography reprinted in his *Literature and Artifacts* (Charlottesville: University of Virginia Press, 1998), Part III, 125–99.

8. William Proctor Williams and Craig S. Abbott, *An Introduction to Bibliographical and Textual Studies*, 4th ed. (New York: MLA, 2009). The introduction seems to define five categories: reference bibliography, historical bibliography, analytical bibliography, descriptive bibliography, textual criticism.

9. Blayney, *The Texts of King Lear and Their Origins*, 1–8.

10. A. W. Pollard and G. R. Redgrave, *A Short-Title Catalogue of Books Printed in England, Scotland and Ireland, and of English Books Printed Abroad, 1475–1640* (1926) = STC 1; 2nd ed., Pollard, Redgrave, Jackson, et al. (1976–91) = STC2; English Short Title Catalogue, www.bl.uk. = ESTC.

11. It is sometimes useful to distinguish STC1 from STC2 as showing the difference between enumerative and descriptive bibliography (so Greetham, *Textual Scholarship*, 21), but the differences in descriptions are minor. ESTC adds only a brief statement of structure (pagination or foliation). The primary example of a descriptive bibliography in English is Greg, *Bibliography of the English Printed Drama to the Restoration*.

12. On the many conceptual and even grammatical ambiguities of this term, see my " 'Ideal Copy' vs. 'Ideal Texts': The Application of Bibliographical Description to Facsimiles," *Papers of the Bibliographical Society of Canada* 3 (1995): 31–50, reprinted in *Abstractions of Evidence in the Study of Manuscripts and Early Printed Books* (Aldershot: Ashgate, 2009), 77–94. See also *What Is a Book?* chap. 11, 188–202. And for what I believe is a caveat on this notion, McKitterick, *Print, Manuscript and the Search for Order*, 80, 151.

13. If only a single copy exists, it still must be interpreted as an abstraction: "Naturally, if the only known copy of a book seems normal, we must infer that it is perfect" (Bowers, *Principles,* 113). Note that if were using the terms descriptive/analytical of manuscript production, they would not mean the same thing, since they would distinguish hypothesized historical events that result in a unique material object.

14. My notion of printer's intentions as the basis of ideal copy has several exceptions, most important I think in the description of cancelled leaves, where both *cancellans* and *cancellandum* must be accounted for. In this case, printer's intentions are not assumed to be static.

15. *What Is a Book*, chaps. 10–11. There are certain catalogues where this distinction is blurred, just as it is necessarily blurred whenever we try to talk about books in the real world. BMC's descriptions of incunables, for example, are of particular book-copies in the British Library, but function in many cases as ideal-copy descriptions: even when the BL owns multiple copies, none necessarily conforms to the printed description. This can lead to confusion, most notably in the case of the Gutenberg Bible, where BMC's description of its copy cannot be mapped onto other library catalog descriptions of other copies. The purpose of ideal-copy description, according to most bibliographers, is that all copies can be evaluated in terms of it (see Bowers, *Principles*, 113).

16. It is harder today than it would have been when this was written to ignore the pious rhetoric concerning the "true spirit of scientific inquiry" and the association of this with "humility" (a word I would not apply to any of the scientists I know).

17. See *Texts of King Lear*, 60 n: "Throughout this chapter frequent references are made to dates of entrance in the Stationers' Register, to Okes's books of 1607–8 and to the several states of ornaments which were damaged during those years. All entrances are transcribed in Appendix I, the books are listed in Appendix II, and ornament damage is described in Appendix IIIC." Appendix I is on pp. 317–33, but the items provide little more than the identification and date of particular books, e.g., "Niccolas Oakes. Entred for his Copy vnder thande of mr Etkins & Th'wardens, a booke called The picture of a true Protestant, or the office & honor. of all true [christ]ians both Ministers & people. (10 November 1609)." App. III is a Checklist of books (334–431). The evidence of Appendices IV–VI is analytical, dealing with ornaments, type, and press-variants.

18. Mark Bland, *A Guide to Early Printed Books and Manuscripts* (Chichester: Wiley-Blackwell, 2010), 8, claims McKenzie reformulates the discipline by moving from Greg's positivism toward a sociology of the text. This seems to be the opposite of what McKenzie implies here. It also belies the amusing characterization of McKenzie as "Prophet of the New Incredulity"; see Jean-François Gilmont, "Printers by the Rules," trans. David Shaw, *The Library* ser. 6, 2 (1980): 126–55.

19. To McKenzie, the analysis of book-copies seems not even "fundamental" to book history: "very little fundamental research has been done on the history of printing" (53).

20. On definitions of external evidence in literary studies, see Joseph A. Dane, *Who Is Buried in Chaucer's Tomb? Studies in the Reception of Chaucer's Book* (East Lansing: Michigan State University Press, 1998), chap. 9, 183–89.

21. I am not certain what "full primary evidence" means in the above statement, since McKenzie does not cite those cases where it has become available. I am assuming, perhaps incorrectly, that he includes his own tables as setting forth that evidence. See 60: "I have stressed the supreme importance of primary evidence," and the call to use "*all* available evidence."

22. See the casual note in Jacques Rychner, "Le Travail et l'atelier," in *Histoire de l'édition française*, tome 2: *Le Livre triumphant (1660–1830)* (Paris: PROMODIS, 1984), 55, on the difference between what the press records of workers and how teams of workers were actually constituted in the STN.

23. Prothero, *A Memoir of Henry Bradshaw*, letter to Dr Furnivall, 349 (corrected from ms.); Needham, *The Bradshaw Method*, 8.

24. Charlton Hinman, *The Printing and Proof-Reading of the First Folio of Shakespeare*, 2 vols. (Oxford: Clarendon, 1963). I am not certain which of the two methods (inductive or deductive) McKenzie sees Hinman as following, since he is associated with both; see "Printers of the Mind," 32 and 35.

25. Harold Love, *Scribal Publication in Seventeenth-Century England* (Oxford: Clarendon, 1993), 90: "[Hinman] presents us with a production-history of an edition so meticulous that it is hard to imagine what might have been added." See, however, *Printing and Proof-Reading* 1:245n1 for Hinman's statements on the number of copies he fully collated and those he only spot-checked, and my notes in *Myth of Print Culture*, 91–92.

26. Note that a compositor in McKenzie's study is a name; in analytical bibliography, it is an abstract system of spelling and setting conventions.

27. "Integrity," a word I have never trusted or understood, is central to the classic New Critical work of Wimsatt and Beardsley; W. K. Wimsatt, Jr., and Monroe C. Beardsley, "The Intentional Fallacy," in *The Verbal Icon: Studies in the Meaning of Poetry* (Louisville: University Press of Kentucky, 1954).

28. This was the purpose of bibliography as stated by Greg (see above, n2), and until recently a core tenet in Anglo-American Bibliography. Cf. the work of early German analytical bibliographers; Paul Schwenke's *Untersuchungen zur Geschichte des ersten Buchdrucks* (Berlin: Hopfer, 1900), on the Gutenberg Bible, had no textual-critical component whatsoever.

29. Maittaire, *Annales Typographici* (1719); Panzer, *Annales typographici* (1793–1803); Hain, *Repertorium Bibliographicum* (1826–1838).

30. Joseph Ames, *Typographical Antiquities, Being an Historical Account of Printing in England*, 3 vols. (London, 1749); Thomas Frognall Dibdin, *Bibliotheca Spenceriana: Books Printed in the Fifteenth Century and of Many Valuable First Editions, in the Library of George John Earl Spencer, K. G.*, 6 vols. (London, 1814–1823); Blades, *Life and Typography of Caxton*; William Lowndes, *The Bibliographer's Manual of English Literature, containing an account of rare, curious, and useful books, published in or relating to Great Britain & Ireland* (London: Pickering, 1834).

31. E.g., Schwenke, *Untersuchungen*, and the many monographs issued in the series Veröffentlichungen der Gutenberg Gesellschaft. Their importance and relation to the seminal work of Bradshaw has been stressed by Needham, *Bradshaw Method*.

32. The work of these bibliographers is ignored by the so-called New Bibliographers (who tended to rely on Curt Bühler) and by the newer ones as well; Blayney, Eisenstein, McKenzie, Tanselle, Darnton, even Febvre and Martin seem minimally acquainted with them and openly hostile to the issues they raised. See my *Out of Sorts*, chap. 1, 17–20; and statements by Lucien Febvre and Henri-Jean Martin, *The Coming of the Book: The Impact of Printing 1460–1800* (1958), trans. David Gerard (London: Verso, 1976), 9. One of the few English bibliographers who seems central to both incunable studies and classical Anglo-American bibliography is A. W. Pollard through his work on BMC (itself growing directly out of the cataloguing principles and assumptions for incunables of Robert Proctor) and on STC, built on those principles associated with the New Bibliography.

CHAPTER 4. HERMAN R. MEAD'S *INCUNABULA IN THE HUNTINGTON LIBRARY* AND THE NOTION OF "TYPOGRAPHICAL VALUE"

1. Herman Ralph Mead, *Incunabula in the Huntington Library* (San Marino, Calif: Huntington Library, 1937). This chapter is a revised version of an article that appeared in *Bulletin of the Bibliographical Society of Australia and New Zealand* 28 (2004): 24–40.

2. Proctor, *An Index to the Early Printed Books in the British Museum* (1898–1906), and Introduction, note 6 above. Other catalogues contemporary with Mead employed

the same system: Francis Jenkinson, *List of the Incunable Collected by George Dunn arranged to Illustrate the History of Printing* (London: Oxford University Press, 1923); Pierce Butler, *A Check List of Fifteenth Century Books in the Newberry Library and in other Libraries in Chicago* (Chicago: Newberry Library, 1933).

3. See, however, Dane, *Myth of Print Culture*, chap. 3.1, "The Cataloguing of Early Book Fragments," 57–75.

4. Konrad Haebler, *German Incunabula: 110 Original Leaves*, 2 vols., trans. André Barbey (Munich: Weiss, 1927); Haebler, *Italian Incunabula: 110 Original Leaves*, trans. André Barbey (Munich: Weiss, 1927); Haebler, *West-European Incunabula: 60 Original Leaves from the Presses of the Netherlands, France, Iberia, and Great Britain*, trans. André Barbey (Munich: Weiss, 1928).

5. William Ludwig Schreiber, *Woodcuts from Books of the 15th Century, Shown in Original Specimens: 55 Leaves detached from Books*, trans. André Barbey (Munich: Weiss, 1929).

6. Henry E. Huntington Library, Institutional Archives. 34.22.4.1; Henry E. Huntington Library, Institutional Archives. 34.22.4.2: "Incunabula." See also Grace Osgood Kelley, "A Report on Problems in Organization and Technique having to do with the Production of a Central or Public Catalog and Shelf-List for the Henry E. Huntington Library" (typescript, 1930) and Donald C. Dickinson, *Henry E. Huntington's Library of Libraries* (San Marino, Calif.: Huntington Library Press, 1995).

7. HEHL, Inst. Arch. 34.22.4.2: "Chronicle Conspectus of the Acquisition of Incunabula."

8. HEHL, Inst. Arch. 34.22.4.2: "Report of H. R. Mead for 1925." Vollbehr sold similar numbers of incunables to the Library of Congress; see Peter M. Van Wingen, "The Incunable Collections at the Library of Congress," *Rare Book & Manuscripts Librarianship* 4 (1989): 85–100.

9. HEHL, Inst. Arch. 34.22.4.1: letter of L. E. Bliss to Max Farrand (Director of Research), asking for permission to acquire more.

10. HEHL, Inst. Arch. 34.22.4.2: "Report of HRM for 1925."

11. HEHL, Inst. Arch. 34.22.4.2: "Incunabula Report for 1927, 16 Jan. 1928," p. 3.

12. HEHL, Inst. Arch. 34.22.4.1: Letter of Max Farrand to Mead, 1931.

13. HEHL, Inst. Arch. 34.22.4.1: "Publications Proposed by HR Mead," 7 Nov. 1927. Reference is to Ernst Voulliéme, *Die Inkunabeln der Königlichen Bibliothek und der anderen Berliner Sammlungen* (Leipzig: Harrosowitz, 1906).

14. H = Hain, *Repertorium Bibliographicum*; GW = *Gesamtkatalog der Wiegendrucke*; Pr = Proctor.

15. HEHL, Inst. Arch. 34.22.4.2: "HRM 25 March 1930."

16. HEHL, Inst. Arch. 34.22.4.2: handwritten note to Memo of 1924–26.

17. HEHL, Inst. Arch. 34.22.4.2: "Report on Incunabula for 1926."

18. HEHL, Inst. Arch. 34.22.4.2: "Report on Incunabula for 1927."

19. Konrad Burger, *Monumenta Germaniae et Italiae typographica: Deutsche und italienische Inkunabeln in getreuen Nachbildungen* (Berlin: Reichsdruckerei, 1892–1913); E. Gordon Duff, *Fifteenth Century English Books: A Bibliography of Books and Documents*

Printed in England and of Books for the English Market Printed Abroad (London: Oxford University Press, 1917).

20. HEHL, Inst. Arch. 34.22.4.2: "Report on Incunabula for 1926."

21. See for example, Anderson Galleries, *Catalogue . . . from the Library of Henry E. Huntington* (New York, March 1916–June 1925). The Library of Congress collection of incunables has a greater number of books, but this reflects only the greater number of duplicates in the collection; see Van Wingen, "Incunable Collections at the Library of Congress," 85.

22. Henry Bradshaw, "List of the Founts of Type and Woodcut Devices Used by Printers in Holland in the Fifteenth Century" (= Memorandum 3) (June 1871); *Collected Papers of Henry Bradshaw* (Cambridge: University Press, 1889), 258–79; Needham, *Bradshaw Method*, 21.

23. "F. L. K." rev. of Mead, *Incunabula in the Huntington Library, The Library* n.s. 19 (1930): 116–17.

24. In the earlier versions of the Check List for the Newberry Library, such type identification is included: *Check List of Incunabula in the Newberry Library, comp. for the use of the library staff* (Chicago, 1919). In the final printed version (1933), which included extensive reference to plates in the Haebler series, the type identification was omitted.

CHAPTER 5. CATCHTITLES IN ENGLISH BOOKS TO 1550

1. Victor Scholderer, BMC V, 573–76.

2. Dane, *What Is a Book*, 34–35. McKerrow notes a variety of forms of catchwords (*Introduction to Bibliography for Literary Students*, 84). In nearly all the English books viewed here, the catchwords were of the same type. Fewer than a dozen departed from this norm.

3. Konrad Haebler, *Handbuch der Inkunabelkunde* (Leipzig: Hiersemann, 1925), 52–53.

4. I thank Randall McLeod for directing me to these books. Some (Grierson's 1912 edition of Donne), contain only a reference to the volume ("VOL. 1.") combined with the signature mark—both printed on the left of the direction line. Others are more like those used in the sixteenth century; they are printed on the left of the recto (the signature mark on the right) and include an abbreviated form of the title, e.g., Zoëga's 1912 *Concise Dictionary of Icelandic* ("ICEL. DICT."). Pulling out books at random from my shelves, I find them in multi-volume books of all periods: a 3-vol. Elzevier edition of Ovid, 1661, Malone's Shakespeare of 1790, Jourda's edition of Rabelais, 1962. Prof. McLeod assures me that Northrup Frye incorporated the catchtitle "W.I.P" (=Work In Progress) into a reading of *Finnegans Wake*, but I cannot find the reference.

5. See above, Chapter 2 and n34.

6. Greg, *Bibliography of the English Printed Drama to the Restoration*, 1: 7. McKerrow, *Introduction to Bibliography for Literary Students*, 81.

7. At HEHL, for example, STC books, although kept together as much as possible, would be in many different locations: incunables (all English incunables are in the vault); folios; early English bindings; and certain autonomous groups of books such as the science books in the Burndy Collection or the Ellesmere Travelling Library of 1600 now part of the Bridgewater Collection. The Huntington once had facsimiles of most of its STC books filed together in the reading room, but going through them only caused distractions for other readers and a reprimand from staff.

8. EEBO = Early English Books On-Line, eebo.chadwyck.com; ESTC = English Short Title Catalogue (1475–1800) (London, British Library), estc.bl.uk.

9. The difficulty of defining an edition or issue is most apparent with the Whittinton grammars, as any cursory reading of the ESTC entries will show. See for example, ESTC notes for STC 25459.9, 25545, 25526. I have not attempted to correct EEBO's often inaccurate records with those in ESTC. By the same token, the units defined by ESTC are often combined in single copies; see, e.g., STC notes to 23180.5: "This may be the same ed. as 23181.2, 23181.3, 23181.5" HEHL notes to this book [RB 59561] notes "Quires B-C are in the same setting as STC 23180.3."

10. What BMC calls "catchtitles" appear in some books printed by Simon de Luere, BMC V, 573–76. In Pr. 5228, they appear beneath col. 2 of each first folio (of bifolium), i.e., in x1rb, x2rb, x3rb, and x4rb but not x5-8. In Pr. 5626.5, a much more eccentrically foliated, quired, and constructed book, they are the only thing that really keeps the three items straight (since both quiring and foliation are eccentric). First item "Scot(us)" then "Jo.ang." then "Mau" again on first folio of each bifolium in the quire.

11. Beatrice White, ed., *The Vulgaria of John Stanbridge and the Vulgaria of Robert Whittinton*, EETS 187 (London: Oxford University Press, 1932), Introduction.

12. See discussion and notes in Pollard and Redgrave et al., STC 2, 1: 420–21: "Statutes: Chronological Series," and 436–37: "Yearbooks," and Katherine F. Pantzer, "Printing the English Statutes, 1484–1640: Some Historical Implications," in Kenneth E. Carpenter, ed., *Books and Society in History* (New York: Bowker, 1983), 69–114.

13. See e.g., the Folger *Sammelband* from the Pembroke collection, whereby these are collected, it seems, as examples of "De Worde grammars," and the Huntington *Sammelband* RB 61711-20 in a contemporary English blind-stamped binding (page opening shown in Figure 4).

14. Only a few of these have the generic catchtitle, e.g., 1512 STC 25541, 25509.3, both with "Whittyn."

15. Dane, *Myth of Print Culture*, chap. 3, 57–75, on the cataloguing of early grammars.

16. The reason for my "sort by title" qualification was my hope to randomize results, in case I did not have the energy to do a comprehensive search.

17. McKerrow, *Introduction to Bibliography*, 298: "roman type first used as a text type by Pynson in 1518 in Pace's Oratio [=STC 19081a], and Italic 1524." My list gives a few earlier examples: STC 12413 (1509); STC 25585 (1512); STC 5545 (1512); STC 735.7 (1512)— all by Pynson; STC 23427a.3 (1511). McKerrow also claims that the first use of pagination

is the Sulpitius of 1494: "After this I have been unable to find any record of an English book with pagination until Leland's *Egkomion tes eiprenes*, Wolfe, 1546." A few can be added: STC 13746 (1509) (in roman); STC 18394 (1534); STC 171 (1535); STC 10661 (and 10662) (1542) STC 24334 (1542) (in roman); STC 14634 (1543).

18. See my *What Is a Book,* chap. 13, 211–38.

19. See, e.g., the histories in the ProQuest website, http://www.proquest.com, and G. W. Cooke, "Eugene B. Power: Father of Preservation Microfilming," *Conservation Administration News* 54 (1993): 5.

CHAPTER 6. AN EDITORIAL PROPAEDEUTIC

1. Roger Mynors, ed., *C. Valerii Catulli Carmina* (Oxford: Clarendon, 1958), x.

2. A. V. C Schmidt, ed., *William Langland: The Vision of Piers Plowman: A Critical Edition of the B-text based on Trinity College Cambridge MS B.15.17.* (1978), 2nd ed. (London: Dent, 1995), lxxi. See the entire and quite bracing section on the text, liv–lxxx.

3. George Kane and E. Talbot Donaldson, eds., *William Langland's Piers Plowman: The B-Version* (London: Athlone, 1975), 45.

4. Lee Patterson, "The Logic of Textual Criticism and the Way of Genius: The Kane-Donaldson *Piers Plowman* in Historical Perspective," in Jerome J. McGann, ed., *Textual Criticism and Literary Interpretation* (Chicago: University of Chicago Press, 1985), 55–91; see also Schmidt's milder version of the same thing: "The basic arguments of Kane and Donaldson can only be accepted or refuted, they cannot be by-passed" (xii). See Charlotte Brewer, *Editing Piers Plowman: The Evolution of the Text* (Cambridge: Cambridge University Press, 1996), "The Athlone Aftermath," 409ff., and discussion in Hoyt N. Duggan, *Creating an Electronic Archive of Piers Plowman*, "A Brief History of the Modern Texts" and notes, www.iath.virginia.edu/piers/report94.html.

5. Producing such an index was purely mechanical, and I thank David Fowler for providing me with one years ago. Others are now in print, e.g., Peter Barney, "Line-Number Index to the Athlone Edition of Piers Plowman," *Yearbook of Langland Studies* 7 (1993): 97–114.

6. Andrew Galloway, "Reading *Piers Plowman* in the Fifteenth and the Twenty-First Centuries: Notes on Manuscripts F and W in the Piers Plowman Electronic Archive," *JEGP* 103 (2004): 232: the Archive "will be the supreme tool for carrying forward textual work on PP"; the Athlone editions are "monuments of daring and shrewd Middle English textual criticism."

7. Edward B. Partridge, ed., *Ben Jonson: Bartholomew Fair*, Regents Renaissance Drama (Lincoln: University of Nebraska Press, 1964), 20.

8. To understand fully an electronic edition requires understanding the computer programs that are at its foundation, a point made by Peter Robinson, "Current Issues in Making Digital Editions of Medieval Texts, or Do Electronic Scholarly Texts Have a Future?" *Digital Medievalist* 1 (2005), www.digitalmedievalist.org/journal/1.1/robinson.

But this was true even for some of the earliest electronic editing programs and theories: see, for example, Vinton A. Dearing, *Principles and Practice of Textual Analysis* (Berkeley: University of California Press, 1974). See the review by Peter L. Shillingsburg of Dearing's privately distributed *A Primer of Textual Geometry* (2005), *PBSA* 102 (2008): 113–15; Peter Shillingsburg, "Hagiolatry, Cultural Engineering, Monument Building, and Other Functions of Scholarly Editing," in Raimonda Modiano, Leroy F. Searle, and Peter Shillingsburg, eds., *Voice, Text, Hypertext* (Seattle: University of Washington Press, 2004), 412–23. For notes on how an amateur can deal with these editions, see my *Who Is Buried in Chaucer's Tomb*, chap. 9, and *Out of Sorts*, chap 6.

9. See, e.g., Alfred Foulet and Mary Blakely Speer, *On Editing Old French Texts* (Lawrence, Kan.: Regents Press, 1979) with useful notes on Old French grammar, and practical advice.

10. See the very amusing review of R. B. C. Huygens, *Ars Edendi: A Practical Introduction to Editing Medieval Latin Texts* (Turnhout: Brepols, 2000), by Scott Gwara, *Speculum* 78 (2003): 531–33, noting Huygens's dicta that editors should be "thoroughly at home in classical Latin Literature," "thoroughly familiar with Paleography," "painstakingly accurate," "your work should aim at being the last word in editing." If this expertise were attainable by the novice editor on the basis of the apparently deficient resources now available, what compelling reason would there be for new resources?

11. See M. G. Carter, on editing Arabic, describing "the perfect manuscript from an editor's point of view," and with much of his editorial homily in the optative; "Arabic Literature," in D. C. Greetham, ed., *Scholarly Editing: A Guide to Research* (New York: MLA, 1996), 546–74; also included are tips such as the following: "One will hope for a clear and accurate hand (Endress, 'Handscriften-kunde' 281, consult also Schimmel for a survey of calligraphy with a sizable bibliography; Gibb et al., s.v. 'Khatt')," 561. I once assumed this section was ironic, but now I'm far from certain. The absurdity of demands placed on beginning editors was noted long ago by Charles Moorman, *Editing the Middle English Manuscript* (Jackson: University of Mississippi Press, 1975), 3–4.

12. My favorite version is the 1977 pamphlet: *The Center for Scholarly Editions: An Introductory Statement* (New York: MLA 1977)—a self-parodying mish-mash of contradictory and vague principles couched in the grandest morality for "editors interested in a CSE emblem" (2), a seal designating "An Approved Edition" (3), not to be mistaken for "'The' Approved Edition" as the writers generously concede on page 4. After all, "the CSE expects editors to think seriously about these features" (3). The more recent statement revises these genially expressed sententiae into about a hundred solemnly numbered principles: "Guidelines for Editors of Scholarly Editions," Committee on Scholarly Editions, MLA (2006) in Lou Burnard, H. Katherine O'Brien O'Keeffe, and John Unsworth, eds., *Electronic Textual Editing* (New York: MLA, 2006), 23–49. Doubtless, most of the absurdities are due not to the thinking of any individual contributor but rather to the fact that this is a committee production; that, however, does not excuse the decision to publish them as a unit.

13. See Jerome J. McGann, *A Critique of Modern Textual Criticism* (1983; Charlottesville, Va.: University of Virginia Press, 1992); Peter Robinson, *The Wife of Bath's Prologue on CD-ROM* (Cambridge: Cambridge University Press, 1996), 10–13; Peter Robinson and R. J. O'Hara, "Computer-Assisted Methods of Stemmatic Analysis" in N. F. Blake and Peter Robinson, eds., *Canterbury Tales Project: Occasional Papers* 1 (Oxford: Office for Humanities Communications, 1993), 53–74; "Cladistic Analysis of an Old Norse Manuscript Tradition," in S. Hockey and N. Ide, eds. *Research in Humanities Computing* 4 (Oxford: Oxford University Press, 1996), 115–37; David Greetham, "Phylum-Tree-Rhizome," *Huntington Library Quarterly* 58 (1996): 96–126.

14. W. W. Greg, "The Rationale of Copy-Text," (1950), in *Collected Papers*, 374–91.

15. Point was raised in an on-line discussion group some fifteen years ago in *Humanist Archives*, 12: "It is a profoundly disturbing comment on the state of the art. Scholars who come into editing from the perspective of their discipline have no idea how to get started" (Charles Faulhaber).

16. See references, n13 above, and Peter Robinson and Robert J. O'Hara, (1992) Report on the Textual Criticism Challenge, rpt. *Bryn Mawr Classical Review* (18 July 1992). The validity of the results of their analysis of the relationships among manuscripts of Chaucer's *Canterbury Tales* was often judged by how closely they resembled the highly problematic results of the Manly-Rickert edition of 1940; John Manly and Edith Rickert, *The Text of the Canterbury Tales*, 8 vols. (Chicago: University of Chicago Press, 1940). There are many statements in the introductory reports to the Canterbury Tales Project to this as well as in the article "Report" cited above.

17. *Losse* for *loffe* of course violates the all-too-familiar and much cited rule of *lectio difficilior*, which in my experience, however widely promulgated, very rarely works in practice.

18. There are a few cases where the textual source of a medieval book or manuscript is known. N. F. Blake, "Aftermath: Manuscript to Print," in Jeremy Griffiths and Derek Pearsall, eds., *Book Production and Publishing in Britain, 1375–1475* (Cambridge: Cambridge University Press,1989), 403–32; "MS Chetham 6709 and Some Manuscript Copies of Caxton Prints," in Claudia Blank, ed., *Language and Civilization: Essays in Honour of Otto Hietsch* (New York: Peter Lang, 1992), 239–54. There are also many cases where the copytext for a modern text is known. The variations that occur have not to my knowledge been studied systematically enough to demonstrate, except in a few cases, what actually occurs in these situations.

19. Zumthor's notion grew out of a relatively simple editorial problem: the versions of *La Chanson de Roland*; see Paul Zumthor, *Essai de poétique médiévale* (Paris: Seuil, 1972), 70–75.

20. The absolute singularity of each textual error or variation was a point made to me many years ago by Jeffrey Henderson, based, I assume on Housmanian principles. But I don't see how any textual or editorial correction or conjecture can be made if this principle is accepted.

21. O′ is not necessarily a coherent text, and the assumption that it is can lead to problems, both in the edition itself and in the way it is read and received. The Manly-Rickert edition of the *Canterbury Tales* and its reception is a clear example.

22. See the classic article on this by E. T. Donaldson, "The Psychology of Editors in Middle English Texts," in *Speaking of Chaucer* (New York: Norton, 1970), 102–18.

23. They are referred to by Paul Maas only as "reconstructed variant-carriers"; Paul Maas, *Textual Criticism* (1927) trans. Barbara Flower (Oxford: Clarendon, 1958), 6. Cf., however, the discussion in Robinson, "Cladistic Analysis," implying that these can be constructed without reference to the original.

PLAYING BIBLIOGRAPHY

1. The best description of this, I believe, is still Paul de Man's 1967 essay "Criticism and Crisis," in *Blindness and Insight: Essays in the Rhetoric of Contemporary Criticism* (Minneapolis: University of Minnesota Press, 1971), 3–19.

III.I BOOK HISTORY AND BOOK HISTORIES: ON THE MAKING OF LISTS

1. N. R. Ker, *Fragments of Medieval Manuscripts Used as Pastedowns in Oxford Bindings, with a Survey of Oxford Binding, c. 1515–1620* (Oxford: Oxford Bibliographical Society, 1954).

2. I am parodying Elizabeth Eisenstein's absurd but psychologically telling claim that when she began to study printing history, there was "not . . . even a small literature available for consultation" on the subject: Eisenstein, *The Printing Press as an Agent of Change*, 1: x.

3. See, e.g., Williams and Abbott, *Introduction to Bibliographical and Textual Studies* (2009), Tanselle, *Textual Analysis: A Historical Introduction* (2009) and even Gaskell's *A New Introduction to Bibliography*, extending McKerrow's *Introduction to Bibliography for Literary Students* into the eighteenth century. See above, Chapter 2.

4. G. Thomas Tanselle, *Introduction to Bibliography*, Seminar Syllabus (nineteenth revision; Charlottesville: Book Arts Press, 2002); *Introduction to Scholarly Editing* (2002). Both available on-line. Greetham, *Textual Scholarship: An Introduction* (1994). It is not feasible to compare Greetham's bibliography with Tanselle's in any detail, but from my spot checks neither seems in any way dependent on or related to the other.

5. *Textual Scholarship*, ix, quoting G. Thomas Tanselle, *A Rationale of Textual Criticism* (Philadelphia: University of Pennsylvania Press, 1989), 46.

6. See introductory statement, xi.

7. I was surprised and somewhat chagrined, reviewing this, to find illustrations of Heywood's *Mery Play* 1533 compared with the edition from the Type Facsimile Society (384–87), illustrations I used several years later. I didn't realize, taking my own obviously

amateurish photos, that I was likely inspired to do so by the photos here. I should also note that a quotation from Febvre and Martin I used as the very basis of my critique of their work in *Myth of Print Culture* appears to be one I wrote myself (an unkind reviewer claims inaccurately that I miscited the page). I have no explanation or excuse for either of these errors.

8. I was recently invited to contribute to one of them, my assignment, "written communications systems before print in China, India, and North America," a subject about which I know absolutely nothing. The editors assured me they were very interested in what I might have to say; I shudder to think what might have resulted had I accepted. I wonder if many of the contributors to these volumes had similar misgivings.

9. As a recent example, the series entitled The Oxford History of Popular Print Culture, gen. ed. Gary Kelly, vol. 1, *Cheap Print in Britain and Ireland to 1600*, ed. Joad Raymond (Oxford: Oxford University Press, 2011).

10. Orietta Da Rold and Elaine Treharne, eds., *Textual Cultures: Cultural Texts*, English Association, Essays and Studies 2010 (Cambridge: Brewer, 2010), 1–2.

11. From *JEGP* review, 2012.

III.2. MEDITATION ON THE COMPOSING STICK

1. The master printer needs this stick, not because it provides "common measure," but rather because more than one composing stick is necessary—it could be two, three, or four.

2. The composing stick shown in Moxon's illustration has two "sliding-measures," and these enable the compositor to set text with marginal quotations. See note in Moxon, *Mechanick Exercises*, Davis and Carter ed., 41: "The 'printers' wood' originally meant these quotations but now refers to spacing-material: the wood (bois de cottations) filling the space between text block and quotation."

3. Hansard, *Typographia* (1825), 487–88, cited in Rummonds, *Nineteenth-Century Printing Practices and the Iron Handpress*, 1: 227.

4. See James Mosley, "Drawing the Typefounders Mould," Typefoundry.blogspot .com (April 2007) on inaccurate illustrations of the hand-mold, and notes above, Chapter 2 n29.

5. Dane, *Out of Sorts*, chap. 1; see refs. above in Chapter 2.

6. Those conventions, as well as the method of setting initial letters of verse lines, are the same whether the text is in italic or in roman. Note that accent marks are constructed from individual sorts: the acute accent between the word unit and the suffix *-que* (numerous cases) is set between these units; the grave accent (*è* for *ex*) also seems to be set following the letter in an individual sort. David Carlson, "Printed Superior Figures in Nicholas Jenson's Lawbooks, 1478–80," *PBSA* 96 (2002): 4–22.

7. Jacques Demarcq, "L'espace de la page, entre vide et plein," in Anne Zali, ed., *L'Aventure des écritures: La page* (Paris: Bibliothèque Nationale, 1999), 89–90. Examples

of both conventions can be seen in the illustrations in David Zeidberg, ed., *Aldus Manutius and Renaissance Culture: Essays in Memory of Franklin D. Murphy* (Florence: Olschki, 1998).

8. The imitations of Aldine books from Lyons use various conventions for setting initial capitals, and apparently did not see this feature as essential to the Aldine aesthetic; e.g., HEHL RB 350834-6, combining an Aldine book of 1502 with a Lyons contrafacture.

9. See, for example, the illustrations in Dutschke, *Guide to Medieval and Renaissance Manuscripts in the Huntington Library*, figs. 114 (EL 34 B6, f 55v, Italy, mid-15th c) and 117 (HM 1031, f. 51, Italy, 2nd quarter 15th c).

10. Even Moxon obliquely suggests this, although I realize the self-contradictory nature of my argument—citing Moxon as suggesting procedures when I am refuting his authority for procedures that are earlier than his text. *Mechanick Exercises*, sec. 22, par. 5: "If *Marginal Notes* come down the side (or sides, If the *Page* have two Columns) he chuses to *Set* them in on the *Stone*, rather than in his *Galley*; because both his *Page* and *Notes* stand safer, being cloathed with the *Furniture*, than they do when they stand Naked in the *Galley.*"

11. RB 443649. See my "Note on the Huntington Library and Pierpont Morgan Library Fragments of Donatus, *Ars minor (Rudimenta grammatices)* (GW 8995, GW 8996)," *PBSA* 94 (2000): 275–82, and *Myth of Print Culture*, 62–65 and fig. 2. On early proofsheets, see most recently Randall Herz, "Three Fifteenth Century Proof Sheets with Manuscript Corrections from Nuremberg Presses," *Gutenberg Jahrbuch* 2011, 56–76.

12. *Out of Sorts*, chap. 1, "The Continuity of Continuity," on the use of the hand-mold.

III.3. THE RED AND THE BLACK

1. *Abstractions of Evidence* (2009), chap. 7: "Formal Perfection and Historical Perfection in the 1476 Boccaccio by Colard Mansion: Note on a Note by Seymour De Ricci," 111–19.

2. That books like this are not anomalous in printing history is the implication of the argument by McKitterick, *Print, Manuscript and the Search for Order* (2003), chap. 3, "Pictures in Motley."

3. Images of the Museum of Fine Arts copy are readily available on the website; http://educators.mfa.org/galleries/slideshow/4178, slide 18.

4. We can call these sub-editions or variant editions if they were produced simultaneously; most bibliographers would refer to this situation as involving two issues, although "issue" more coherently implies a difference in time.

5. E.g., "A Ghostly Twin Terence (Venice, 21 July 1475; IGI 9422, 9423)," *The Library* ser. 6, 21 (1999): 99–107.

6. Nor, for the record, can I find a match in any of the other recorded copies.

7. On Haebler leaf-books, see above, Chapter 5.

8. See, e.g., McKerrow, *Introduction to Bibliography for Literary Students*, 329–36, whose description is largely the same as those of his contemporary incunabulists, e.g., Haebler, *Inkunabelkunde*, 109. See also Rummonds, *Nineteenth-Century Printing Practices*, 2: 617–31. There are other ways of printing in two colors, several dating from the fifteenth century: the methods of Mansion, Caxton, or Schoeffer's *Canon Missal* do not require two pulls at press.

9. Margaret M. Smith, "Fragments used for 'Servile' Purposes: The St. Bride Library Frisket for Early Red Printing," in Linda L. Brownrigg and Margaret M. Smith, eds., *Interpreting and Collecting Fragments of Medieval Books* (Los Altos Hills, Calif.: Red Gull Press, 2000), 177–88; also noted by Smith in the St. Bride Journal *Ultrabold* 3 (2007): "The Red-Printing Frisket at St. Bride Library."

10. Having said that, I have an exception ready to hand: the unbound fragment shown in my Figure 8, where the extent of red printing results in black islands, which cannot be produced under this standard method.

11. "Two-Color Printing in the Fifteenth Century as Evidenced by Incunables at the Huntington Library," *Gutenberg Jahrbuch* 1999, 131–45.

12. I thank David Becker and other staff members at the Museum of Fine Arts whose names I failed to record.

III.4. FRAGMENTS

1. *Quincuplum Psalterium gallicum, romanum, hebraicum, vetus conciliatum* (Olivier, 1515).

2. The distinction is Bradshaw's. Henry Bradshaw, "List of the Founts of Type and Woodcut Devices" (1871), in *Collected Papers*, 262–63. This does not quite cover the possible categories; see Goldschmidt, *Gothic and Renaissance Bookbindings*, 1: 120, and my *Myth of Print Culture*, 61.

3. For example: the content of endpaper is irrelevant, but orientation of print must match or be perpendicular to lines of print in the book.

4. "An Example of Netherlands Prototypography at the Huntington," *Huntington Library Quarterly* 61 (1999): 401–9.

5. See discussion in III.2 above.

6. That shelf location for incunables should represent or reflect the history of typefonts used by specific printers is the cataloguing principle established by Robert Proctor for the British Museum; Pollard, "Memoir," in *Robert Proctor: Bibliographical Essays*, xxii–xxx.

7. Paul Needham, "Fragments in Books: Dutch Prototypography in the van Ess Library," in Milton McC. Gatch, ed., *"So Precious a Foundation": The Library of Leander van Ess at the Burke Library of Union Theological Seminary in the City of New York* (New York: Grolier Club, 1996), 85–110.

8. *Abstractions of Evidence*, chap. 9: "Leander van Ess and the Panzerization of Early Books and History," 139–43.

9. "Note on American Fragments of Grammatical Texts from the Oxford Press of Theodoric Rood (STC 315 and 695)." *The Library* ser. 6, 20 (1998): 59–61. The text is from Anwykyll, *Compendium totius grammaticae* (Oxford: Rood, 1483); several other examples of this text exist. It is contained in J. Angeli, *Astrolabium* (Venice: Emerich, 1494). There are notes on this book by Nicolas Barker, and it was first described by Richard Rouse, "Copy-specific Features of the Printed Book: What to Record and Why," in Lotte Hellinga and John Goldfinch, eds., *Bibliography and the Study of 15th-Century Civilisation*, British Library Occasional Papers 5 (London: British Library, 1987), 206–7, 213. The classic study on books similar to the UCLA volume is Ker, *Fragments of Medieval Manuscripts used as Pastedowns in Oxford Bindings*, (1954), *Corrigenda and addenda*, comp. David Rundle and Scott Mandelbrote (2004).

10. The database is not published. See Scott Husby, Bookbindings on Incunables in American Library Collections, www.biblsocamer.org/BibSite/Husby/ (2011), and "Bookbindings in American Library Collections: A Working Census," in Bettina Wagner and Marcia Reed, eds., *Early Printed Books as Material Objects* (Berlin: De Gruyter, 2010), 205–15; Dutschke, *Guide to Medieval and Renaissance Manuscripts in the Huntington Library*, 2:723, HM 41785.

11. Ibid., and illustration #39. These fragments were pastedowns in HM 41761, "removed and catalogued separately in 1975." Likely, the criterion for catalogue entry is the separation of the fragments from the book containing them; this may not be entirely logical, but it is certainly rational. Note that of twenty-seven entries in the new "Supplement," six are of single leaves or a fragment of a leaf, none earlier than the thirteenth century. *Supplement to the Guide to Medieval and Renaissance Manuscripts in the Huntington Library*, comp. Peter Kidd, *Huntington Library Quarterly* 72, 4 (2009).

12. Ptolemaeus, *Quadripartitum* (Venice: Ratdolt, 15 Jan. 1484) BMC V, 283. See my "A Shadow Edition in Ratdolt's 1484 Ptolemaeus," *Gutenberg Jahrbuch* 2002, 90–93.

13. To determine that, I need access to a second copy. The leaf is also yet another exception to the ordinary methods I once believed in concerning the methods of two-color printing. See III.3 above.

III.5. THE NATURE AND FUNCTION OF SCHOLARLY ILLUSTRATION IN A DIGITAL WORLD

1. William Kuskin, ed., *Caxton's Trace: Studies in the History of English Printing* (Notre Dame, Ind.: University of Notre Dame Press, 2006). See my review, *Speculum* 82 (2007): 204–6. I should note without any irony that I know and admire many of the contributors to this volume, as well as those who saw it through press.

2. *What Is a Book*, 7–11, 188–202.

3. There are exceptions to this general rule, and annotations can be considered part of the project of producing an edition; see my " 'Si vis archetypas habere nugas': Authorial Subscriptions in Politian, *Miscellanea* (1489)," *Harvard Library Bulletin* 10 (1999): 12–22, on mass-produced hand-corrections from errata sheets.

4. STC 5088, in the next set of illustrations, is just as difficult: the illustrations are so poor that it is almost impossible to collate them optically. However, I am almost certain the copy I am looking at (Harvard) is the source of the one in the illustration. That's what EEBO says: UMI Collections 149:02. (There are many other copies).

5. W. J. B. Crotch, ed., *The Prologues and Epilogues of William Caxton* EETS, OS 176 (London, 1928). On this edition, see my *Abstractions of Evidence*, 132–37.

6. See my "Linear Perspective and the Obliquities of Reception," in Sandra Pierson Prior and Robert M. Stein, eds., *Visions and Voices: Essays on Medieval Culture and Literature in Honor of Robert W. Hanning* (Notre Dame, Ind.: University of Notre Dame Press, 2005), 428–53, and *Out of Sorts*, "The Representation of Representation," 141–63.

7. Examples can be found by looking through any recent issue of *Huntington Library Quarterly*; in Figure 4 above, I have asked specifically that the structure of the book remain visible, even at the cost of the clarity of the image.

8. Compare, for example, the photographic conventions used for both bindings and individual pages in a catalogue from Phillip J. Pirages, Fine Books and Manuscripts, Cat. 61: *Historically Significant and Decorative Bindings, 1536–2010*.

9. For a brief history of the microfilm collection that is the basis of EEBO, see the ProQuest website http://www.proquest.com., and G. W. Cooke, "Eugene B. Power: Father of Preservation Microfilming," *Conservation Administration News* 54 (1993): 5.

III.6. ART OF THE MIND

1. Suzanne Muchnic, *Los Angeles Times*, 7 August 2011.

2. Jean-Pierre Cuzin, *Jean-Honoré Fragonard, Life and Work: Complete Catalogue of the Oil Paintings*, trans. Anthony Zielonka and Kim-Mai Mooney (New York: Abrams, 1988), 97n1.

3. This zero-degree of rare-book binding is remarkably similar to trade-bindings of the eighteenth century, a continuity that overleaps, somehow, a century of cheap pasteboard binding characteristic of the way run-of-the-mill "old books" were rebound in the nineteenth century.

4. See www.bobross.com and the special series "Wildlife."

PRINCIPAL SOURCES

Aers, David. "A Whisper in the Ear of Early Modernists: or, Reflections on Literary Critics Writing the 'History of the Subject'." 1991. Rpt. in David Aers, ed., *Culture and History (1350–1600): Essays on English Communities, Identities, and Writing.* Detroit: Wayne St. University Press, 1992. 177–202.

Alston, R. C., and M. J. Jannetta. *Bibliography, Machine Readable Cataloguing, and the ESTC: A Summary History of the Eighteenth Century Short Title Catalogue.* London: British Library, 1978.

Ames, Joseph. *Typographical Antiquities, Being an Historical Account of Printing in England.* 3 vols. London, 1749.

Belanger, Terry. "Descriptive Bibliography." In Jean Peters, ed., *Book Collecting: A Modern Guide.* New York: Bowker, 1977. 97–115.

Blades, William. *Life and Typography of Caxton.* 2 vols. London: Lilly, 1861.

Bland, Mark. *A Guide to Early Printed Books and Manuscripts.* Chichester: Wiley-Blackwell, 2010.

Blayney, Peter W. M. *The Texts of King Lear and Their Origins.* Vol. 1, *Nicholas Okes and the First Quarto.* Cambridge: Cambridge University Press, 1982.

Bowers, Fredson. *Principles of Bibliographical Description.* Princeton, N.J.: Princeton University Press, 1949.

Bradshaw, Henry. "List of the Founts of Type and Woodcut Devices Used by Printers in Holland in the Fifteenth Century" (= Memorandum 3). June 1871. In *Collected Papers of Henry Bradshaw.* Cambridge: Cambridge University Press, 1889. 258–79.

Brown, Julian. "Names of Scripts: A Plea to all Medievalists." In *A Palaeographer's View: Selected Writings of Julian Brown,* ed. Janet Bateley, Michelle Brown, and Jane Roberts. London: Harvey Miller, 1993. 39–46.

Burger, Konrad. *Monumenta Germaniae et Italiae typographica: Deutsche und italienische Inkunabeln in getreuen Nachbildungen.* Berlin: Reichsdruckerei, 1892–1913.

Carter, Harry. *A View of Early Typography Up to About 1600.* Oxford: Clarendon, 1969.

Catalogue of Books Printed in the XVth Century Now in the British Museum. 13 vols. London: British Museum, 1908–. (= BMC)

Dane, Joseph A. *Abstractions of Evidence in the Study of Manuscripts and Early Printed Books.* Aldershot: Ashgate, 2009.

———. *The Myth of Print Culture: Essays on Evidence, Textuality, and Bibliographical Method.* Toronto: University of Toronto Press, 2003.

―――. *Out of Sorts: On Typography and Print Culture*. Philadelphia: University of Pennsylvania Press, 2011.

―――. "Two-Color Printing in the Fifteenth Century as Evidenced by Incunables at the Huntington Library." *Gutenberg Jahrbuch* 1999. 131–45.

―――. *What Is a Book? The Study of Early Printed Books*. Notre Dame, Ind.: Notre Dame University Press, 2012.

Darnton, Robert. *The Business of the Enlightenment: A Publishing History of the Encyclopédie, 1775–1800*. Cambridge, Mass.: Harvard University Press, 1979.

DaRold, Orietta, and Elaine Treharne, eds. *Textual Cultures: Cultural Texts*. Cambridge: Brewer, 2010.

De Ricci, Seymour. *A Census of Caxtons*. Oxford: Bibliographical Society, 1909.

Derolez, Albert. *The Palaeography of Gothic Manuscript Books from the Twelfth Through the Early Sixteenth Century*. Cambridge: Cambridge University Press, 2003.

Dibdin, Thomas Frognall. *Typographical Antiquities, or the History of Printing in England*. 4 vols. London: W. Miller, 1810–19.

Dickinson, Donald C. *Henry E. Huntington's Library of Libraries*. San Marino, Calif.: Huntington Library Press, 1995.

Duff, E. Gordon. *Fifteenth Century English Books: A Bibliography of Books and Documents Printed in England and of Books for the English Market Printed Abroad*. London: Oxford University Press, 1917.

Dutschke, C. W. *Guide to Medieval and Renaissance Manuscripts in the Huntington Library*. 2 vols. San Marino, Calif.: Huntington Library Press, 1989.

Early English Books On-Line. eebo.chadwyck.com. (=EEBO)

Eisenstein, Elizabeth. *The Printing Press as an Agent of Change: Communications and Cultural Transformations in Early Modern Europe*. 2 vols. Cambridge: Cambridge University Press, 1979.

Encyclopédie, ou dictionnaire raisonné des sciences, des arts et des métiers. 10 vols. Paris, 1751–72.

English Short Title Catalogue. www.bl.uk. =ESTC.

Febvre, Lucien, and Henri-Jean Martin. *The Coming of the Book: The Impact of Printing, 1460–1800*. 1958. Trans. David Gerard. London: Verso, 1976.

Figgins, Vincent. *The Game of the Chesse, by William Caxton, Reproduced in Facsimile from a Copy in the British Museum, with a few remarks on Caxton's typographical productions*. London: John Russell Smith, 1860.

Fournier, Pierre-Simon. *Manuel typographique utile aux gens de lettres, & à ceux qui exercent les différentes parties de l'art de l'imprimerie*. 2 vols. Paris, 1764.

Gascoigne, Bamber. *How to Identify Prints: A Complete Guide to Manual and Mechanical Processes from Woodcut to Ink-Jet*. New York: Thames and Hudson, 1986.

Gaskell, Philip. *A New Introduction to Bibliography*. New York: Oxford University Press, 1972.

Gesamtkatalog der Wiegendrucke. 10 vols. Stuttgart: Hiersemann, 1928-. www.gesamt katalogderwiegendrucke.de/.

Goldschmidt, E. Ph. *Gothic and Renaissance Bookbindings.* 2 vols. London: Benn, 1928.

Greetham, David C., ed. *Scholarly Editing: A Guide to Research.* New York: MLA, 1996.

———. *Textual Scholarship: An Introduction.* 1992. Rev. New York: Garland, 1994.

Greg, W. W. "Bibliography—An Apology." 1932. In *Collected Papers*, ed. J. C. Maxwell. Oxford: Clarendon, 1966. 239–66.

———. *A Bibliography of the English Printed Drama to the Restoration.* 4 vols. London: Bibliographical Society, 1939–59.

Gumbert, J. P. "A Proposal for a Cartesian Nomenclature." In J. P. Gumbert and M. J. M. de Haan, eds., *Essays Presented to G. I. Lieftinck.* Vol. 4. *Miniatures, Scripts, Collections.* Amsterdam: Van Gendt, 1976. 45–52.

Haebler, Konrad. *German Incunabula: 110 Original Leaves.* 2 vols. Trans. André Barbey. Munich: Weiss, 1927.

———. *Italian Incunabula: 110 Original Leaves.* Trans. André Barbey. Munich: Weiss, 1927.

———. *Handbuch der Inkunabelkunde.* Leipzig: Hiersemann, 1925.

———. *Typenrepertorium der Wiegendrucke.* 5 vols. Leipzig, 1905–24.

———. *West-European Incunabula: 60 Original Leaves from the Presses of the Netherlands, France, Iberia, and Great Britain.* Trans. André Barbey. Munich: Weiss, 1928.

Hain, Ludwig. *Repertorium bibliographicum.* 4 vols. Stuttgart: Cotta, 1836–38.

Hellinga, Lotte. *William Caxton and Early Printing in England.* London: British Library, 2010.

Hellinga, Wytze, and Lotte Hellinga. *The Fifteenth-Century Printing Types of the Low Countries.* 2 vols. Trans. D. A. S. Reid. Amsterdam: Hertzberger, 1966.

Henry E. Huntington Library. Institutional Archives. 34.22.4.1-2.

Hinman, Charlton. *The Printing and Proof-Reading of the First Folio of Shakespeare.* 2 vols. Oxford: Clarendon, 1963.

Howard-Hill, T. "Enumerative and Descriptive Bibliography." In Peter Davison, ed., *The Book Encompassed: Studies in Twentieth-Century Bibliography.* Cambridge: Cambridge University Press, 1994. 122–29.

Husby, Scott. *Bookbindings on Incunables in American Library Collections.* www.biblso camer.org/BibSite/Husby. 2011.

Isaac, Frank. *English and Scottish Printing Types, 1501–58, 1508–58.* 2 vols. London: Oxford University Press, 1930–32.

Johnson, A. F. "The Classification of Gothic Types." 1929. In Percy H. Muir, ed., *Selected Essays on Books and Printing.* Amsterdam: Van Gendt, 1970. 1–17.

Kane, George, and E. Talbot Donaldson, eds. *William Langland's Piers Plowman: The B-Version* London: Athlone, 1975.

Ker, N. R. *Fragments of Medieval Manuscripts used as Pastedowns in Oxford Bindings, with a Survey of Oxford Binding, c. 1515–1620.* Oxford: Oxford Bibliographical Society, 1954. *Corrigenda and Addenda*, comp. David Rundle and Scott Mandelbrote. 2004.

Ker, W. P. *The Dark Ages.* New York: Scribners, 1904.

Kuskin, William, ed. *Caxton's Trace: Studies in the History of English Printing.* Notre Dame, Ind.: University of Notre Dame Press, 2006.

Lerer, Seth. "Caxton in the Nineteenth Century." In Kuskin, ed., *Caxton's Trace: Studies in the History of English Printing*. 325–70.

Lieftinck, G. I. "Pour une nomenclature de l'écriture livresque de la période dite gothique: Essai s'appliquant spécialement aux manuscrits originaires des Pays-Bas médiévaux." In B. Bischoff, G. I. Lieftinck, and G. Battelli, eds., *Nomenclature des écritures livresques du IXe au XVIe siècle. Premier colloque international de paléographie latine. Paris, 28–30 April 1953*. Paris: CNRS, 1954. 15–34.

Lowry, Malcolm. *Nicholas Jenson and the Rise of Venetian Publishing in Renaissance Europe*. Oxford: Blackwell, 1991.

Maas, Paul. *Textual Criticism*. 1927. Trans. Barbara Flower. Oxford: Clarendon, 1958.

Maittaire, Michael. *Annales typographici ab artis inventae origine ad annum MD*. The Hague, 1719.

McGann, Jerome J. *A Critique of Modern Textual Criticism*. 2nd ed. Charlottesville, Va.: University of Virginia Press, 1992.

McKenzie, D. F. "Printers of the Mind: Some Notes on Bibliographical Theories and Printing-House Practices." *Studies in Bibliography* 22 (1969): 1–75.

McKerrow, Ronald B. *An Introduction to Bibliography for Literary Students*. Oxford: Clarendon, 1927.

McKitterick, David. "Not in STC: Opportunities and Challenges in the STC." *The Library* ser. 7, 6 (2005): 178–94.

———. *Print, Manuscript and the Search for Order, 1450–1830*. Cambridge: Cambridge University Press, 2003.

McMurtrie, Douglas C. *The Book: The Story of Printing and Bookmaking*. 1927. New York: Oxford University Press, 1943.

Mead, Herman Ralph. *Incunabula in the Huntington Library*. San Marino, Calif.: Huntington Library, 1937.

Modern Language Association. *Center for Scholarly Editions: An Introductory Pamphlet*. New York: MLA, 1977.

Mores, Edward Rowe. *A Dissertation upon English Typographical Founders and Founderies (1778), with a Catalogue and Specimen of the Typefoundry of John James (1782)*. Ed. Harry Carter and Christopher Ricks. Oxford: Oxford Bibliographical Society, 1961.

Morison, Stanley. *John Fell: The University Press and the "Fell" Types*. Oxford: Clarendon, 1967.

———. *Selected Essays on the History of Letter-forms in Manuscript and Print*. Ed. David McKitterick. Cambridge: Cambridge University Press, 2009.

Mosley, James. " 'So du die chrift abformen wilst': Abklatschen, clichage, Dabbing and the Duplication of Typographical Printing Surfaces." In, *Rationalisierung der Buchherstellung im Mittelalter und der frühen Neuzeit*, ed. Peter Rüch and Martin Boghardt Marburg: Institut für Historische Hilfswissenschaften, 1994. 197–204.

———. *Typefoundry: Documents for the History of Type and Letterform*. Typefoundry .blogspot.com.

Moxon, Joseph. *Mechanick Exercises on the Whole Art of Printing (1683–4)*. Ed. Herbert Davis and Harry Carter. 2 vols. Oxford: Oxford University Press, 1958.

Muchnic, Suzanne. "Lichtenstein's Three Brushstrokes Gets a Brush Up." *Los Angeles Times*, 7 August 2011.

Myers, Robin. "George Isaac Frederick Tupper, Facsimilist." *Transactions of the Cambridge Bibliographical Society* 7 (1978): 113–34.

Needham, Paul. *The Bradshaw Method: Henry Bradshaw's Contribution to Bibliography*. Chapel Hill, N.C.: Hanes Foundation, 1998.

———. "Fragments in Books: Dutch Prototypography in the van Ess Library." In Milton McC. Gatch, ed., *"So Precious a Foundation": The Library of Leander van Ess at the Burke Library of Union Theological Seminary in the City of New York*. New York: Grolier Club, 1996. 85–110.

———. "Palaeography and the Earliest Printing Types." In Holger Nickel and Lothar Gillner, eds., *Johannes Gutenberg: Regionale Aspekte des frühen Buchdrucks*. Berlin: Staatsbibliothek zu Berlin, 1993. 19–27.

Nineteenth Century Short Title Catalogue. www.proquest.com/pdpq/19thcen_stc. (=NSTC)

Painter, George D. *William Caxton: A Quincentenary Biography of England's First Printer*. London: Chatto & Windus, 1976.

Pankow, David. *The Printer's Manual: An Illustrated History: Classical and Unusual Texts on Printing from the Seventeenth, Eighteenth, and Nineteenth Centuries*. Rochester, N.Y.: RIT Cary Graphic Arts Press, 2005.

Pantzer, Katherine F. "Printing the English Statutes, 1484–1640: Some Historical Implications." In Kenneth E. Carpenter, ed., *Books and Society in History*. New York: Bowker, 1983. 69–114.

Panzer, Georg Wolfgang. *Annales typographici ab artis inventae origine ad annum MD*. 11 vols. Nuremberg, 1793–1803.

Parkes, M. B. *Their Hands Before Our Eyes: A Closer Look at Scribes*. 1999. Aldershot: Ashgate, 2008.

Patterson, Lee. "The Logic of Textual Criticism and the Way of Genius: The Kane-Donaldson *Piers Plowman* in Historical Perspective." In Jerome J. McGann, ed., *Textual Criticism and Literary Interpretation*. Chicago: University of Chicago Press, 1985. 55–91.

Pettegree, Andrew. *The Book in the Renaissance*. New Haven, Conn.: Yale University Press, 2010.

Pollard, Alfred, G. R. Redgrave, et al. *A Short-Title Catalogue of Books Printed in England, Scotland & Ireland and of English Books Printed Abroad, 1475–1640*. 2nd ed. 3 vols. London: Bibliographical Society, 1976–1991.

Proctor, Robert. *Bibliographical Essays*. London: Chiswick, 1905.

———. *Index to Early Printed Books in the British Museum . . . to the year 1500*. London: Kegan Paul, 1898.

Prothero, G. W. *A Memoir of Henry Bradshaw*. London: Kegan Paul, 1888.

Robinson, Peter. "Cladistic Analysis of an Old Norse Manuscript Tradition." In Susan Hockey and Nancy Ide, eds., *Research in Humanities Computing* 4. Oxford: Oxford University Press, 1996. 115–37.

————. "Current Issues in Making Digital Editions of Medieval Texts, or Do Electronic Scholarly Texts have a Future?" *Digital Medievalist* 1 (2005).

Robinson, Peter, and R. J. O'Hara, "Computer-Assisted Methods of Stemmatic Analysis." In Norman F. Blake and Peter Robinson, eds., *Canterbury Tales Project: Occasional Papers* 1. Oxford: Office for Humanities Communications, 1993. 53–74. www .digitalmedievalist.org/journal/1.1/robinson.

Rummonds, Richard-Gabriel. *Nineteenth-Century Printing Practices and the Iron Handpress*. 2 vols. New Castle, Del.: Oak Knoll, 2004.

————. *Printing on the Iron Handpress*. Newcastle, Del.: Oak Knoll, 1998.

Savage, William. *A Dictionary of the Art of Printing*. London, 1841.

Schmidt, A. V. C., ed. *William Langland: The Vision of Piers Plowman: A Critical Edition of the B-text based on Trinity College Cambridge MS B.15.17*. London: Dent, 1995. 2nd ed. 1978.

Schreiber, William Ludwig. *Woodcuts from Books of the 15th Century, Shown in Original Specimens: 55 Leaves detached from Books*. Trans. André Barbey. Munich: Weiss, 1929.

Schwenke, Paul. *Untersuchungen zur Geschichte des ersten Buchdrucks*. Berlin: Hopfer, 1900.

Snyder, Henry L., and Michael S. Smith, eds. *The English Short-Title Catalogue: Past, Present, Future*. New York: AMS Press, 2003.

Steinberg, S. "Medieval Writing Masters." *The Library* ser. 4, 22 (1941): 1–24.

Tanselle, G. Thomas. *Bibliographical Analysis: A Historical Introduction*. Cambridge: Cambridge University Press, 2009.

————. *Introduction to Scholarly Editing*. Seminar Syllabus. 18th rev. Charlottesville, Va.: Book Arts Press, 2002.

————. *Introduction to Bibliography*. Seminar Syllabus. 19th rev. Charlottesville, Va.: Book Arts Press, 2002.

Timperley, C. H. *Encyclopaedia of Literary and Typographical Anecdote*. London, 1842.

Updike, Daniel Berkeley. *Printing Types: Their History, Forms, and Use: A Study in Survivals*. 2 vols. Cambridge, Mass.: Harvard University Press, 1937.

Veröffentlichen der Gesellschaft für Typenkunde des XV. Jahrhunderts. Berlin, 1907–39.

Vervliet, Hendrik D. L. *The Palaeo-Typography of the French Renaissance: Selected Papers on Sixteenth-Century Typefaces*. 2 vols. Leiden: Brill, 2008.

Voulliéme, Ernst. *Die Inkunabeln der Königlichen Bibliothek und der anderen Berliner Sammlungen*. Leipzig: Harrosowitz, 1906.

White, Beatrice, ed. *The Vulgaria of John Stanbridge and the Vulgaria of Robert Whittinton*. EETS 187. London: Oxford University Press, 1932.

Williams, William Proctor, and Craig S. Abbott. *An Introduction to Bibliographical and Textual Studies*. 4th ed. New York: MLA, 2009.

Wroth, Lawrence Counselman. "Corpus Typographicum." In *Typographic Heritage: Selected Essays*. New York: Typophiles, 1949.

Zedler, Gottfried. *Die älteste Gutenbergtype, mit 13 Tafeln in Lichtdruck*. Veröffentlichungen der Gutenberg Gesellschaft, 1. Mainz: Gutenberg Gesellschaft, 1902.

INDEX

ACKNOWLEDGMENTS

An earlier version of Chapter 4 appeared as "Herman R. Mead's *Incunabula at the Huntington Library* and the Notion of 'Typographical Value'." I thank the Bibliographical Society of Australia and New Zealand for permission to reprint the revised version here. For photos and photo permissions, I thank the George J. Mitchell Department of Special Collections at Bowdoin College, the Henry E. Huntington Library in San Marino, and the William Andrews Clark Memorial Library, University of California, Los Angeles. Jerry Singerman and everyone else at the University of Pennsylvania Press have been consistently helpful and generally amusing; so too the anonymous reviewers who markedly improved their skills at writing readers' reports after my many revisions. I thank also Dulcinea Circelli, Andrew Durkin, Sidney Evans, Mary Farley, Alexandra Gillespie, the Greens, Paulina Kewes, Amelia Kunhardt, Seth Lerer, Paul Needham, Michael Peterson and Michaeline Mulvey, Sandra Prior, Margaret Russett, Laura Scavuzzo Wheeler, Scott Staples, Irene Wang, and especially Linda Carpenter, my favorite professor. Finally, I will never accept the fact that she I call my darling Eloise is not here to see this book, nor those others, hers as well, in which she still lives.